Master of the Ocean Giants
An Autobiography

Master of the Ocean Giants

An Autobiography

Captain Donald Hindle

ATHENA PRESS
LONDON

Master of the Ocean Giants: *An Autobiography*
Copyright © Captain Donald Hindle 2004

All Rights Reserved

ISBN 1 84401 323 5

First Published 2004 by
ATHENA PRESS
Queen's House, 2 Holly Road
Twickenham TW1 4EG
United Kingdom

Printed for Athena Press

This book is dedicated to the memory of my Parents, who made it all possible.

Contents

Foreword

OCTOBER 25TH 1971 was a day forever printed in my mind – the culmination, as I thought then, of a long and dedicated career in the Merchant Navy, by commanding South Africa's biggest ship, MT *Gondwana*, a huge tanker nearly a quarter of a million tons deadweight, and one of the biggest ships ever built in the world at that time.

We were standing at the dockside beneath a striped awning at the naming ceremony of the *Gondwana*, in the shipbuilders' yard of Ishikawajima-Harima Heavy Industries Co. Ltd. (IHI) in Küre, Japan, originally the principal construction centre for the Japanese Navy, which did, in fact, build the huge Japanese battleship, *Yamamoto*. This was the day for the naming ceremony; a strong wind was blowing from a nearby typhoon but the few drops of rain did not spoil the atmosphere as the IHI band, resplendent in their red tunics, struck up a lively tune. When the ship was named, a hanging sphere opened and a flock of white pigeons flew out and scattered, perhaps bewildered by the thunderflashes which exploded at the same time. I was standing there in my full dress uniform, together with the officials from Safmarine, the owners, and IHI. I must confess that I had some difficulty seeing through moistened eyes, casting my mind back to a boyhood which, thanks to my parents, I had survived; and during which, thanks to my mother, the money had been found to give me some sort of education, despite my frequent absences from school due to hospitalisation for bouts of pneumonia and my ever-present asthma and bronchitis.

Apprenticeship

One

It was June 1948.

'You're on your own, now.' So spoke my mother as we stood outside the small boarding house she ran, in Holmfield Road, Blackpool.

I gave her a perfunctory kiss on the cheek and hoisted granddad's old leather suitcase into the taxi, and off we drove to Blackpool North Station. It was the first time in my life I had ever been in a taxi; Dad was out at work, starting up an upholstery business again, trying to overcome the post-war difficulties everyone had to face, and certainly not available to ferry children to the station.

Travelling across country before motorways existed was a tiresome affair. First I changed trains at Preston, then Manchester, then Newcastle to High Shields station; but the time had passed quickly, my mind full of pictures of what my first appointment would be like, and whether it would be worth all the striving to get this far, even though it was only the beginning of my career.

It had been a struggle, no doubt about that. I left Blackpool Grammar School aged sixteen to become a student at Fleetwood Navigation School, and then started writing to shipping companies for acceptance as an apprentice. By perusing the pages of the *Journal of Commerce*, I had obtained the names and addresses of thirty-five shipping companies. To these I wrote, full of hope and confidence, only to be shattered when those that did reply turned me down.

My next-door neighbour, Ray Morgan, had already managed to sign on as an apprentice with King Line, but they had no more vacancies; another friend, Peter Bone, had managed to obtain an apprenticeship with Sir William Reardon Smith and Sons, a tramp company whose head office was in Cardiff. It was Mrs Morgan who had passed on this information to me, and, really as a last-ditch effort, I wrote to Smith's of Cardiff – and to my amazement, they accepted me!

At last, I thought, I was not on life's scrap heap at sixteen. This spurred me on to learn as much as I could at the Navigation School and also at the Sea Cadets that I had joined. Although what I learnt was, at that stage in my career, very basic, it was nonetheless very helpful.

I had passed my seventeenth birthday in November 1947 and still had not heard anything about a definite appointment from Smith's of Cardiff. In those days, there was no one to advise about careers; my parents had left me to my own devices, thinking – perhaps rightly – that they had done all they could by nurturing me through childhood and educating me, and now it was up to me.

It came as a bombshell when I received a reply back from Smith's that they no longer had any vacancies for apprentices. I just could not believe it. I'd had a letter telling me that I was accepted and then here was a letter saying I wasn't! As I had already written to all the companies I could find, and as I was now really too old to start out as an apprentice, at the age of seventeen I just knew intuitively that I was fighting for survival; so I wrote back to Smith's in the following vein:

18th April 1948

Dear Sirs,

I am in receipt of your letter of the 18th October 1947 accepting me as an apprentice, and now you write that there is no vacancy. Accordingly, if I am not now accepted, I have no option but to take legal action against your company.

Yours faithfully,

Donald Hindle

I don't know how many seventeen-year-olds would have taken such a step, but as far as I could see, I had nothing to lose and my whole future was in the balance.

To my eternal delight, Smith's wrote back that they had accepted me as an apprentice and that I should join the *Indian City* at Redheads' Dry Dock, South Shields, on the 10th June 1948.

Life was taking a turn for the better, or so I thought – that is, until I took my mandatory eyesight test, which I could not take earlier because it was an MOT test to be taken upon appointment to a vessel and whenever sitting for examinations.

The test was taken in the same building as Fleetwood Navigation School; it wasn't the standard card test, but a sequence of lights coloured white, red or green or in combinations, made more difficult by using an oil lamp which gave the white light a reddish hue, the lights themselves decreasing in size down to pinpricks as the examiner turned the control knob. The upshot – failure!

I couldn't believe it. After eight months at the Navigation School, to be appointed at long last and then to fail a test that I knew I shouldn't have done, because there was certainly nothing wrong with my eyesight.

What to do? Surely I could not give up that easily; surely there must be something and somehow, somewhere that I could do – and then I thought of a solution;

The 'time served officers' studying at the Navigation School had often mentioned taking various parts of their examinations at Liverpool – including their eyesight test – that pointed me in the direction of a possible solution.

Without more ado, I took a train to Liverpool next morning and presented myself for an eyesight test at the MOT office. Giving my name and address to the clerk, he asked me why I'd come all the way to Liverpool when I could have taken the test at Fleetwood; thinking quickly I was able to glibly tell him that I was now living with my grandmother in some street in Liverpool. Of course it was a lie, but I was fighting for survival and not thinking too much about ethics.

I passed this test but, perhaps because I was not as good a liar as I thought, the clerk had phoned Fleetwood, only to be told that I had failed the test the week previously. The clerk did not throw me out of the office, but sympathetically told me that a certificate could not be issued.

Again I was down and thought I was on life's scrap heap, but the kindly man helpfully suggested that I should take the Special Test in London, designed to cater for those who had failed; but it would be a more stringent test.

The next week I took the early morning train from Blackpool to London, for my afternoon appointment with Captain Quick, Principal Examiner of Masters and Mates. He was a stern-looking man, and thorough in his tests, but declared that there was no colour blindness and gave me a certificate there and then. I was overjoyed, and could hardly wait to set out on my sea career.

Two weeks before I was due to join the *Indian City* I received a list of clothing that I should take with me and, as a sort of afterthought, a form to be filled in by my doctor.

Of course the family doctor knew me well by this time and so I had no worries presenting myself to him and asking him to sign the form; imagine my desolation when he refused. 'I couldn't let you go to sea,' he said, 'not with your chest condition.'

I didn't know which way to turn; I thought of forging his signature but there was space on the form for a stamp and his NHS number – could I really be on the scrap heap this time? No, never, I thought. There must be a way. There was – Liverpool again!

Remembering what I had heard of conversations by seasoned mariners during coffee and lunch breaks at the Navigation School, I recalled some mention of medicals by the 'Pool' doctor at Liverpool. I didn't hesitate; the very next day I was on the early morning train to Liverpool, having ascertained the exact location of the Shipping Office.

My enquiries resulted in the clerk pointing to a door marked 'Doctor', and my rather timid knock on the glass brought forth an encouraging 'Come right in' from a jovial-looking man who turned out to be the doctor. He looked at the form and immediately asked why I hadn't given it to my own doctor to be filled in.

'I have never needed a doctor in my life,' was my quick response, praying beneath my breath that I would be forgiven for telling such a barefaced lie.

He accepted what I told him and began his perfunctory examination, and I knew now that if I breathed through my nose instead of my mouth, it limited the amount of wheezing from my chest; but just to be on the safe side, I told him that I was just recovering from a cold that had gone on my chest, but was now almost 100%. I don't know if he believed me or not but he signed and stamped the certificate.

My determination to be a success in life and not to be a failure was now being justified.

I was feeling a little self-conscious in my brand new apprentice uniform, complete with cap and brass buttons, as I lugged my heavy leather suitcase down the steps from High Shields station. There was no waiting taxi but I would not have taken one anyway. I was used to walking or running everywhere, and even though my suitcase was heavy, it was the sort of day when everything was light.

The ticket collector at the station had pointed me in the general direction of Redheads' Shipyard. It was a dull, drizzling day. Some of the bomb damage still remained from the war, and the rest of the homes I passed seemed to be old and the worse for wear, but my eyes were looking ahead, because I could see the jibs of cranes in the distance, and knew that my destination was now within easy walking distance.

The green double door barring the entrance had 'Redheads' Shipyard' painted on it in white, and a smaller door for workers to be clocked in and out past the gatekeeper.

I had not come across a broad Geordie accent before, and when I asked the gatekeeper the way to the *Indian City* it took me some time to make out what he was saying. Once again I was pointed in the right direction and made my way through the heaps of scrap, old rusty chains, planks, empty paint drums and the general dirt and debris of the shipyards of that era; but beyond that I saw a ship which, when I came a little nearer, bore the name *Dallington Court* on her stern, and when I asked one of the workers – there were plenty walking around, cigarettes in mouths, wearing dirty greasy suits of yesteryear, as uniforms were not in vogue – he pointed to the gangway with his thumb.

With this limited direction, I climbed on board the *Dallington Court* and then across her deck to a ship moored alongside with a big black 'S' on her red funnel. That must be her, I thought, the *Indian City*. I asked again and with a nod, it was confirmed that that was the name of the ship.

There was no connecting gangway that I could detect, but I saw that there was a plank across from the boat deck of the *Dallington Court* to that of the *Indian City*.

I had no idea where to go or whom I should report to, but that dilemma was soon resolved because after negotiating the gangplank dragging the heavy suitcase behind, a voice said, 'Hello, you must be the new apprentice!' And there was this young fellow, dressed in working gear of blue linen shirt and dungarees (now known as jeans), with a welcoming smile and a handshake.

'My name is Turner,' he said. 'They call me "Dagwood" or "Dag". I was the junior apprentice till you arrived. Welcome on board, bring your case inside.'

We were on the boat deck, a lifeboat on each side, and in between was the accommodation: two double berth cabins for the apprentices and a mess room, all on the after side of the accommodation; and on the forrard side, three single berths for the chief cook, carpenter and bosun, with a shower room at the end shared by seven of us.

Dagwood showed me where to stow my gear. This was mainly working kit with one suit for the hoped for shore excursions and a couple of books – *Nicholl's Concise Guide, Vol. 1* and *Nories' Nautical Tables*. I quickly changed from uniform (which no one ever wore) into my dungarees (which I always wore).

Dagwood showed me round and advised me about the shipboard routine; we shared the scrubbing of cabin and brass polishing for Sunday inspection. And I, as junior apprentice, was primarily responsible for keeping the mess room clean and collecting our food from the galley, or, in nautical terms, I was the 'Peggy'.

I was introduced to Johnny Hughes, a tall, dark-haired good-humoured fellow, who was the senior apprentice, and Charley Gower, tall, fair-haired, a Welshman with a typically melodious voice. By the time we had all been introduced and had a cup of tea, it was time for the four of us to 'turn-to' and go about whatever work had been given to the senior apprentice by the mate or by the bosun; at this time, we were clearing up the 'tween decks, stowing and lashing shifting boards so that they wouldn't move in bad weather; the shifting boards had been slotted into steel girders in the centre of the lower hold to prevent the previous cargo of grain from shifting.

Fortunately, due to my years in the Sea Cadets and the Scouts, I was very handy with knots, splices and lashings and so had no trouble, which seemed to surprise the bosun, who was watching me closely, being from Norway, where everyone learns to sail at a young age, he probably did not expect much from an English first tripper.

We knocked off for the day at five, and Dagwood showed me how to take the enamel round kits down to the galley for our evening meal. It was a routine that never varied. First the officers' food was given to the pantry boy; next the engineers' food was given to the mess room steward; next the sailors' food was given to the deck boy; then the Arab firemen were given theirs, and lastly the apprentices were given theirs.

We were rationed with certain foods, so whatever we were given was never enough. Although we were served last, we finished first. No matter what it was, we ate it, barely tasting it in our haste to polish it off and dash back to the galley to see if there was any left. Usually there wasn't anything, but when any surplus was not put in the deep freeze, we could have it and we wolfed that down as though we had never been fed in our lives. Greedy? Not really; we worked very hard physically from 7 a.m. until 5 p.m. if we were on day work, but until 8 p.m. if we were on overtime for six days per week, and then in our spare time we had to scrub our cabins, mess rooms, do the 'Peggy' and study by taking a correspondence course issued by the Merchant Navy Training Board.

If we were on watch, it was the three-watch system: 4-8, 8-12, 12-4, four hours on, eight hours off, seven days per week, except when overtime was worked, which was usually another three hours per day. When there were three on a watch, it would be an AB, an ordinary seaman, and an apprentice. We would rotate our duties so that at night one would be 'first wheel' – that is, steer for two hours, one hour 'standby' and one hour 'lookout'; 'second wheel' – that is, one hour 'lookout', one hour 'standby' and two hours 'wheel'; or 'farmer' – that is one hour 'standby', two hours 'lookout' and one hour 'standby'.

In the daytime, the lookout and standby men would work on deck with the day workers. By this time, most ships were already fitting automatic steering, so this reduced the three-man watches to two-man watches.

There was no sophistication on any of the ships around that time. So many ships had been sunk during the war and been replaced by ships churned out by the United States under the Lend-Lease agreements between our countries. This meant that ships were mass-produced to the same design as those built in the Twenties and Thirties, mainly smallish cargo ships of around 10,000 tons deadweight, with steam reciprocating engines which, although slow and uneconomic, never failed, chugging along at 64 rpm, and lubricated by hand, and with steam winches on deck, also lubricated by hand (apprentice's hand, I should add) – two winches to each hatch. As these revolutions were so slow that there was little or no chance of overheating; it ran forever.

On the main deck were five hatches and underneath five more hatches from the 'tween decks down to the lower hold, and beneath the lower hold were the double bottom tanks for fuel or water.

All the ships of that era had a raised fo'c's'le under which were the bosun's store, paint locker, 'Chippy's' shop and rope store. Underneath that, at the bottom, was the forepeak tank for fresh water storage or water ballast. Amidships was the bridge, saloon and officers' accommodation, and in ships with a centre hatch, the accommodation around the engines was for the engineers, with the 'half decks' above for the apprentices and petty officers. Down aft was the poop deck, housing the crew.

By the time I had cleaned up after the evening meal and washed the tin plates, mugs etc., I had had little time to absorb this new world in which I found myself. It was very confusing, mainly because our crew had not yet signed on and the ship was swarming with dockyard workers who seemed to spend an inordinate length of time chalking up bets on the bulkheads – and, like we all seemed to do at that time, smoking their heads off!

We had been brought up in wartime and were used to discipline, so when I was told that the flags must be hauled down at sunset, it was done as a routine and accepted by everyone. As we were a British ship in a British port, then we had only the ensign or 'Red Duster' flying over the stern and the Reardon Smith house flag at the truck of the mainmast.

The time of sunset was calculated every day and the duty officer would check the chronometer and blow a whistle at sunset, whether you could see the sun or not, and at that time, both flags were hauled down together. On this, my first day, I was given the task of hauling down the house flag and 'Dag' the ensign. The whistle blew and we both hauled away; unfortunately, the wind had wrapped mine, which was tied on top of a pole that in turn extended the flag above the truck, so that when I tried to lower it, the flag fouled the truck. No amount of tugging would release it so I reported to the mate, who was the duty officer, that it was stuck and would not come down. Although he was small in stature the mate was fierce looking; he glared at me.

'Better climb up there, free it and bring it down then!' he ordered.

For a moment I was stunned.

'Er, yes sir, aye-aye sir,' was my somewhat uncertain response.

I was not afraid of heights but climbing up to the truck of the mainmast, about 100 feet up, was no joke. The lower mast was easy enough, with steel rungs; but on the topmast there was only a flimsy ladder with wooden rungs spliced through wire, which became narrower the higher you climbed. Frankly, it was dangerous – not the climbing, but the wire at the topmost ladder was badly corroded due to the sulphur dioxide and other chemicals belching out of the funnel and invariably enveloping the main topmast. I managed to free the flag and haul it down in one piece, but I had learnt a lesson, and one I would never forget; as I became Mate and then Master, I always inspected and maintained my ships, even in places not easily accessible.

Two

THE CREW WERE signed on, on the 15th June 1948, and I also joined them at the shipping office to sign on as apprentice.

Now it was already feeling more like a ship, with a full complement of forty-two of us, Master, Mate, Second Mate, Third Mate, Radio Officer, Chief, Second, Third, Fourth, Fifth, and Sixth Engineers, Bosun, Carpenter, four ABs, two Senior Ordinary Seamen, two Ordinary Seamen, two Junior Ordinary Seamen, Deck Boy, five Firemen, one Donkeyman, one Chief Steward, Second Steward, Officers' Steward, Mess Room Steward, Pantry Boy, four Apprentices, Chief Cook, Second Cook, Galley Boy.

The apprentices would work either under the bosun or 'chippy' (the carpenter). First we had to clear and secure the timber in the 'tween decks, then fit the hatch boards to the hatches to the lower holds, then on to the main deck, clearing all the rubbish left by the dockyard workers, fitting the hatch boards, covering the hatches with just one tarpaulin and wedging the steel side battens with hardwood wedges.

The rubbish left lying around the main deck was enormous; it was roughly swept and piled in heaps by the rails.

Watches were set and stores came on board: deck stores, engine stores and, of course, cabin stores, mainly food. With about thirty willing hands, the stores were shipped and stowed very quickly, in no more than two days – and that was to last us nine months!

Pilot on board, tugs made fast, single up fore and aft, let go! The tugs pulled us slowly into the River Tyne, turning to head downstream, tugs away! We slowly steamed with the tide until we reached the river mouth – pilot boat alongside. Pilot away – heave up the pilot ladder – and we were off, the fresh smell of the sea replacing the smog, dirt and noise of the Tyneside shipyard.

Water on deck! Hoses washing down everything in sight, a job loved by every sailor, getting rid of all the dockyard rubbish, over the side it went (no plastic to pollute in those days) planks, chippings, wrappings, empty drums, broken wires, dunnage, over it went and the high pressure of the hoses combined with the energetic scrubbing with deck brooms made the *Indian City* appear shipshape in no time at all.

The next day it was out with the holystones to take the dirt and stains off the teak decks; hard, boring work, but when completed the ship was almost gleaming.

A ship is a busy place. We always have to keep one thing uppermost in our minds – the cargo. We were bound for Margherita di Savoia on the Adriatic cost of Italy, near Barletta, to load a full cargo of salt for Japan.

The very thought of it was exciting. In those days, not many people had travelled except some of the armed forces, who had fought in the Desert or on mainland Europe; but to go to Italy, then through the Suez Canal, Red Sea, and Indian Ocean to Japan, was the epitome of travel: 'Go to sea and see the world' was certainly a very apt saying.

The *Indian City* was looking clean and shipshape, and now we were down in the holds again. All the shifting boards, steel uprights etc. were properly lashed and stowed in the 'tween decks, now we had to sweep the whole of the 'tween decks and lower holds, haul up the rubbish and dump it overboard. Once this was going full swing, the mate appeared on deck in a white boiler suit and summoned the apprentices to work with him to limewash the inside of all holds and 'tween decks to help nullify the corrosive effect of the salt upon the bare steel of the holds' internal structure.

We quickly picked up the procedure; it was basically simple. Mix powdered lime with fresh water in a forty-gallon drum on deck, lower this down in five-gallon drums to the mate and two apprentices assisting down below. The apprentices down below would put the suction end of a stirrup pump into the five-gallon drum of lime, and the mate clambered over the side stringers, spraying lime over everything (and everyone!).

It was hard work pumping all day, and with leaks from the pump spraying lime all over us, by the end of the day we were covered in lime and quite badly burnt. We didn't complain, it was all in a day's work, and the dirtier and tougher the job the more the apprentices were called upon to do it!

The mate himself worked all day whilst his day watch was shared by the other two mates or the Captain himself. It took us eleven days to reach Margherita di Savoia at our normal speed – between nine and ten knots – which was just time to complete the limewashing of all five holds and the 'tween decks.

Margherita di Savoia was an open roadstead. We anchored about a mile and a half offshore and awaited the shore officials to board and clear the ship inwards for customs, immigration and health before we could carry out our cargo loading.

Three

EARLY THE FOLLOWING morning, the apprentices and the crew cleared the hatch boards off the 'tween deck hatches and removed just one of the hatch boards on each of the main deck hatches. Then the derricks were 'topped' and rigged in 'union purchase' so that one plumbed over the main hatch and the other plumbed over the side, with both the runners joined to one hook and hooked on to a cargo net.

The salt was brought out in small barges propelled by sweeps, pushed by the crew standing on top of the salt, which was bagged in very small sacks. Once alongside, the salt bags were loaded into the cargo net, which, when full, was heaved straight up and then across to the hatch where the net was lowered on to the hatch top, the bags taken out and the empty net heaved back for another load.

Whilst they were filling the next net with bags of salt, the men on top of the hatch were opening up the ties on each sack of salt and tipping the contents into the empty hold below. The work was very labour-intensive and it's probably not done in this way today, but we were at anchor there for about twelve days loading our full cargo of 10,000 tons of salt.

The weather was glorious, with the hot sunny cloudless days of a Mediterranean summer and the blue sea sparkling. We only worked sunrise to sunset, an easy job for us apprentices, one of whom was designated as the cargo winch oiler. This job was always given to apprentices, probably because they were more conscientious than most of the crew. The art of the job was to pour oil in all the oil cups and holes without stopping the winch from operating; otherwise it would slow down the cargo operation. We became quite adept at pushing our can amongst the drive shafts and cogwheels without losing any hands! We used gallons of oil, as we would oil all the winches at least once every hour, but as we used old oil from the main engine sump, which we hauled up by the five-gallon drum from the boiler room, it really didn't cost the company anything; but we ended up with oil streaming off each winch and down into the scuppers.

The shore labour who operated the winches and actually loaded the cargo stopped for a short break at lunch time, and every one of them ate the same lunch – bread and tomatoes! It really was not so surprising because the tomatoes grew out in the open and they grew easily so that it was a very cheap meal; and Italy, just after the Second World War, was a very poor country indeed.

One evening, when the last of the cargo had been loaded for that day and as some of them were waiting on board for the last barge to take them ashore, the fishermen were returning to Margherita di Savoia after a day's fishing. They also were using sweeps but with a simple square sail to help them on their way. One of the hatch men, a big, handsome man with muscular arms and chest, was waiting outside our boat deck accommodation, and he cupped his hand to his mouth and hailed the passing boats, who hailed him back. He then leapt on to the rail at the side, with one arm reaching up to the awning spars and as he stood there, nicely balanced, he started singing a kind of chant, and after every cadenza, paused for the response, which drifted over to us across the water from the fishing boats. It was the sort of natural spontaneous singing that the great composers try to emulate in their operas; but they never, I believe, achieve such a moving scene as was enacted before us with such spontaneity and depth of feeling; it is still clearly imprinted in my mind, fifty-four years later.

The excitement of being at sea and visiting foreign ports in those days lay in the opportunity of going ashore. This was not always possible because of our on-board duties and desperate shortage of money, especially as a junior apprentice, earning the princely sum of six pounds per month (old pounds), from which was deducted an amount for Social Security. But we did have one big advantage at that time: cigarettes were the international currency; they were very cheap on board and a packet or tin of fifty cigarettes could buy a meal and perhaps some wine.

On the second day we had so arranged our duties that Dagwood and I could go ashore together along with the second mate and a very diminutive radio officer – 'Sparks'. We went ashore in one of the empty barges, discovering that the calm sea was not so calm when viewed from the bottom of one of these small boats.

We were dressed for the shore, me with my one and only suit on (no casual gear in those days), for once without working clothes. Glad to get through the breakers and into the calm waters of the creek-like small boat harbour, we landed safe and sound on terra firma, we looked around and saw – nothing!

We were miles away from anywhere, no habitation in sight, no exciting 'bright lights' but just a dusty coast road leading... we didn't know where! But we had seen, in the distance, our Chippy with one of the crew, so we just followed, not knowing really what to do or where to go.

We trudged a mile or two along the road, passing fields full of tomatoes and melons, until we came across a couple of stone dwellings. One, obviously with an eye to other seafarers who may occasionally pass by, had written a notice, hanging on the doorpost, with just one word, instantly recognisable, internationally – 'VINOS'.

Yes, there was our Chippy and two of the crew, imbibing happily as the wine must have been as cheap as water in those days, but we apprentices were not to be lured into such habits, in the middle of a hot Mediterranean summer day; so we continued walking until we caught up with the second mate and Sparks who were some way ahead.

As we debated how far to walk, a group of eight young men approached and started demanding (we presumed) money, and becoming increasingly aggressive when none was forthcoming. They were obviously demobilised Italian army personnel, as they wore parts of army fatigues and, like a lot of Italians then, would be extremely poor and probably unemployed.

We didn't know the language but kept walking slowly along the track, which we now learnt lead to Barletta. This was not good enough for the local down and outs, who hurled stones at us, one cutting the second mate on his forehead. I don't know how this little fracas would have ended because, at this juncture, a middle-aged man, riding a bicycle, appeared on the scene. We stopped him and by use of my schoolboy French were able to make him understand what was going on.

The man shouted at our assailants, waving his arms in good Italian style; whatever he told them had some effect because they gradually drifted away, leaving us in peace to continue our walk to Barletta, which took us around three hours altogether.

Barletta was a small place in those days (and maybe still is). We didn't have much money, so we just sort of marched around until we came across the one and only cinema… advertising a film in English! We thought that this was too good an opportunity to miss, so we paid our money and sat down in the dark expectantly, only to find that the film, although it had an English title, was in Italian!

We did not feel like sitting through an Italian lesson so exited quickly and decided to make the long walk back up the dusty road to Margherita di Savoia, some five miles distant.

It was still hot, and having lost the others, just Dagwood and I walked slowly through the afternoon heat made more tolerable by a pleasant sea breeze that had sprung up. Walking back was not as slow because we were more familiar with the way and not delayed by assailants or 'vino' sellers, so within about 2½ hours we were back at the harbour side in Margherita di Savoia to join one of the salt barges back to our floating 'home' – or so we thought!

Barges there were, men there were, but we didn't need any knowledge of Italian to understand what they were saying – it was too rough to make it safely through the breakers out to the ship. Now what do we do? Nowhere to go, nobody to help us and no money to speak of… We were also very worried about what the Captain might think of his apprentices if we didn't return to the ship – it was thirty-four years later before I really found out what the Captain thought!

It was already evening and as no one was holding our hand and telling us what to do, we decided we had to find somewhere to sleep and hope that the next day would be calmer and safer for small boats to operate.

We looked around for some shelter. I found a heap of straw in the shelter of a hedge; Dagwood found a half-ruined stone building, which looked uncomfortable, but as we were tired we slept, the heat of the Mediterranean summer night keeping us relatively warm until morning.

Came the dawn, and as I extricated myself from the straw, I discovered that it was an old dungheap that had stained my one and only suit appropriately. Dagwood came out of his shelter with a crick in his neck, two others of the crew appeared from under a pile of empty canvas salt bags in the barges; one or two others drifted in as we looked around for a boatman willing to take us out to our ship, but as there was no reduction in the force of the wind, not one could be induced to risk it, even though we offered them considerable amounts of cigarettes once we returned to the ship.

We figured that the wind would only increase as the day wore on so our thoughts turned to the more practical things in life, such as food! Of course we were not starving after a day without food, but as we were looking at one more day at least without nourishment, we were not feeling very happy about our situation. By now, there were six of us stranded, so we decided to pool what money we had and Dagwood and I being the youngest and fittest, would walk back to Barletta to see what a few lire could buy.

We took the now familiar track to Barletta, no taxi, no buses, no cars from whom to thumb a lift, just the two legs we were born with to get us there. Fortunately, our few lire bought us a couple of loaves of bread, which we took back with us to share amongst the group stranded at Margherita di Savoia. Between us, we scavenged in the fields for tomatoes and melons and so had enough to eat that day. But we were more choosy where we slept that night.

The wind had died down a little, on this our third day ashore, and by bartering with the boatmen they agreed to take us out to our ship – they were brave because they knew how difficult it was; we, being passengers, just trusted in their good judgment.

There were six strong men on the sweeps, and the six of us passengers were told to crouch in the bottom of the barge. As soon as we were clear of the little harbour, the full force of the breakers hit us and we seemed to be completely under water. As the oarsmen pushed with all their might, the water cascaded on board and we poor mortals, crouched in the bilge, tried our best to bale out the water.

The boatmen knew their trade all right, and we made it through the surf into the comparative safety of the sea, heading at an angle across the waves to keep as much water out as possible. In this way we made it back safely to the *Indian City*, soaking wet as we crawled up the gangway, with the Captain and everyone else, peering down at these bedraggled specimens of humanity making their way to the safety and comparative comfort of their 'home'.

The boatmen were well rewarded with the only currency we all had – cigarettes – and pulled themselves back into the harbour.

Only two more days of loading salt were needed to load us to our Plimsoll marks and to batten down all the hatches with three tarpaulins on each, steel side battens firmly in place and steel crossbars bolted on top of each section of hatch boards. We had to make it as watertight as possible, even if the tarpaulins were ripped by the wind or seas we could experience on our long passage to Japan.

Four

IT WAS EASY TO leave our loading port of Margherita di Savoia, just heave aweigh the anchor and full ahead on the engines, and head more or less straight for Port Said, about five days' steaming away.

The on-board routine soon established itself. We washed down the decks and scrubbed the woodwork to rid ourselves of the dirt accumulated during loading, and with derricks dropped and firmly secured, we were able to strip all the guys and runners and stow them under the fo'c's'le, just leaving two of the derricks rigged for use in the Suez Canal.

Four days on passage, we were happily devouring our midday meal, when all of a sudden there was a bang and the whole ship shuddered, to the extent that our plates jumped up about four inches on the table. We hadn't the faintest idea what was going on but we were out of our seats in a flash and ran out on deck, as did everyone else down aft and amidships. We saw the Captain, 'Ginger' Harris, running out of his cabin and up the ladder to the bridge; I figured that anything that makes the Captain run must be really serious!

The mate had called for the 'Chippy', and they were immediately engaged in sounding all the double bottom tanks to see if we were making water. Everyone on board had memories of the war, and there were still lots of floating mines being reported and so that was our first thought. Then we wondered if it could be a semi-submerged wreck, still floating around, even though hostilities had ceased two or three years before.

We were not making water, and did not find out the cause of our unidentified 'shock', 'explosion', 'collision' – call it what you will – which occurred in deep water miles away from land, until the next day, when we arrived at Port Said. After the usual officials had boarded, the agent brought a newspaper for the Captain, always welcome. In it was an account of an earthquake in about the area we had passed through the day before; so what we had felt was the hydraulic shock – mystery solved!

Port Said was an exciting place. Of course, we could not go ashore. What each ship did was to tie up to the dolphins or buoys to one side of the canal, to form a convoy. During the few hours we were there the agent brought the mail and we hoisted on board two mooring boats that were used to tie us up to the canal bank if we experienced heavy fog, or to let another northbound convoy pass.

The boatmen had all kinds of souvenirs to sell to us: stuffed camels, prayer mats, brassware, 'dirty' postcards, 'naughty' books. They used to sidle up and whisper, 'You buy dirty postcard?' or, 'You buy Spanish fly?' It all added to the colour of the place, the smells and the sounds of Port Said as it was.

There was one other bonus – girls! Not, I regret to say, on board, but on the northbound passenger liners. They lined the rails, waving happily at the crews of ships who never saw a girl from one month's end to the next. Sailors and apprentices alike were swinging from the awning spars, whistling, shouting, and promising eternal happiness to anyone who fancied them!

As soon as the northbound convoy passed, we let go the moorings and followed the ship ahead, the pilot taking great care to keep our distance in case she slowed down, or, as occasionally happened, broke down. It took the best part of a day to navigate the canal, even though we steamed through the night, the darkness illuminated by aid of a powerful searchlight hoisted on to the bow. The pilots changed halfway through.

When the convoy entered the Bitter Lakes, all of them anchored, until the northbound convoy passed, as many of them were fully laden tankers and so had priority. In those days, most of the ships flew the Red Ensign. The familiar outlines of a Blue Funnel ship was always in evidence, the two red bands of a Clan liner, the well-known funnels of Shell and BP, Harrison's tramp ship with two white bands and one red in the middle ('two of fat and one of lean'), and occasionally a Smith's tramp would be encountered, easily recognisable by the big black 'S' on the funnel ('S on the funnel, f— all on the table!') and then there was the white 'H' of 'hungry' Hogarths, and many, many others. They are nearly all replaced now by 'box' ships carrying containers and unrecognisable funnels belonging to Taiwanese, Korean, Japanese etc.

We dropped the pilot, the searchlight and both mooring boats at Suez, usually whilst still under way, and then set our course down the Gulf of Suez, with the Sinai Peninsular to port and Egypt to starboard.

Out of the Gulf of Suez, with the Gulf of Aqaba to port, we entered the Red Sea; it was July and very, very hot. There was little or no wind, what wind we made at our maximum speed of 10 knots was either nullified by a following wind or heated up by wafting the very hot fumes out of the open engine room skylights through the forrard portholes of the boat deck accommodation. Of course, there was no such thing as air conditioning in those days; it was really unbearable.

We soon rigged the canvas awnings over the awning spars; this gave us a bit of shade, and the only way to have any chance of sleep was to sleep on deck, under the awning, either on a settee cushion or slung from a hammock tied to the awning spars. All the apprentices made their own hammocks, using a piece of old canvas about six feet long, sewing a seam at each end, punching eyelets in and eye splicing boat lacing to an eye splice in a lashing each end. We were tired after a hard day's work and usually slept like logs in the Red Sea, despite the heat, because, being in sheltered waters, the ship was not rolling around.

Watches continued as usual and day workers had the unenviable task of descaling and oiling the main decks; this could only be done satisfactorily in very hot weather in waters sheltered from the seas and heavy spray; the Red Sea, especially southbound, was ideal for this work.

We released the heavy rust by pounding it with a long-handled, heavy Munday hammer, we then scraped the loose rust with a long-handled triangular scraper, and finally wire-brushed it with a long-handled wire brush. When the steel was rust-free and shiny, it was swept and covered with fuel oil from the engine room, not by slapping it over with mops but by kneeling down and rubbing the oil into the steel by hand, minimising the surplus oil and giving it chance to dry in the hot sun. We could only do it this way by tying burlap round our knees to prevent them burning, as we only wore shorts and working shoes, no socks, shirts or vests. Yes, we were exposed to radiation day in and day out; nobody told us about skin cancer and we were burnt black by the sun.

With all this heat, combined with extremely hard physical work for long hours, at least from seven in the morning until five in the afternoon, we could drink a bucket! The only drink available to us in any quantity was water, this was lukewarm, slightly rusty and pumped by hand out of the after peak tank, into a bucket, which the 'Peggy' would carry back to the mess room. Such luxuries as iced water, refrigerators etc., were not heard of in those days; nothing had changed at sea for about fifty years. Anyway we drank the water, and nobody fussed over us with salt tablets. We not only survived but also grew strong and fit – no fat crew on any ship of that era! We did find that by filling an empty Chianti bottle with water and hanging it under a lifeboat in the shade, whatever breeze there was cooled it marginally and made it slightly more palatable, but we were so thirsty that we didn't really bother about what we drank. Of course we could make tea in pint mugs, but with the addition of tinned condensed milk, it was not a drink I could stomach.

Five

ALTHOUGH WE WERE bound for Japan, we had to call in to the port of Aden for fuel oil bunkers; this was quite normal in those days because ships entering and leaving the Red Sea actually had to pass Aden, so no deviation was required, and it was also known to be a cheap source of bunkers as well as a good shopping place for the passenger ships, which used to call every time they passed.

We tied up to the buoy and waited for the bunker barge to come alongside. With the sizzling hot weather and sheltered waters, it was ideal for us to continue our battering and oiling of the main deck. Imagine my surprise when the second mate, who was on watch on the bridge, hailed me.

'Hey, you!'

'Who, me sir?'

'Yes, you!'

This was the normal form of address to someone as lowly as a first trip apprentice.

'Do you know anyone on that ship over there?' he shouted, pointing to a ship in the distance.

'Oh, no sir, not me! Nobody knows me, it's my first trip.'

'Well there's someone calling your name on the Aldis Lamp – can you read Morse?'

Much to his surprise, I was able to answer in the affirmative.

'Better come up here and talk to whoever it is.'

I rushed up to the bridge, pointed the Aldis and sent, 'Don Hindle here', and much to my astonishment, received a reply.

'How are you, Don? This is Ray Morgan here!'

Well, you could have knocked me down with a feather. What a coincidence, that my next-door neighbour should be in the same place as me at the same time, thousands of miles from home. It was unbelievable.

I quickly rattled off a message inviting him on board, because I was good at Morse, as most of us were in those days, when VHF

35

radios were non-existent and mobile phones hadn't been thought of. All communication was by Morse light or flag signals.

Ray replied that he would come across in the lifeboat shortly. Of course I carried on with my work and stopped only when I saw the lifeboat from his ship, the *King Neptune*, come alongside.

I could hardly contain my excitement, somewhat dampened by the Captain, who happened to be around, asking why I couldn't be smart 'like them' – Ray and his shipmate, Jack Apsey, resplendent in whites, and me in my dirty shorts, working shoes and covered in rust. I suppose I could have asked for time off to spruce myself up but, as a humble first tripper, the thought did not enter my head.

I'd nothing to offer them, really, but a mug of our lousy tea but it was an incident forever printed in my memory and recalled when I met Ray, fifty-two years later, when I called at his home in New Zealand, whilst my wife and I were on holiday there.

There seemed to be a lot of incidents on my first trip; just after Ray and Jack had returned to the *King Neptune* we let go and headed out of Aden, when I was hailed from the bridge to check around for stowaways. I hadn't a clue what to do so I just sort of looked around quickly in the kind of places not visited frequently by the crew. I didn't find anybody and as a last resort, thought I would look into the side pockets where coal used to be stowed before the boilers were converted to burn oil. I entered down the steel-runged ladder of the fiddley, above the boilers and through a steel door, and then went into an area that was pitch black. I had no torch, but when I got used to the gloom, illuminated slightly through the fiddley door, I tripped over something, pushing a pile of empty forty-gallon drums over. The noise elicited a scream and two dark forms dashed out from behind the clattering drums and bolted to the open door. I don't know who was more terrified – them or me!

Stowaways they were, and as they emerged into the strong sunlight the pilot was just leaving, so they were able to scramble down the pilot ladder to join him. After that little incident, I was feeling very pleased with myself, although it was more by good luck than good judgement that I found them.

Six

WE WERE BOUND for Yokohama with a full cargo of salt and fully replenished with fuel oil in the double-bottom tanks. After dropping the pilot just outside harbour limits, we were heading through the sheltered waters in the Gulf of Aden – and it was hot!

Within a couple of days we passed the island of Socotra to starboard, identified in the Pilot Book as an island to avoid, not only because of the strong currents flowing between it and the Horn of Africa, but because cannibals had been reported. Exactly when, the Pilot Book did not indicate, but it was certainly not a place, at that juncture, where one would like to loiter; even the passenger ships avoided it!

Now we were in the Arabian Sea, with a strong wind from the south-west as it was the time of the year when the south-west monsoon blows, all the way from Africa, across the Arabian Sea and Indian Ocean.

This strong monsoon made an easy passage for us, no holds to prepare for cargo, but the bad weather made our routine maintenance work difficult, so we were mainly overhauling derrick running gear and, of course, keeping the routine watches round the clock, seven days per week; but there was plenty of heavy spray and seas pouring over the decks. By now I was completely settled in to my new world; on this passage, I was just on day work. I turned-to at seven a.m., and knocked off at five, unless overtime was worked, and then we worked through until eight at night. Of course, it was physically hard, but just what a young man of seventeen needed. The discipline of the job, combined with back-breaking labour, meant that we slept like a log – no matter what the weather.

The standby man called us at six-thirty, time to make a cup of tea before our Norwegian bosun turned us to, with a curt, '*Ja*, to again!'

On this particular morning, half awake, as I sat on the steam pipe casing, drinking my pint mug of tea, I thought I was seeing things, because there were two lines, almost four inches wide, leading from the chief cook's cabin, which was directly behind me, all the way alongside number three hatch, and disappeared into the saloon pantry, amidships. On closer inspection, the two lines proved to be ants, one black line going to the pantry, and the other white line coming back towards the chief cook's cabin! I bent down hardly believing what I was seeing, and discovered that the white line was composed of ants carrying a grain of sugar on their heads!

Actually I had solved a mystery. Like most ships, the *Indian City* was infested with cockroaches. These loathsome creatures were everywhere; they would eat soap, woollen socks, everything, in fact. Our cabins were kept spotlessly clean, thoroughly scrubbed and polished, but the only cockroach killer available at that time was Flit; we used to carry it in forty-gallon drums and then spray it over everything with an old type pump-action spray gun – the cockroaches loved it! Like I said, they were loathsome creatures, and whenever we opened the food locker in our little mess room, there was a rustling sound as they all fled from the light. I quickly learned that when we punched a hole in both sides of the sweetened condensed milk, we must immediately insert a wooden plug, otherwise, as we tried to pour the viscous liquid, a drowned cockroach would inevitably block the hole – ugh!

Anyway, to get back to the ants. Never have I seen ants on board a ship, except the *Indian City*. Whenever we clobbered a cockroach, as we sat down to eat, out the ants crawled all over the place; then we would see a platoon of them march out and carry the dead cockroach away on their heads.

Now we could investigate further, Chippy had come on deck to see what all the fuss was about, and between us we discovered that the black and white lines marched over the storm step and right into the chief cook's cabin!

It was such a major issue that the Captain himself became involved and he instructed 'Doc' (the nickname for all chief cooks, from when they used to be the doctor on board) to vacate his cabin, and Chippy to demolish all the furnishings; I was his assistant.

It didn't take long to remove the bunk, drawers and hanging locker, and then take the linoleum off the teak wood deck – but no sign of ants. Chippy then removed the wooden dowels covering the steel nuts which secured the 4-inch-thick planks. Then he used a hammer and crowbar to prise them off. No need; they collapsed in a splintered, dust ridden heap. It was one huge ants' nest. This really did solve the mystery as to why the chief cook was always complaining about ants in his cabin.

A spray of Flit was obviously useless, so we poured Flit from a 40-gallon drum to flood the cabin – this was effective, because even if the chemical didn't poison them, they drowned in it!

Yes, the mystery was solved, the ants disappeared for three months and then we saw a line of them appearing out of the engineers' duty mess. Fortunately, I never was troubled with ants again, but cockroaches were shipmates on every ship.

One of the more pleasant aspects of steaming across the Arabian Sea was that we attracted a school of dolphins. At night, if I was on watch, part of that watch was spent on the fo'c's'le head, as lookout. Usually, there was little to see on an ocean passage, just the occasional light of a passing steamer, which we would report to the bridge, by ringing the bell – one stroke, light to starboard; two strokes, light to port; and three strokes for light dead ahead. There was nothing else to do during the one or two hours of lonely vigil except to peer over the bow itself and watch the dolphins, like torpedoes, weaving in and out around the bow, their tracks easy to follow because of the phosphorescence they made as they swam through the water.

Nearly every morning, breakfast could be found on deck. There are plenty of flying fish in tropical waters. They can be seen skipping from wave top to wave top; but at night they are attracted to the lights of passing ships, perhaps thinking that it is sunlight. However, sadly for them, they have a hard landing on the steel deck and knock themselves out. Sometimes the cook would oblige and fry one or two, which, as far as the ever-hungry apprentices were concerned, was manna from heaven, fresh as could be and tasting like herrings, a really tasty snack.

This passage took us thirty days, chugging along at about 9½ knots – not fast – but one thing about the old-fashioned steam reciprocating engines, they never broke down! We passed close enough to see the lighthouse on the island of Minicoy, one of the Lakshadweep Islands, then we headed for the southern coast of Ceylon (Sri Lanka) and navigated through the island-strewn Malacca and Singapore Straits before steaming through the South China Sea, passing close to Palawan, Luzon and Formosa (Taiwan), before we made our landfall on the Japanese coast and into Tokyo Bay, to anchor off Yokohama.

Of course there was the usual excitement when the mail arrived on board, but our minds were set on going ashore, where a 50 box of cigarettes was the passport to a seafarer's heaven.

I was unlucky at this port; it was my turn to be night watchman. This duty was always given to an apprentice because, for one thing, we were company men; and for another, we were always reliable and trustworthy.

We used to spend the night inspecting moorings, checking that nothing was being stolen, helping the drunks on board and, at about five in the morning, lighting the coal stove so that it would be nice and hot when the cooks turned-to at six thirty. For this little chore, the cook would leave out something to cook, perhaps bacon and eggs; or, if we were lucky, a few potatoes and lard to cook some chips.

I was lucky that first night; potatoes were left out so I was sure that the fire was good and hot to cook my mouth-watering breakfast. Concentrating fully on the food, I didn't hear a quiet footstep behind me but felt a tap on my shoulder. I jumped about two feet in the air, and the frying pan with scalding fat tipped over and down my left leg – bare because I was wearing shorts. I never did find out what the little obsequious Japanese worker wanted because I was busy trying to tie a cloth round my leg in some considerable pain, and it was at that juncture the chief cook – 'Doc' – arrived on the scene.

I was helped to the chief steward's cabin – he in fact acted as doctor on board. He took one look at my leg, now covered in blisters, and told me that I would have to go ashore to the hospital.

That was the one and only time I went ashore during our

week or so in Yokohama. I walked, with some difficulty, in the direction I had been given by the agent, where I would find the US Military Hospital – Japan was still occupied by the USA in 1948. The staff quickly fixed me up by bursting the blisters and putting a clean dressing on, and with that I walked back to the ship, wearing my uniform because my one and only suit was stained. Imagine my surprise when an elderly Japanese man bowed low to me in the street, perhaps thinking that I was one of the occupation forces. Well, for a lad of seventeen it was a boost to one's ego, thinking that I must look much older than my years.

Although the discharging of our salt cargo was slow by modern standards, there were no delays due to strikes or working 'unsocial' hours. Work continued round the clock, high days and holidays included, so that we were completely discharged in the comparatively short time of five days.

Each hatch had two derricks to work cargo, both operated by steam winches, oiled, every hour or so, by an apprentice. The salt was shovelled on to 'save-alls', which were cargo nets, about three metres square, lined with canvas. When the salt was piled high, the four corners of the net were hooked on to the cargo hook and hauled straight up out of the hatch, which had been cleared of its covering of tarpaulins, hatch boards and steel H-section girders. Once clear of the hatch, the salt was hauled over the side by the second derrick, which was plumbed over the waiting barge. The salt was then lowered on to the barge; the net released on one side and then hauled up, empty, back on board and down the hatch – most of the digging in the holds was done by women.

Because the salt was not really sensitive to a drop of water, a light shower or rain would not stop the discharging and it is amazing that by constant working of five hatches you can actually discharge ten thousand tons of bulk cargo so quickly; mind you, compared with the biggest ship in the world, *Globtik London*, a tanker of nearly half a million tons deadweight, which I was later to command, it was a trivial rate of discharge. I can remember loading crude oil at Kharg Island (Iran) at 40,000 tons *per hour*! So compare that with the hourly rate of around eighty tons achieved by the *Indian City*.

41

Seven

As ALWAYS, IT WAS good to get back to the good clean, fresh air of the high seas. We left the murky air of Tokyo Bay astern with all hatches battened down. Derricks had been lowered into their steel crutches and bolted securely in place, and all the running gear, that is the wire runners, guys, head and heel blocks, were taken down and stowed underneath the fo'c's'le, where they were greased and overhauled ready for the next cargo. The threefold wire purchases of the topping lifts were left in place, unless it was a long passage, when they were sent down and stowed underneath the fo'c's'le to reduce the exposure to salt water.

Our next destination was Sydney, some three weeks' steaming away through good weather all the way, no typhoons to disturb us; the sea off Japan was warmed by the Kuro-shio, so the weather was warm and good for all the heavy work we now had to do.

It took only one day to stow all the running gear and wash down the decks. The main work was in the cargo holds, which had to be properly prepared for our next cargo of grain – the surveyors would not allow loading into a dirty hold, and on top of that there were the very stringent safety regulations which had been adopted internationally, to prevent bulk grain cargoes from shifting during bad weather, as the grain settled. This would make the vessel list, and heavy seas could broach the hatches and the vessel would flounder.

If a vessel was expected to carry bulk grain, she would be so designed that heavy steel girders could be rigged in the lower holds along the centre line. These were slotted into steel shoes at top and bottom and then further secured by two wire spans on either side, which were shackled to the ship's side and then tightened with bottle screws. Once the steel uprights were in position, heavy shifting boards about 6 metres by 0.2 m x 0.05 m were slotted into position; usually the apprentices did this independently.

When you consider that each of the steel uprights weighed about two tons, and they had to be positioned at sea, and the ship would always be rolling to some extent, you can appreciate that high standards of seamanship were required to heave these uprights out of the 'tween decks and lower them into the lower hold safely; it was dangerous work, and in those days there were no safety hats, harnesses, safety shoes, etc. We never had any accidents; we took pride in our ability and the strong muscles we developed over the years.

Once the uprights were positioned, we would haul out the shifting boards, one at a time, using steel pincer-like 'dogs' to clamp them and two heaving lines rove through blocks one on each side of the 'tween deck.

Usually at least three of us would fit the shifting boards, two on the heaving lines and the third one standing on top of the boards as they were slotted into the steel uprights. As the height of the boards grew, so the man clutching hold of the steel upright with one hand would step up on top of the board, as it was slotted. The top board would be almost ten metres above the deck.

It was not easy work. It was tiring physically, as well as dangerous, but there was some satisfaction in actually 'building' something; whilst we were thus employed, the crew would be sweeping out the holds and hauling up the rubbish to be dumped over the side – no pollution, really, as all the material was biodegradable. It was mostly the residue of previous cargo, stained dunnage, frayed ropes, rags, but no plastic, as it was not yet widely used.

Once the lower holds were fitted with their shifting boards, we then had to build 'feeders' in the 'tween decks. Essentially, this was a square box built over the hatchway, lined with burlap and divided into four sections, so that as the grain in the lower hold settled during the passage, grain would be fed from above to keep the lower hold topped up and thus prevent any chance of the grain cargo shifting during bad weather.

Again, the apprentices would usually build the feeders but this time the ship's carpenter or Chippy would be in charge, especially on ships which were not fitted with steel uprights to slot the feeder boards. In these cases, heavy baulks of timber, suitably tommed off, would be used to provide strength to the structure.

There was definitely job satisfaction in being able to build the total structure; although we didn't give much thought to it at the time, our thoughts were more mercenary – overtime! How much could be earned to spend at the next port? As a first tripper I earned only £6 per month. This was very little, even in those days, but we didn't have to pay travelling expenses to go to work, and our food and accommodation were free. By this time we had paid our Social Security contributions, which had just come into vogue, and by the time we had bought our duty-free cigarettes (we all smoked) there was little left, so overtime was our spending money.

I was well used to the shipboard routine by this time, working hard all day, sleeping like a log when not on watch, doing 'Peggy', 'dhobi' (washing clothes) or scrubbing the decks and polishing the brass for weekly inspection by the Captain. There was one other routine, essential but carried out with little enthusiasm by all apprentices – studying!

We had all started out with a reasonable standard of education, usually supplemented by a spell at some Nautical College or other like Pangbourne, Conway, or, in the case of many apprentices who found their way on the 'tramp' ships, with no training at all.

Perhaps it would be as well, at this juncture, to better describe what were known then as 'tramp' ships. One dictionary describes them as follows: 'cargo steamer that is not confined to any particular run or to any particular cargo, but carries cargo that is profitable and convenient'. In the period of my apprenticeship, Britain had the biggest merchant fleet in the world, with an abundance of 'tramp' ship companies, such as Ropners, Runcimans, Hogarths, Court Line, King Line, Smith's of Cardiff, etc. None of these companies had regular runs and they would all be employed on the carriage of lower freight bulk cargoes, as the higher freight cargoes such as machinery, canned goods, heavy lifts, etc. would be carried by the Liner companies with regular runs to specific destinations, e.g. Clan Line to South and East Africa and India; Harrison Line, British India, Port Line, Blue

Star Line, South American Saint Line, Shaw, Savile and Albion, Stag Line, Blue Funnel (Alfred Holts), and so on.

No matter what type of company an apprentice or cadet served his time with, we all had to serve at least three years and five months actually at sea during our four years' apprenticeship, and during that time we were expected to study. Usually, in the Liner companies, there would be time on board allotted as study time, but on 'tramp' ships, apprentices' time was for working, it was what has become known as a 'chipping hammer' apprenticeship. Whatever the type of ship, we all had to complete a correspondence course from the Merchant Navy Training Board. These courses were sent out to each apprentice through the Head Office, then to the Captain, who would ensure that the work was completed in time and returned to the MNTB. At the end of each year, there would be an examination on board, invigilated by an officer, and the resultant progress sent back to the MNTB. When they were marked, these papers would be returned to Head Office for their comments before sending them back to the Captain, and he in turn would summon the apprentice and demand explanations if results were too bad. It was not a perfect system, but by the end of our four years, we did know something about navigation, chart work, ship construction, seamanship, meteorology, mathematics, lifeboats, signals, etc.

How long would we spend in Sydney? That was the burning question of the moment. One of the ABs laughed when I asked him. 'One thing I can guarantee is that there will *always* be a strike in Aussie,' was his comforting reply; after all, we just lived for the excitements to be found at the next port, which, as far as most of us were concerned, was the receipt of mail from home. Although I wouldn't admit it to anyone, I was homesick, and I suppose most of the younger ones were until they became more used to the seaman's way of life – the highs when homeward bound, and the lows on leaving home for anything up to two years. Many of the old timers were not married so it made little difference; but to those who were, it was always harder to leave a wife and children behind.

Sydney is probably the best natural harbour in the world,

completely enclosed and with comparatively deep water so that fairly large vessels can enter. We were piloted to a position near Tauranga close to the Sydney Harbour Bridge; there we were to stay for five weeks, moored to a buoy, whilst the 'wharfies' settled their latest strike!

Of course time in port is not a holiday. We still had our work to do, and as we were in sheltered waters, we had a good chance to work over the side on stages to chip the rust off the ship's side and to paint her from bow to stern with black gloss, cutting in with red boot-topping and painting the name and draught marks in white.

We painted all the black topsides, which included the areas directly under the scuppers from the washbasins and toilets; these scuppers were just open pipes with a steel flap to prevent the waves from blowing back the discharge into the toilets, and were a kind of non-return valve. Everyone working over the side knew that they were there; accordingly, we would lash the handles of the toilets to prevent them being used, and/or hang a notice saying, 'DO NOT USE – MAN WORKING UNDERNEATH'.

One of the deck boys, a first trip Scot with no experience, was happily painting over the side, from a stage. No one had told him about the potential threat of working under open scuppers without taking precautions; predictably, someone flushed the toilet over him and I can still hear his choice language – with his strong Scottish accent – as he climbed back on board to find the culprit and wash off the results!

A lifeboat left the ship every evening at six, and then we were expected to either hire a launch back from Circular Quay or take our own lifeboat back at a fixed time of 10.30 p.m. As I was on day work, I had the chance to go ashore in the evening and then again at weekend, but with very little money and knowing no one, it wasn't so much fun really – until that is, I met Nola Dillon! No, this is not a developing love story, but she and her friend took Dagwood and me around to see more of Sydney than we would have done otherwise. We went out to the National Park and the girls took a picnic. I did splash out to see Mario Lanza in *Be My Love*, which broke me for a while; but, like a gentleman, I took Nola Dillon back home. One problem though, she lived out of town, and getting back made me late for the lifeboat back to the ship. I was counting my pennies, wondering how to get back on board as it was nearly midnight and no launches available until morning. Then, out of nowhere, came the ship's lifeboat! Unbelievable good luck, or so I thought at first, until I saw the Captain standing there looking very stern. Then I quickly realised that my good luck was rapidly turning into bad luck.

Apparently the firemen had been having a bit of a fight and one of them had ended up with a badly gashed head wound, and so he was being brought ashore for hospitalisation – hence the lifeboat.

When the injured fireman had been dealt with, the Captain was free to return to the ship and, glaring at me, wanted to know what I was doing out at this hour. I don't know if he believed my story, but the very next day I was put on night watch for the rest of the stay in Sydney; maybe just as well, because I was broke anyway!

We had been nearly five weeks at the buoys before finally mooring alongside to load. It was a simple procedure, all we had to do was open the hatch and let chutes blast the grain in from big storage silos; it took only three days to load, which is not bad considering that the unions would not allow night work at that particular time; but by the time all our hatches were full and the ship loaded down to her summer Plimsoll marks, we were restless and ready for off.

Quickly we battened down the hatches. With a pilot on board we slowly left the berth with the aid of the two tugs. By the time the tugs were let go and the pilot disembarked we had already stowed the mooring ropes safely below decks, secure against the head seas we could expect as we crossed the Great Australian Bight towards Fremantle, where we were to take on board fuel oil bunkers for the passage home.

Eight

THE GREAT AUSTRALIAN Bight lies just above the roaring forties, so we did not experience really bad storms, but plenty of swell and with our low powered, steam engine, it took us all of nine days to reach Fremantle, with the mainly head winds and sea, there was plenty of heavy spray being shipped so most of our work was inside, overhauling running gear, cleaning and painting storerooms and accommodation.

Our stay in Fremantle was short, less than twenty-four hours, filling all our double-bottom fuel tanks with oil that was cheaper than in many other places in the world. This did not require any work by the apprentices, so we were given half a day off. I decided to go and have a look at Perth, taking a local bus because taxi fares were well beyond my limited means.

It was interesting to view the parched countryside, just to see something different from our watery world. Perth itself was a revelation, perched as it was on the banks of the Swan River. I walked around just looking at the sights and decided to walk across a park on the other side of the river. Walking and listening was about all I could afford at the time; looking at the sights had perhaps taken my concentration off the people, because I bumped into a man going in the other direction. He didn't stop to hear my apology and it was a few minutes before it dawned upon me that I had had my pocket picked – not that there was much in it anyway, but it really was every penny I possessed in the world! Fortunately I had purchased a return ticket and was able to travel back to Fremantle, somewhat poorer but certainly a lot wiser!

The next day we completed bunkers, and cleared the Australian coast setting course for Cape Guardafui on the Horn of Africa.

It was a really fine-weather passage. We had the south-east trade winds pushing us along gently at our maximum speed of ten knots, and then the benefit of the north-east monsoon, so we could maintain our speed and with good visibility were able to make a landfall on Ras Hafun on the Horn of Africa.

Now we were on familiar waters back up the Gulf of Aden, the Red Sea and, finally, the Gulf of Suez. We had excellent weather to wash and paint any steelwork that needed painting, and a good opportunity to have a go at the main deck again, rubbing in the used engine oil and drying it a little by spreading the ashes out of the galley fire.

This was also the passage when we painted the masts and derricks, and then we were heaved up to the topmast to white lead the shrouds and stays, using a mixture of white lead and tallow, and then lowering ourselves down the rigging by slipping the special hitch that secured the bosun's chair which was, in turn, made fast to the rigging by a shackle. It was not for the faint-hearted, swinging around in a little chair nearly one hundred feet in the air, but I quickly became used to it and never feared the heights.

Seven days of lovely hot sunny weather, no heavy seas or spray, time to top up on the suntan! Actually, whenever possible we wore only working shorts – it saved washing!

As usual, we anchored in Suez Bay to take on board the two mooring boats and the searchlights to hang over the bow, but we were mainly interested in our mail from home. Once this was read, we went to have a look at whatever the bum boats were selling; there were always some in attendance.

This being the last port of call before we returned to the UK, we all bartered as best we could to buy wooden carvings, rugs, brassware and anything interesting which was not too expensive, because I always bought something for my parents and sisters – not expensive, certainly, but the best I could do on the very small pay I received.

The Suez Canal was always reckoned to be a good place to take on water, so we always welcomed the water barge just to freshen up the rust-coloured de-aerated water we had left in the afterpeak tank; strangely enough, we never had upset stomachs from the Egyptian water, despite the lack of hygiene ashore.

Pilot on board, anchor aweigh and off we sailed in convoy. We didn't stop to anchor in the Bitter Lakes, as we were northbound, but we did tie up to the canal bank for a few hours when fog descended on us. Then a few hours later we dropped the mooring boats and searchlight, and finally the pilot; then we were well and truly HOMEWARD BOUND!

We had been away six months but the way we behaved you would think it was more like six years. Of course I realise that six months is a long time, but on tramp ships for every new voyage, everyone had to sign on Ship's Articles and this, legally, bound you to that ship until you returned to the UK or a near Continental port, for two years and three months. The longest time I was on one ship was for eighteen months, but all officers and apprentices who served in Bank Line, for example, did two years every trip, because they traded mainly in the Far East and South East Asia and seldom came back to the UK. Of course, this was hard, but we really had no choice; it was not long after the war and National Service was mandatory – unless you chose to go to sea or down the mines – and this continued until about 1955.

The excitement of being homeward bound was very real. There were lots of smiling faces and fooling around because, in the seafaring parlance, we had 'the Channels'; this term was used because most voyages ended by our steaming up the English Channel. Everything was cleaned and painted, all the cabins, alleyways and storerooms, and on the day of arrival, we polished the brass binnacle on the upper navigating bridge ('Monkey Island', we called it), the brass steam whistle and the brass bell on the fo'c's'le head, and that was really hard work because they were not cleaned very often so needed plenty of elbow grease.

The excitement reached fever pitch when we received orders by radio to discharge our cargo at London; prior to that, we had been given 'Land's End for Orders' or, as it was abbreviated by radio, 'LEFO'.

We picked up the pilot off Dover, changed him for a river pilot at Gravesend and were locked into Victoria Docks with the aid of two smoky coal-burning tugs.

The doctor boarded immediately, who then granted us Free

Pratique, and this was the signal for the agent and customs and Immigration officers to board. Within minutes the mail was passed down to the chief steward and sorted into piles for deck, engine and catering departments, to be passed around immediately and read avidly. As it was late in the afternoon, the 'signing off' at the Shipping Office would not be until the next morning.

All the pent-up excitement, built up during the previous days was quickly dispelled when I read my letter from home: my father had suffered a heart attack and was dangerously ill.

My immediate 'boss' was the mate, who promised to see what he could do for me the following day when we 'paid off' at the Shipping Office in Dock Street. There were no phones on board that could be used but I managed to use a payphone outside the dock gates and determined that my father had been instructed to stay in bed for three months and to *stop smoking*!

The next day I was given leave of absence for five days by the mate, so after signing off, I made my sad way to Euston Station and took the next train home to Blackpool.

Nine

WE STEAMED OUT on a murky day in early January, 1949, leaving the wintry smog of London astern. I was still feeling anxious about my father's condition but he was having specialist treatment and was told that, if he took care, he could eventually return to a reasonably active life; and he did just that – living for another twenty-seven years. The routine on board was completely familiar now, although one or two faces had changed. We still had Charlie Gower and 'Dagwood' Turner as second and third apprentices, but Johnny Hughes had left to study for his Second Mate's (Foreign Going) Certificate; his replacement was Chris Barlow, also on his final voyage as senior apprentice.

There was no excitement as we left Britain's cheerless shores, some sadness here and there at leaving loved ones, but once we had cleaned up the ship, we started thinking about our next port – Port Arthur, Texas – to load a full cargo of grain for Calcutta.

Out into the western ocean we steamed, rolling to the mighty swells of the Atlantic. As usual, our work was in the holds, preparing for our next cargo, sweeping out the remains of the previous grain cargo, clearing the bilges by removing the old burlap, lifting the limber boards and clearing out remains of grain and other noisome residues, and finally clearing out the hold wells, which were there to pump out water if the hatches were breached. The wells, or 'hatboxes' as we called them, were covered with burlap to prevent the grain filling the well through the perforated steel covers; this cover was then sealed round the edges with cement.

As the shifting boards were still in place from the previous cargo, there was no need to touch them, and some 'feeders' were used so, all in all, it was a comparatively easy passage for us – except, of course, for the renowned bad weather of winter in the North Atlantic. We pitched and rolled all the way across, not feeling seasick, but definitely queasy. The sun barely shone, making it difficult to obtain a sun sight to fix the vessel's position. But despite that, with skilful navigation, we made our landfall on the Turks and Caicos Islands, no doubt as did Columbus, centuries earlier, transitting the Windward Passage east of Cuba, avoiding the strong east-going Gulf Stream, and made our way through the Caribbean to Port Arthur.

Port Arthur was a small port on Lake Sabine, approached through the port of Galveston and the connecting canal. There was not much to see but I just had to walk ashore and see the sights – we were miles away from anywhere. As I walked along a dusty road from the port, I was the only person in sight, but I turned back after a police car drew up alongside me and asked what I was doing! So much for walking in the not so friendly USA!

Turning back, I came across a mobile pizza outlet. Not having ever sampled such exotic food before and, being ever hungry, I asked for a large pizza. The fat lady serving looked at me dubiously and told me that it was very big; so, thus cautioned, I changed my order to 'medium' – just as well, the 'medium' size would have fed four of us!

Our ship's carpenter, the burly, florid-faced 'Chippy' Kavanagh, knew his way round though; he found a poker school somewhere, and although he didn't clean them out he made enough dollars to see him through the rest of the trip.

Actually I should not have been so surprised at Chippy's luck, because he spent most evenings on the passage in the crew's mess room playing poker for cigarettes – and never lost! Once, after much persuasion, Chippy had played poker with the four apprentices, and we were cleaned out in quick style. We were really watching a professional at work; he remembered the sequence of cards but never cheated. Anyway, after that one and only lesson, he wanted to give us our cigarettes back, but we were men enough to refuse, thinking that we had learned a good lesson at relatively little cost.

It only took us three days to load our full cargo at Port Arthur before we steamed out of Lake Sabine and Galveston, heading for Calcutta.

The first few days we were near enough to the United States to pick up the local radio stations, on medium wave, which was relayed by Sparks through the ship's loudspeaker system, which was a useful hangover from the war, as none of us could afford radios. It was the first time I had heard commercial radio, and some of the jingles were sung around the decks for days afterwards: 'LSMFT – Lucky Strike means fine tobacco!' and 'Use Camay like the lovely ladies do-o-o!' etc.

It was a slow steady passage back across the North Atlantic, but this time we were at a lower latitude, south of the Azores, which meant that the weather was better. As all the holds were full, we spent most days working on deck, cleaning, greasing, overhauling topping lifts, etc. One day, I was helping to free the spare anchor shackle by the use of number one derrick when the runner was let go and shot up to the derrick head, about forty feet above the deck. We could lower the derrick but that was not easy with the ship rolling around, so an ordinary seaman called Geery shinned up the derrick without a second thought, leaned over the derrick head to heave the runner, but slipped with the grease combined with the ship rolling, lost his grip and fell straight down. Unbelievably, a first trip deck boy sprang across and caught him, or at any rate arrested his fall as they both ended up flattened on the hatch top. The quick thinking of that sturdily built deck boy certainly saved Geery's life, and not even a bone broken as they scrambled up on their feet grinning all over their faces.

It was a long passage to Calcutta, via the now familiar waters of the Mediterranean. What was a surprise to me, with my limited experience, was how cold it was in the Mediterranean, bearing in mind that the last time I sailed through was November and it was still comparatively warm. Now, in February, we were feeling the worst of the northern winter, with strong northerly winds all the way through.

As we neared Pantelleria, an island between Sicily and Tunisia, west of Malta, the wind was stronger than ever, strong gale to storm force from the north; the *Indian City* was a low-powered vessel and, without ballast in her double bottom tanks and with no other ballast tanks, she was bobbing around like a cork, her stern raising the propeller clear out of the water at times, causing the steam engine to race, momentarily, until the governor reduced the revs.

There were snow flurries through the night and I remember being on lookout, looking *up* at the lights from Pantelleria; although I was young and inexperienced, I didn't need to be a genius to work out that we were on a lee shore and having difficulty keeping off it.

Captain 'Ginger' Harris had ordered us to fill up the two aftermost double bottoms, numbers four and five, so that the centre plate keel would act as a breakwater and prevent the ballast water rushing all to one side, which would cause us to capsize. The action to run sea water ballast into these two aftermost tanks certainly saved what was a parlous situation from becoming a disaster; the propeller was kept sufficiently in the water long enough to give us the necessary power to claw off the lee shore.

The rest of this long, 54-day passage was broken up by the Suez Canal passage and the ever-welcome letters from home.

To make a landfall at the entrance to the River Hooghly is not easy because the delta of the river is low-lying, and if the weather is hazy it's not easy to take a sun sight because of the uncertain horizon. We did have one weapon in our armoury, so to speak: the depth of water. We didn't have any electric sounding machine (echo sounder) but we did have a sounding machine, right aft, which when the heavy lead weight was released, plunged down to the bottom as the ship steamed slowly ahead. An officer would feel the wire with a metal feeler, so that when it went slack it would be on the bottom, and it was then hauled back up on deck. A tube attached to the lead weight and coated with chromate of mercury helped to give a more or less accurate reading, if held against a boxwood scale. This method was somewhat cumbersome and seldom used, but at times it was useful; in this case, it showed the depth, which, if a single position line of the sun was available, gave a reasonably accurate position from where we could set our course to the known location of the pilot cutter. In really bad visibility, we could use the radio direction finder to give us a bearing of the cutter.

Calcutta is one of the most densely populated areas on earth, as evidenced by the number of bodies floating downriver; but it was the first truly exotic port I had so far visited. Everywhere was teeming with people. All the cargo was discharged by hand, employing hundreds of people, who scooped the grain through their legs using the woven split bamboo scoops, scooping it into large sacks held open by two men who dragged the full hessian sacks to one side, secured the open end of the sack and then piled it on top of others, which were hooked up by our winches, ten sacks to the rope strop; this was then landed on the quay, where two men lifted each sack with billhooks onto the head of another, who was enveloped in the huge heavy sack so that only his spindly legs were visible. The sacks were then carried into a godown, away from potential rain showers.

Every grain of wheat was swept with short split bamboo brooms off the quay; it was a job for women of the lowest caste only.

Across the dock a ship was loading coal. There was an endless stream of labourers climbing up ridged planks with woven bamboo baskets on their heads that were then tipped into the hold of the ship; this work went on night and day such that, in a surprisingly short time, the ship would be fully laden.

On the dockside cranes, numerous vultures were perched. These carrion eaters are the most ugly of all birds; no doubt their profusion indicated that there was plenty of carrion available, but by waiting near a ship, they would always find some garbage dumped in a forty-gallon drum hung over the stern rails which was good feeding for them!

Because labour was so readily available, it was also very cheap. Swarms of men would come on board offering their services whilst we were in port. Always there was help for the cook in the galley, and the dhobi wallahs were everywhere, offering to wash all our clothes; then there would be mess boys willing to scrub and clean mess rooms, alleyways and cabins. On deck there would always be the gully-gully man, who would get up to all sorts of tricks, like swallowing a large stone and regurgitating it. Another would produce a poisonous snake out of one bag and a mongoose from another, holding them apart until enough of us had been persuaded to part with a few annas, but when released, the mongoose always won and snapped the snake's vertebrae behind the head.

The fortune-tellers were everywhere, and they used a lot of persuasive techniques to get you to hear their spiel – they were surprisingly good; I believe that they used hypnotism to elicit information which was later imparted to the astonished subject.

Ideally, the ship needed to be kept clear of all these various categories of labourers and indeed, a full rota of guards were employed to stop them boarding; but nothing was stolen and they didn't seem to cause any harm. No doubt they had bribed the guard in the first place, but that was the way of India: everyone who was employed paid the man above a small portion of their meagre pay.

It was cheap to have clothes tailor-made in Calcutta. There was a 24-hour service. Both Chris Barlow and myself had a set of khaki shirts and shorts made – useful, because they could be worn later as working gear. We both went ashore in our new outfits, fascinated by the sights and sounds of Calcutta as it then was – hordes of rickshaw wallahs, 'sacred' cows meandering across the main thoroughfare of Chowringee, beggars everywhere, many with limbs missing, blinded, or with other terrible afflictions, most in rags, and very many just sleeping and living on the pavements.

Of course, we didn't have much money to spend; but we did enjoy this simple pleasure of looking and absorbing all that was around us. None of us were hard drinkers and, in any case, all the Smith's fleet were 'dry' ships, so we were not led into bad habits, except, of course, smoking, which was the only bad habit we could afford anyway!

We resisted the temptation to hire a rickshaw, so we just walked our legs off in the heat of the Calcutta dry season. It wasn't very exciting, perhaps, but the feeling, the smells, the sights and sounds of Calcutta as it was then are still with me now, fifty years later.

Only a week was needed to discharge all our cargo so we then took the river pilot back down the Hooghly River, lowering the derricks, battening hatches and stowing mooring ropes below decks as we steamed downriver at our full ten knots, plus a strong current speeding us on our way to the pilot cutter.

Ten

IT WAS A STRAIGHT course to Geraldton in Western Australia, just north of Perth, helped with a fair weather monsoon through the Bay of Bengal and not hindered by cyclones. With only a light south-east trade wind to hinder us in the southern part of the Indian Ocean, we made good time – if you could call ten knots good time!

As always, we looked forward to the next port. No one on board had been to Geraldton before, but we knew it to be a small port, mainly for the export of grain. The one thing that was much talked about was the cheap wine – Aussie plonk, as it was known – Penfolds special, as cheap as ninepence (about four new pence) per bottle, so even us impecunious apprentices could afford it.

Three things I remember about Geraldton. The first was the sight of our Norwegian bosun, Thorsten Svenson, waylaying a lady in a shop doorway and serenading her with an imaginary violin. He was quite harmless, just drunk out of his mind, but the lady looked terrified until she managed to squeeze past him and escape down the main street.

The second was the apprentices' visits to the local Seamen's Mission; frankly, we were broke so we could afford nothing else; but, as always, these missions provided a haven for any seaman, of whatever nationality, who had no money or did not know where else to go. It was somewhere to meet; usually tea was served, or soft drinks – definitely no alcoholic beverages!

The vicar in charge was very friendly, taking three of us on Sunday in his car to two remote country church services, miles away from anywhere, but it did give us a look at a very small portion of life in the outback. It seemed to be the highlight of the week, because well-dressed ladies took pleasure in serving us with tea, sandwiches and cakes after the service.

The third thing I remember about Geraldton was that there was a thriving crayfish industry around Rotnest Island, and we talked about 'jumping ship'. This was quite common and an accepted way of emigrating to Australia then, but of course we didn't. Later on I learnt that Chris Barlow had actually emigrated there; whether he went crayfish fishing or not I don't know.

It took us a week to load our cargo and then we were homeward bound again back to England's green and pleasant land – it would be summer – to take some leave after serving nearly thirteen months on my first ship – the *Indian City*.

Although this story is my autobiography, I will just write here of my seeing the name of my first ship appearing again some twenty-five years later. I saw an article in a newspaper referring to the *Indian City*, obviously by this time a newer version. One of the apprentices on board was missing in the middle of the Pacific Ocean. This ocean is so vast, about 9,000 miles across, that one can steam for days without seeing a single ship, yet this lucky apprentice was spotted by a passing ship twenty-four hours after falling overboard. He was rescued and taken safely to Canada.

He must be the luckiest man alive!

Eleven

MY NEXT SHIP WAS the *Orient City*. I joined her at Avonmouth in August 1949; she was discharging grain.

All the ships on which I served during my apprenticeship were very similar, all about 10,000 tons deadweight, all steam reciprocating engines, all with raised fo'c's'le, midships accommodation, engine room and poop accommodation, with five hatches, two on the foredeck, two on the after deck and one in between the midships accommodation and engine room, which was formerly the cross-bunker before the ships were converted from coal burners to oil burners.

The one main disadvantage of converting the ships from coal to oil was that the double bottom tanks could no longer be used for water ballast; accordingly, when the ships were travelling light, if they were low on bunkers, they were very light and used to roll heavily; additionally, as the propeller would be partly out of the water, it would race when the stern lifted, even though there was a governor on the engine to try to prevent this.

Apart from the major problems because of the shortage of ballast, one drawback struck me the moment I boarded the *Orient City*. It was the accommodation. We slept all four of us in the same cabin that opened right out on to the boat deck; there was an adjoining mess room – but no running water. Whenever we wanted a wash or shower, we had to go outside, down the after ladder from the boat deck, and into the bathroom that we shared with the stewards. It was not an ideal arrangement. In fact it was uncomfortable, and during periods of bad weather, intolerable. The 'Peggy' responsible for collecting meals, washing dishes etc. had a difficult job with no water to help. The only way we could manage was to fill a bucket with water from the steward's bathroom, carry it up to the mess room and, during bad weather, lash the bucket to the bench seat; and when we were in very bad weather, lash the bench to the legs of the table! As this chore was done three times per day, it was irksome to say the least.

The comparative discomforts of accommodation were rapidly put to the back of our minds. We had work to do!

We left the locks of Avonmouth on a fine summer's day in August 1949, heading down through the Bristol Channel and passed between Land's End and the Scilly Islands to our next destination – Falmouth; this short trip took us about a day and then we dry-docked in Falmouth for six weeks.

This was my first experience of dry-docking. It was a relaxing time, really; the crew had been paid off and we left the overside and bottom painting to the dockyard workers, but we still had work to do in the holds, to prepare for our next cargo. Together with the mate, we dismantled all the feeders and shifting boards, stowing them all, securely lashed, to the sides of the 'tween decks. It was hard work but we were proud of our strength as we hauled and handled the heavy boards from seven in the morning until five in the evening, and then – ashore! No seaman worth his salt ever stays on board if he can go ashore, and we were no exception to that rule!

As usual, we were hard up, although by now my pay had increased slightly as I was in my second year. Furthermore, I was old enough to legally go into public houses and sample the odd pint or two!

I never really developed the habit of drinking heavily; it was more a learning process rather than a craving. One night I had gone ashore with 'Oscar' Hardcastle, the third apprentice – I was by this time second apprentice – and after a few drinks, we walked slowly back towards the ship, only to be accosted by a 'lady' on the way. She offered us food! Would you believe it, she actually cooked us a mixed grill. It was marvellous, especially after our appetites had been sharpened by the beer. Actually she was obviously lonely, because she gave Oscar and myself a slip of paper with her name and address on it, but we never contacted her again.

No, this is not going to be a salacious account of a seafarer's love life; all I will say on that score is that it was neither better nor worse than most others I sailed with; and surprisingly, to most people, seafarers in those days, anyway, were for the most part celibate. Certainly this was true on 'tramp' ships and tankers, but perhaps less so on the liner trades.

Twelve

WE WERE READY for sea, already we'd been too long in port, which had lost its glamour, as we were always hard up. The crew signed on in October 1949 and we were off again across the western ocean, heading for the Turks and Caicos Islands, where we were to load a full cargo of salt for Japan.

We anchored off the Caicos Islands in an open roadstead; the salt was rowed out, partially assisted by a single sail in each barge, helped along by the wind from the north-east trades. It was similar here to Margherita di Savoia, where salt water was evaporated from small lakes, or salt pans, then dug out bagged and landed on to the barges. Once alongside, the ship's derricks were used to haul it on top of the hatches, the sacks were opened and the contents tipped down into the hold.

Oscar and I were oiling winches, and the chief was happy as he puffed at his pipe to see the oil streaming off the winches and down into the scuppers. To keep him puffing away happily, we used to put a drop or two of the lubricating oil in his tobacco tin that he left on the hatch, as we passed by – evil-minded apprentices!

Dressed only in working shorts and shoes, we relished the hot sun on our backs, but apart from our work there was not a great deal to do in our spare time. We could see the fish in the clear waters, just below us: sharks, devilfish and many others. We caught a couple of small sharks and made sharkskin belts and I made a sheath for my deck knife, but there was nothing ashore. The Caicos Islands had virtually no habitation that we could see – just a flat, sandy coral-strewn vista.

To make life a bit more exciting, I decided to make a canoe. I had no idea how to make one, no one to show me or guide me, but that was the way it was at that time; one used one's own initiative.

I found a piece of 4x4 in the 'tween decks; it was slightly bent, but, beggars can't be choosers; it was suitable, I thought, to be the keel. We had an old saw used to build feeders and a hammer, and with these basic tools I cut two slots in the 'keel' and fitted two boards as 'bulkheads'. Next I fitted a stem and stern post, nailed these to the 'bulkheads' with battens and then covered the whole with an old piece of canvas, nailing a rubbing strake along the keel and then coating it all with two coats of bitumastic. Believe it or not, it actually looked like a canoe.

Within two days, the whole job was completed, the bitumastic dried and ready for the test! I lashed a shifting board across the awning spars on the boat deck, with a tail-end block lashed at the end and a gantline rove through and then, using a cargo strop, slung the canoe over the water, lowered it down. To our delight, it actually floated – and, what was more important – did not leak!

I secured a painter to the stem post and made a couple of paddles, and then Oscar and I set out to explore the islands.

We knelt on two boards that protected the outer canvas covering and found that, by crouching down, we made the canoe stable and quite manoeuvrable. We could paddle right into the harbour waters and on to the white sandy beaches.

We found plenty of huge, colourful conch shells, and the best of these we piled into our canoe; and on later trips we were able to collect sponges that we used in the shower, but we never really managed to rid the sponges of their grit, which clung to them no matter what we did.

The canoe was a diversion, a bit of fun, and I heard later, was used for two years on the *Orient City*, long after I had left, before it was loosely secured to the gangway in New York's East River and drifted away.

After about three weeks, we had exhausted the stock of dried salt at the Caicos Islands, so we weighed anchor and steamed round to the nearby Turks Islands, one dark moonless night. We took the population of the Caicos Islands with us – about one hundred, if memory serves me right, men and women. They were all sat around number five hatch; difficult to see because of the blackness of their skins, only their eyes and teeth flashing white in the darkness.

One of the crew – Paddy – had managed to buy some of the local rum, which had inspired him to think that he was a latter-day Fred Astaire, and he started to tap dance on top of some empty oil drums, stowed by the mast house. The islanders loved it and were clapping and shouting encouragement, when Paddy's enthusiasm got the better of him and he slipped heavily between the wobbly oil drums – he was quite badly hurt.

That was not the end of the Paddy saga. He was carted off to our two-berth 'hospital' where a doctor from Grand Turk pronounced that he was suffering from exhaustion and malnutrition! The exhaustion bit I could understand – too much rum, too much hot sun and not enough water; but the food on board was not that bad to make him undernourished. He was supposed to rest in hospital and be fed lots of food, but we forgot all about him and I remember as I was oiling number three winches a couple of days later, Paddy burst out of the hospital, thoroughly rested, sober and shouting, 'The bastards, they forgot to feed me!' So all was back to normal. Paddy gorged himself back in the crew mess room, and decided he was better working than awaiting 'treatment' in our 'hospital'.

Once anchored off Grand Turk, we had to have a pilot on board because of a hurricane nearby. He slept in the hospital, now vacated by Paddy.

Within a few days, we had to weigh anchor and steam away from the islands, to keep clear of the hurricane that was passing too close for comfort; but within three days, we returned to our anchorage, keeping the pilot on board in case the hurricane recurred.

The crew had managed to purchase bottles of the local rum by some means or other. The apprentices were not included in whatever was going on. Nobody had any money because no sub had been given, and our supplies of cigarettes had long run out.

Eventually, following some kind of turmoil outside the hospital, which resulted in the pilot 'abandoning ship'; we found out what had been going on. Apparently the chief steward had noted that our stock of potatoes – stowed below decks in one of the coal bunker side pockets – was depleted. The mate and the

Captain carried out an investigation and it was discovered that the crew had been selling sacks of potatoes for rum! Of course this was immediately stopped, but the actual culprits were never discovered.

Some of the crew, crazed with rum, went round everyone on board to try and determine who was the 'squealer' – who had told the chief steward about the potato scam! They never did find out. It was probably one of the stewards, but I did learn that they had crept into the hospital one dark night and held a knife at the pilot's throat whilst trying to determine if he was the 'squealer'!

Apparently the pilot was terrified; hence his rapid departure the following morning.

There was another source of rum, as I was to find out, quite by accident. As explained earlier, we had nothing to drink except lukewarm, rust-coloured water (boiled, it made lousy tea!). There were no cans or bottled drinks, no cold water fountain etc., but we were used to it and didn't complain. After all, it was a long time ago, and the average house in Britain did not possess a refrigerator, and bottled drinks were only for birthday parties.

I had started up a friendship with the second cook, George Smith. He was a quiet Geordie who just got on with his work, usually peeling potatoes or baking bread, without any fuss. One night he invited me to his cabin to sample some punch he had made; there was a big stainless steel bowl used for mixing dough, which he had filled with the punch. At that stage in my life, I did not know what punch was, but I was always thirsty, working out in the hot sun all day, and George produced this gorgeous-looking bowl full of iced punch, with slices of orange, and ice cubes floating on top. Of course, George had daily access to the large, walk-in main refrigerator, which was stacked up with nine months' supply of meat, so cooling something to drink was no problem.

I tasted a glassful of this liquid; it was like nectar of the gods! Dehydrated after my day in the sun, I couldn't get enough of it; we drank glass after glass – and that was the last I remember until I woke at six the next morning still on George's settee, whilst he had turned-to in the galley! What woke me was not a hangover, surprisingly, but the rustle of cockroaches as they crawled out of my mouth! Ugh!

To this day I squirm when I think of it. All ships were infested with cockroaches, but because for the first time in my life I had drunk too much, which, combined with my state of dehydration had knocked me out, I can't have moved all night; but whether it was the rum or the cockroaches, I have never drunk rum from that day to this!

Where did George get the rum? I asked myself. Surely he would not be selling ship's stock of food? No, he was trading pork fat, which the locals loved, for rum. Not only that, I learnt that the quiet George had also made an arrangement with the shore-side nightwatchman, that he would trade pork fat for his wife's favours! Well, the islanders were friendly, and they really did like pork fat!

One other thing has stuck in my mind, whenever I recollect our sojourn in the Turks and Caicos Islands. I paddled over to one of the islands and decided to walk some way across to see if there was any habitation, eventually I did find one hut, but what surprised me then was to see a huge sign on the side of it advertising Coca-Cola! This was in 1949, not a time when one expected advertising to have spread to such a remote part of the world; and, not only that, there was not a soul in sight to read it, only me!

After six weeks, you can well imagine that our stay at the islands had palled. We were more than ready for the sea again and when we weighed anchor, heading for Panama, we were as happy as schoolboys at holiday time.

Down came the derricks, hatches were secured and battened, running gear stowed away, all vestiges of the cargo and shore-side activities washed away with our saltwater hoses, and deck brooms used as long-handled scrubbing brushes – it was good to be at sea again.

Thirteen

WE WERE HEADING now through the Caribbean bound for the Panama Canal. The canal was much talked about because, unlike the Suez Canal, which was, in basic terms, a ditch connecting the Red Sea to the Mediterranean, the Panama Canal had to cope with different heights, and there were three sets of locks to be negotiated, as it was built in sections – hailed as a great feat of engineering when it was built around 1914.

Already looking forward to mail that we had not received for nearly two months, we arrived at Panama and anchored to take on board bunkers and, of course, receive mail.

The Americans controlled the Panama Canal and they provided all the pilots and officials so, as one would expect, it was efficiently run. In a matter of hours, we had completed the formalities, weighed anchor and proceeded into the locks at Panama, aided by a tug.

The ships were positioned in the locks by four 'mules' as they were called – engines on tracks, one connected to each corner of the ship by flexible steel wire hawsers which were kept under tension as the water poured in or out of the locks at a tremendous rate. The forty nautical miles of canal were a pleasant surprise; we steamed through jungle on both sides, such a variation from the sand of the Suez Canal or the more usual expanses of featureless sea that was our natural environment.

It took us about twelve hours to transit the canal, time for us to trade with a small boat, a full stand of bananas for some of our coffee grain – which we never drank because of the water, which made it taste like dishwater when made into coffee! But we really relished those bananas; we didn't have much fresh fruit, and bananas were never on the menu because they didn't keep long enough.

Now we were heading across the vastness of the Pacific to Moji, on the southern tip of Honshu. The Pacific was so named by Vasco de Balboa, who discovered it in 1514 and, of course, it did look like its name – 'Pacific' – and indeed for most of its vastness the weather is fine. However, the northern part is notorious for its typhoon winds, which can reach 280 k.p.h. Luckily on this particular passage, the weather was fine, virtually all the way – all fifty days of it! The ocean seemed never ending, not another ship in sight, perhaps two only, sighted at a distance, the whole way across.

There was always a little bit of a buzz around the ship when the lights of another ship were sighted at night; out would come the Aldis lamp, and flashing the other ship with 'AA' – 'AA' – the call sign, answered by 'T' and then the message, in Morse code: 'What ship, where bound?' Back would come the reply, '*King Neptune*, Kobe to London.'

If the ship was known to us, for example; if it was one of our own company ships, we would ask about the people on board; or if there was bad weather around, we would ask about the weather; or if bound for Australia, we would ask about the delays due to strikes, etc. This form of communication by Aldis lamp and Morse was the norm, all ships used it because there was no VHF radio or satellite communication then. We did have short and medium-wave radio, operated by Sparks but he would be mainly listening to the traffic lists to see if our call sign was on the list with a message from the owners or agents at the next port. The Captain would also send his ETA at the next port and request various services and supplies from the agent.

Of course on long passages we had the opportunity for a really good maintenance programme, so that was a plus, as far as the mate was concerned; but as far as the apprentices and crew were concerned, it gave us the opportunity to complain (quietly!) about the food – although, actually, it was not too bad. We had three meals per day, which we ate very rapidly because we were always hungry. We also had a ration of bread; if I remember rightly, it was two loaves per week. They did not last long. For one thing, the ration of butter was so small, and most of the time it was so hot that the weekly supply of butter had melted by the time we had carried it from the pantry to our own mess room; accordingly we ate the bread and butter on the one day only; for the rest of the week it was dry bread with our meal. We did not have anything other than the daily issued meals – no luxuries such as biscuits, cake or cheese. Perhaps, in retrospect, this was good for us; we didn't have an ounce of fat on any of us and we were always in good health.

However, perhaps because the long passage had caused us to grumble more than usual and dry bread was not what we wanted to eat, I decided to ask the chief steward for some cheese, because we knew that the officers were eating such a luxury – daily – in the saloon! I marched with boldness towards the chief steward's cabin, but sheered off before reaching it, decided instead to go with less boldness to the pantry door and ask the second steward if we could have some cheese.

The second steward was in charge of the pantry and not enthusiastic about giving extra stores away, so he bellowed, 'Chief, the apprentices want cheese!' I felt like Oliver Twist asking for more! I did hear the chief steward's reply though, and it was not printable! I slunk back to our mess room, 'cheeseless', and duly put in my place by the stewards. After all, we apprentices were the lowest form of shipboard life, weren't we?

We were more than usually excited to reach Japan. It was almost two months since we left the Turks and Caicos Islands, so whatever was on offer in Japan would be more than welcome!

We moved to a buoy and started discharging our salt cargo right away – no strikes here! The agent had brought the mail and the money. We queued up for our sub, and those who were not on watch took the first boat ashore. I was one of the lucky ones. My duty was oiling winches in the daytime only for this port, so I had every night off, as we worked twelve-hour shifts, six to six.

I hadn't a clue where to go or what to do. Although we had been paid, I didn't have much money, and all I could think of was buying some tea sets to take home for my mother and sisters. These were very delicate and packed in straw-packed wooden cases which were brought to the ship for us – they only cost £1 each, then!

I decided to have a haircut; this was easy because the Japanese displayed a white and red pole outside the little wooden shop where they cut hair; what I did not anticipate was that the hair was cut by a girl! This was certainly different; every barber in UK at that time was a man, and every haircut was the same – short back and sides!

Having decided to have my hair cut, I thought it would be a bit discourteous to turn and run when I saw a girl wielding scissors! She smiled, pointed me to the chair. '*Dozo*,' she said, meaning, 'please'. I have never liked women cutting hair ever since that day; they snip with little scissors and mess around endlessly, and whereas in England at that time it would take about ten minutes, in Japan it took forty minutes! It was not so much the cutting of hair bit by bit that irritated me, but the shaving of my forehead! Now I ask you, who grows hairs on their forehead! I was somewhat mollified by the hot towel placed on my face and the massage of my neck and shoulders, but certainly glad to be out of the door when the ordeal was over.

I made my way back to the area where the launches were, stopping at another little wooden building advertising beer in English; from the street, I could see one or two familiar faces inside. It was a gathering of six of the crew and junior engineers just enjoying a beer or two at the 'First and Last' that is, the first pub outside the dock gates, which often turned out to be the last!

It was evening and we enjoyed our drinks, poured in typical fashion by the Japanese bar girls, who would top up every glass the moment even a sip was taken, crying, '*Hai, dozo!*' – 'Yes; please.' We were all enjoying this attention – until, that is, the American Military Police came in. It was then and only then that we found out that (a) this area was out of bounds to foreigners, and (b) there was a curfew, and we were out after hours!

We were herded out on to the street; one of our number, a tough Australian AB called, predictably, Ossie, also predictably started to remonstrate with the large-sized American MPs, one of whom, weighing about 150 kilos, gave Ossie a good punch on the jaw, sending him sprawling to the ground. The rest of the crew scattered, and I hadn't a clue where to go; only by the fortuitous intervention by one of the bar girls was I able to find my way back to a launch which would take me back to the ship. Actually it was a sampan, propelled by one oarsman standing up in the stern and pulling the single oar from side to side.

I only went ashore twice in Moji because all my money (it wasn't much) was spent either at the barber's or on buying presents to take home, but it was a pleasant interlude to see Japan as it then was. All the buildings were low-rise and built of lightweight wood with opaque paper over the windows and sliding doors, except for the business premises, which would have glazed windows.

There were no flushing toilets, only the hole in the ground type, which were dug out at regular intervals and the contents taken out into the countryside and spread over the ground to fertilise the crops. This meant that we did not normally eat ashore in Japan!

Despite the lack of flushing toilets, the Japanese themselves were very clean, bathing every day and wearing clean clothes every day. I also found them to be very friendly, polite and generous; they loved giving small gifts or 'presentos'.

The Japanese worked night and day discharging our salt cargo, and in less than a week it was all finished.

Once again we lowered the derricks, loosely covered the hatches, because we were going to work in the holds; we let go the buoys, heading out to sea, stowing and securing everything, and sailed back out into the Pacific.

Fourteen

WE WERE HEADING for Vancouver in Canada to load a cargo of grain for UK; on passage we would be working to clean all the holds of the remains of the salt cargo and, of course, fit all the steel uprights, shifting boards and feeders to pass survey for the grain cargo.

As she was in light ship condition, we would not expect to ship heavy seas because without ballast, we would just bob around like a cork, instead of being plunged beneath any heavy seas we may encounter. Accordingly, to facilitate our work down below, the hatch boards were not fitted, and only one tarpaulin was loosely wedged along the steel batten to keep the wind from blowing it away.

The third night out from Japan, an unusual event happened. I had been on watch. I was first wheel, and as I changed over at 10 p.m. – four bells; I remember making the bells, ding-ding, ding-ding, as I left the bridge, but by the time I had reached our accommodation, the wind was already blowing gale force.

It was unusual because any bad weather is usually forecast, and if it is not, the officer on watch will notice a rapid falling of the barometer, or if the storm is of great intensity, then its approach would be heralded by an increase in the height and length of the swell, at right angles to the storm centre.

In this particular case, the only reason we could come up with for such a storm of such intensity to come, virtually out of nowhere, was that it must be a typhoon, spawned in the doldrums, which tracked in a north-westerly direction, as they normally do before either (a) dissipating over mainland China, or (b) recurving up the Sea of Japan, speeding up and intensifying back out into the Northern Pacific.

I don't know what Beaufort force it was, but it was the only time, in all my years at sea, when all the sailors and apprentices were called out on deck for the safety of the ship.

The wind was on the port beam, screaming and howling through the rigging, the tops of the waves being whipped off and flung horizontally across the hatches to disappear into the blackness of the night.

All the tarpaulins were ripped off, and some of the very heavy iron-bound hatch boards were whisked off the hatch tops and hurled like match-sticks in to the night.

The apprentices were ordered to secure number two hatch; I ordered our junior apprentice, 'Chunky' Jones, to go to the fo'c's'le and bring back a gantline with which to lash the hatches because I was busy with something else. 'I can't,' he said, 'I'm frightened!' Poor Chunky... maybe he didn't realise that we were all frightened, but there was still a job to do. I went forward with him, and we crouched in the lee of the hatches to avoid flying hatch boards and being blown overboard!

We brought the gantlines back and lashed the remaining hatch boards in place by zigzagging the lashing across the hatch. We moved on all fours, crouching in the lee of the hatches to the saloon, where all the crew were sitting around on the deck, dead tired, soaking wet, but knowing that the ship was safe, as a pale dawn filtered through the saloon port holes. The mate, Johnny Hughes' elder brother, dished out a double tot of rum to all hands; although I had no fondness for rum, at that particular time I was glad of anything!

When daylight came, we were able to look out on to the main deck and take stock of the 'damage' – there wasn't any! The storm, although very intense, had ripped off the tarpaulins and some of the hatch boards, all of which had been caught by the lee rails, so that nothing was lost overboard; we were able to go back on deck, replace the hatch boards and re-cover the hatches with tarpaulins before wedging the battens.

It was a longish passage to Vancouver – three weeks, at our leisurely speed of around nine knots – but when we approached the port, the spectacle was breathtaking. The Rockies dominated the vista; all covered in pine trees and snow everywhere, just like a Christmas card.

For the first time I was to experience the kind of heating the North Americans experienced. All the shops and offices were heated to such a high temperature as to be suffocating! I bought a book in one of the stores and then, in company with Oscar, visited an all-day diner for something to eat. We stuffed ourselves with doughnuts, they were absolutely mouth-watering, tasting all the better because we never had such luxuries on board.

Then, as now, Vancouver was a modern city and seemed very prosperous, we just looked wide-eyed at everything. I have been back recently, and it is still enjoying prosperity – perhaps having a Chinese mayor has something to do with it!

We only loaded part cargo and then moved to New Westminster City to top up before leaving the scenic environment of British Columbia, heading south again for Panama and then to our discharge port of Avonmouth, in the Bristol Channel. After discharging we steamed up to Barry in South Wales, where our ship was to load a full cargo of coal for Argentina; but I left then on 25th March 1950, for a spell of home leave.

The day before I left, I had my 'revenge' on the chief steward who thought that giving us apprentices such luxuries as cheese and biscuits would be akin to sacrilege. I was instructed by the mate to go into that holy of holies, the steward's store, beneath the pantry, to sew up two sacks of flour that had gone bad; the reason for this was so that one of our superintendents could take the flour with him to feed to the pigs on his farm. No problem for me, it was an easy job, nice and warm and dry – then I espied a bolted steel door and realised that this opened into the 'tween deck… opportunity knocks infrequently in an apprentice's life!

During the morning smoko, I planned with the rest of the apprentices what we could do with this golden opportunity. Then, with our plans laid, I returned to my sewing in the steward's store. A few moments later, there was a gentle tapping at the steel door, within seconds, the bolts were drawn and the steel doors, although stiff, were prised open – wide enough for me to pass through the four tins of biscuits stacked on a shelf in the store!

We feasted on biscuits as though we had not been fed for months, and by the next day they were all gone! As I was leaving the ship to go on leave, an irate chief steward was waving a meat cleaver out of the pantry door threatening to 'part 'is 'air in the middle' if he found the thief!

Fifteen

MY SPELL OF LEAVE extended to four months because I tore my cartilage playing football; although I was fit in the arms and chest, my legs were no longer up to playing football!

I joined the *Bradburn* at Birkenhead in July 1950. She was a pre-war ship, one of the few to escape the U-boats during the war. She was similar to the other ships in appearance, but of course much older. One thing in her favour, though, she had good accommodation, and I had a cabin all to myself – real luxury.

She was in dry dock at Birkenhead, having her annual survey by Lloyd's and the usual bottom scrape and paint, with anti-fouling below the water line to keep the weed and barnacles at bay. These creatures, if they were allowed to grow, greatly reduced the speed – not that it was fast to start with!

This was the first time I had seen a woman on board ship; the Captain was allowed to take his wife, and as they did not have any children to consider Captain Fisher was always accompanied by his wife – not that it made any difference to us because she kept strictly to their own accommodation and didn't interfere at all with the running of the ship.

From Birkenhead, we steamed down to Barry to load a full cargo of coal for Buenos Aires, Argentina. Loading coal was a messy business; the rail trucks were lifted into the air then tipped into a chute that poured it into the different holds, with clouds of coal dust accompanying each truck-load.

There was no way we could keep clean. All the accommodation, all our clothes and bodies were black with coal dust, so it was a great relief when the last hold was full and everything battened down. We started washing down whilst we awaited the pilot's arrival.

This was the job sailors like best, washing the ship clean after loading was finished; we were no exception. The apprentices were given the midships house to wash and scrub from top to bottom. We were, as always, exuberant, jumping down from one deck to the next, grabbing handrails but scorning ladders – and this was my undoing! I landed on my right leg, still weakened from my cartilage problem, and the searing pain let me know that I had torn it again; the pain was so severe, I let out an involuntary scream as I lay writhing on the wet deck, right outside the Captain's door!

Captain Fisher came out to see what all the commotion was about, saw me writhing in agony and helped drag me into his day room. Despite my coal-dirty, sodden self, he seated me in his plush armchair. It was a comic situation, really, because the end of the hose was flailing about on the bridge as I was no longer holding it and eventually, it wedged itself under a mushroom ventilator, just above deck level, which helped to ventilate the Captain's day room, and as I sat there water started pouring in through the deck head ventilation. Both the Captain and his wife were running this way and that, trying to comfort me and at the same time stop the water pouring in from the deckhead.

Eventually, order was restored, and he turned his attention to me, trying to determine what had happened. I explained about the cartilage and he was adamant that I would have to pay off. I pleaded with him to let me stay because I knew that in order for me to complete the requisite sea time of three years and five months during my four years, I could not afford any more time off. I assured him that no matter what I would not be any trouble whatsoever, and that whilst my knee was healing again, I would be able to steer, even if I could not clamber about and do the things one was normally expected to do.

I must have been persuasive, for he let me stay; partly I suppose, because it might have delayed the ship slightly, as the pilot was just boarding. Anyway, I was eternally grateful to him. The Captain must have had second thoughts as he helped me out of his cabin – I could not put any weight on my leg.

Somehow, I managed to clamber down to see the chief steward and had him bandage my knee really tight, so to the Captain's surprise, I re-appeared on the bridge as we were leaving the berth with the aid of tugs, just in time to take my watch at the wheel.

Steering a ship was not normally too hard a job because we only did a two-hour 'trick' at the wheel, but as I couldn't do any other kind of work, my 'trick' had been extended to a full watch – four hours! Normally, ships were steered by hydraulic operation of the steam steering gear, but as this was an old ship, she was equipped with a rod and chain steering mechanism, which meant that it had to be pulled from side to side, using some muscle power to overcome the friction of all the cogs and bearings in the total system, about 80 metres long. No stool or seat of any kind was ever provided, so that my watch of four hours was spent on one leg. Heaving the wheel from side to side, especially when the ship was rolling, as she was most of the time, was tough work; but I was determined not to give in and I managed to keep it up for three months until my knee had healed enough for me to resume near normal duties. Initially, I had to crawl along alleyways up to the bridge, but now I could stand upright, and when there was work in the holds later on, I was strong enough to climb up and down the hold ladders, using my arms and one leg.

I was shipmates this trip with Terry Dancy. We got along fine; and also Vernon 'Bill' Bailey, who was senior apprentice. In fact, I suppose all the apprentices got along together on all the ships I served because, frankly, we were literally in the same boat, and so we learned quickly how to get along together. For example, it wouldn't do for anyone to make a noise during someone's watch below, because we always worked twenty-four hours. The ship never stopped at sea, and we even worked round the clock in most ports.

It was a long passage down to Buenos Aires, or BA as we called it, but it was mainly fine weather and with good accommodation we found nothing to complain about; but naturally, we always had a grouse about the food – primarily that there wasn't enough!

Nearly a month after leaving Barry, we picked up the pilot to take us up the River Plate and then the harbour pilot into *Dique Sud*, or South Dock, where we discharged our full cargo of coal, using shore cranes.

It took us two weeks to discharge the coal, so we had plenty of time for sightseeing. I could walk again with a bit of a limp, but a bus ran from outside the dock to the main street of Corrientes, so that was very convenient – and not too expensive. Usually I would go ashore with Terry Dancy; I remember having a couple of beers in one bar and hearing the waiter sing. It was wonderful; he was a former opera singer.

It was obvious from the posters, and what we could glean from the newspapers and the people who spoke English, that Eva Peron was the darling of the people. This was perhaps the reason why, when I saw the musical *Evita* in London many years later, it was so meaningful.

As always, money was a problem, so I quickly found my way to the Seamen's Mission, which was very active there; I remember that they had regular boxing matches amongst the seafaring community, but my leg was still not up to such strenuous activity... well, that's my excuse!

There was another free show, it was by radio to the USA in English, of course, and for the first time, I realised that a lot of the laughter on Commercial Radio was 'on demand' – that is, the producer would hold up a card reading 'APPLAUSE' and frantically jump up and down until he had heard enough.

When all the coal was discharged, we had to sweep the whole ship thoroughly, because our next cargo was grain, which we were to load further upriver at San Lorenzo.

Of course, it was dirty work. The more we swept, the more the dust rose, and then we had to heave it up on deck and then on to lorries on the quayside. Once the 'tween decks and lower holds were swept clean, we then had to pressure hose them to wash every last particle of coal from the sides and frames across the tank top and into the 'hatboxes' at the after end of the hatch. Then the engineers would pump the water out into the dock, dirty though it was.

When all the holds were cleaned, we hauled out the steel uprights which were rigged along the centre line as usual, but only slotted three metres of shifting boards, as the amount of loose grain only came to that height. The rest of the grain was loaded in bags, as this eliminated the chances of the grain shifting in bad weather.

All the grain was loaded at San Lorenzo, a small town just north of Rosario. As the berth was a long way out of town, no sub was given and we didn't go ashore.

Altogether we were a month in Argentina, and ready to put to sea again for the longest of long passages, about five weeks to Bombay.

Sixteen

WE HEADED DUE east, just north of the roaring forties and near enough to feel the huge swells developed in the Southern Ocean; but as all the winds, sea and swell were from the westerly direction, they didn't hold us back, and in fact helped us to maintain our top speed of ten knots. The south-west monsoon was still strong in the northern Indian Ocean and Arabian Sea, but, again it was helpful, as it pushed us along steadily. The only complaint we had was that the weather was humid, with mediocre visibility much of the way, but that did not stop us singing happily as we were working – 'From BA to Bombay is a hell of a way' – or words to that effect!

Bombay was reminiscent of Calcutta: hot, dirty, noisy, with people sleeping out on the pavements. Dancy and I went ashore, this time feeling more affluent, and we hired a horse-drawn gharry. I don't know if our instructions to the driver were properly understood, because we had told him to take us round the main city area for about an hour – that was all we could afford – and then back to the ship. We ended up in a street with large cages, like huge birdcages, hanging from the second floor of the houses on both sides of the street – they were used to harbour prostitutes, who thrust out their emaciated arms to all the passers-by. By this time, I suppose we could count ourselves 'men of the world'. At least, we had travelled all round it, but both Dancy and I found the scene disgusting and we were glad to find safer and less disquieting vistas through the city, with its colonial buildings still intact.

Discharging was completed within seven days and we headed out to sea, this time back to Geraldton in Western Australia, to load a full cargo of grain for Madras.

There were two recollections of our second visit to Geraldton. The first was the medical inspection on arrival. Usually, the port health officials asked the Captain to fill in a form asserting that there were no communicable diseases on board; but this time, the doctor had every one of the officers and crew on deck in a large circle as he went round looking every one of us in the face; if I remember rightly, there had been an outbreak of typhus in India recently, and perhaps he was looking for signs of that. In any case, we were always having vaccinations for one thing or another at most ports – smallpox, cholera, typhus, yellow fever – and had to carry the certificates with us.

The second incident concerned our bosun; he was a tall, burly man, who had been everywhere, done everything. He had helped to build the Panama Canal in his youth, and been in the Hong Kong Police and the Irish Guards, but now he was our bosun, who brooked no nonsense from the crew and was much respected by all. However, shortly after our arrival in Geraldton, he disappeared.

It was not unusual for sailors to 'jump ship' in Aussie, in fact it was half expected, but this was normally associated with the younger element and usually occurred just before the ship sailed, not when it first arrived.

We carried on with our loading and one or two trips to the Seamen's Mission, the local shops and a pub or two, and thought nothing more about the bosun until we were due to sail ten days later. Then, who should appear, climbing up the gangway, jacket over his shoulder, but our erstwhile bosun.

The mate had words with him once we were at sea and clear of Geraldton, heading for Madras, India, in the Bay of Bengal. Very quickly we found out the reason for his disappearance and dramatic reappearance – he had been to see his wife! No one had any idea that he was married, as many older sailors were not, but our bosun was one of life's enigmatic characters: tough as teak and a man unto himself.

Seventeen

WE WERE INTO the north-east monsoon by now, so we had a fine-weather passage all the way to Madras. The Admiralty Pilot Book had warned us of the climate to be expected in Madras – three months hot, and nine months hotter! And so it proved to be.

By now, I was familiar with the Indian scene, the gully-gully men, dhobi wallahs, the beggars, the poverty, vultures, and large cockroaches known as Bombay Tigers; the pavements strewn with people sleeping out in the open. We had seen enough, and ended up in the Seamen's Club or Mission, where it was clean and comparatively cool; no air conditioning, of course, but slow-moving ceiling fans stirred the air behind the bamboo blinds.

I have never been a heavy drinker, but India, at that time, enforced some kind of prohibition, the only way we could buy a cool beer was in the Seamen's Club, and then we were rationed to two bottles per man. Actually it was enough, we enjoyed the cool, the company of other seafarers and, in fact, I met a lad I knew from my days in the Blackpool Sea Cadets. It was a change of environment, a safe haven for those of us who had little money and no local contacts.

I remember buying one or two small presents for my sisters and my mother, haggling because we needed to! But at least had something to show for our ten days alongside in one of the hottest ports on earth.

We headed out into the comparative cool of the Bay of Bengal, which was very welcome, this time heading for Aden, where we were to load a full cargo of salt for Japan.

The passage only took nine days, but they were nine very busy days because we had to dismantle all the shifting boards and feeders then stow and lash them in the 'tween decks, sweep the holds and then, joy of joys, spray all the steel with limewash.

We had to work hard to complete everything so that the ship

was ready to receive her cargo, but we didn't mind because the weather was fine and we were earning overtime every day and especially at weekends.

Once at Aden, we could relax a little, as the loading took ten days. Now for the first time I was able to have a look round the shops at Aden, especially developed to entice the travellers ashore from the numerous passenger ships which called there for bunkers both outwards and homeward bound. Not only were the oil bunkers cheaper than anywhere else at that time, but the stop also provided something of interest for the passengers to look forward to and, in fact, it was the main source of revenue for the country.

During our ten days moored to the buoy off Steamer Point, we had time to paint the ship over the side so that by the time we sailed she looked like new; her black topside shining and her name freshly painted in white.

We knew that we had a twenty-six-day passage ahead of us, mainly in fine weather, ideal for deck maintenance and the usual chores of 'Peggy' – scrubbing out, dhobi and our pet hate – studying!

By this time, I had completed more than half of my correspondence course and had begun to receive the papers back from Head Office, duly marked in red where I had been below standard! The Captain was not very pleased with me, but it did spur me on to greater efforts with no overtime being worked and no bad weather to use as an excuse!

Eighteen

WE WERE HEADING now for Hakodate at the southern tip of Hokkaido, Japan's northernmost island. None of us had given much thought to the weather in that part of Japan; it was February, so we knew that it would be winter, but we had given no thought to the fact that Hakodate was out of the influence of the warming Japan current, the Kuro-shio, so we were not prepared at all for the intense cold as we slowly steered up to the buoy in the sheltered waters of Hakodate Harbour.

To facilitate shackling the anchor cable to the buoy, we had knocked out the joining link of the anchor cable and then led the heavy anchor chain through the Panama fairlead right in the bow, and this was then hove out to the buoy, to which it was shackled, so that we were securely moored – or so we thought, but more of that later.

I said it was cold. It was freezing; the wind blew from the mountains in the north, from around Sapporo, where they sometimes have winter sports; even the sea froze!

The tugs and barges managed to break the ice so that we could keep discharging the salt but it was so cold that our saltwater sanitary tanks froze and we even had difficulty flushing toilets, as the non-return valves were freezing.

Despite the intense cold I remember a barge owner washing himself down from a bucket of fresh water on the deck of his barge alongside: whilst I always believed in keeping clean, that was absolutely madness, but he smiled up at us as we gazed down at him, stripped to the waist, as he completed his ablutions with icy water.

By now I had saved up enough money to make going ashore worthwhile, so the morning after arrival, a group of us went ashore with the agent to sample the sights of Hakodate, and to see if there were souvenirs worth buying to take home.

I will mention the cold again – it was freezing, there was ice everywhere. The women pulled little sledges behind them on the icy pavements and we, muffled though we were, really felt the chilly blast from the north. Actually I did find one or two souvenirs to buy. I still have the silver cigarette case I bought (sensibly, I stopped smoking shortly afterwards!), and a lighter shaped like a small revolver and a few trinkets to take home.

As the agent's boat would not be returning to the ship for a few hours, I found a small bar-cum-restaurant (they were all small) which provided some respite from the cold; on sliding back the paper-covered light wooden lattice door, the inside did not promise much, just a couple of very low tables in the centre, about 20 cm off the tatami matting. Taking off my shoes at the door, I was given open slippers to wear and then sat down at the table, feet into the well beneath, which contained an *habachi*, or charcoal burning pot. If this was supposed to give out heat, it was a waste of time, for despite a tablecloth which covered one's thighs, my feet gradually froze, and the only thing warm was the hot *sake*, or rice wine, they poured for me.

It did make me realise how hardy the Japanese people are. All the buildings then were low-rise, thin wooden structures with opaque paper or thin glass over the windows and doors, and no heating whatsoever inside, except for the *habachi*, which really was useless. Most of the food was served cold, and the minimal cooking was carried out over a charcoal stove. Life was very primitive in Japan at that time!

Back on board, it was, of course, freezing. Fortunately, we had steam-heated radiators in the accommodation, so we were warm inside, but on deck there was ice everywhere. We had to keep the steam winches moving all the time to prevent any part of them freezing and to prevent the condensed water in the steam exhaust pipe from freezing. As the steam pipes went all the way forrard to give power to the anchor windlass, the drains were left open to let the condensation out and so that the windlass could be kept slowly turning, but this meant that the whole of the fo'c's'le and foredeck was thick with ice.

As we were in a fairly crowded area, with all ships moored to buoys close by, we all swung together as the wind shifted but, as I mentioned earlier the *Bradburn* was an old ship; not only that but there was little or no knowledge at that time about the effects of extreme cold on steel, and the fact that the molecular structure could change at around 0°C. The corroded and weakened brake band on the windlass, now feeling the full force of the wind as it clamped the mooring cable, parted. With a roar, the anchor chain went flying out, taking the steelwork round the Panama fairleads with it.

I was on deck and dashed forward, or at least slithered over the ice, as did the third mate, who had been on anchor watch on the bridge; between us, we managed to let go the other anchor, bringing up the *Bradburn* only feet from the ship astern.

We looked over the bow, and saw that the section of the bow with its two Panama fairleads was swinging round the anchor cable! Without the aid of shore tugs we were able to heave the ship back up to the buoy, hang off the other anchor, re-secure the anchor cable to the buoy and then heave on board the part of the bow that had been torn off. Next day a shore repair squad welded the steelwork back together and took the brake band off the starboard windlass, to be renewed ashore and then bolted back in position.

Nineteen

WE WERE GLAD to be clear of Hakodate, back into the warmth of the Kuro-shio and south through the islands, enjoying tropical weather until we reached our next port – Fremantle, Western Australia – for bunkers, and then across to Durban in South Africa, to load a full cargo of grain for Hamburg, Germany.

We enjoyed the weather and the work, preparing the holds with shifting boards and feeders for their next cargo of grain, all familiar tasks, in fine weather and not too much overtime, just enough to keep us out of mischief!

Durban was then, as now, what we could describe as a civilised port: plenty of shops, bars, restaurants and fine weather to see the sights. At the entrance on the port side was the bluff, and I will always remember the sight of the red-shirted prisoners, shackled with leg irons, moving along the top; perhaps moving towards their shift in the coal mines; and then, close by, in the water, to port, two huge whales, which had been caught offshore and were being flensed of their flesh for meat and oil.

The loading was carried out alongside, comparatively quickly for that period – seven days, as I recollect; but by now we were really glad to see the hatches battened down because we were now heading back to Europe, and by the time we arrived maybe we would be given leave.

Our passage round the Cape of Good Hope and up through the Atlantic, the English Channel and North Sea to Hamburg, went without major incident; it was a fine-weather passage, giving us a chance to clean and paint the ship from top to bottom, and as she was over twenty years old, the chance to put a few patches here and there, because she was due for Special Survey upon arrival in Europe.

We didn't interfere with the main structure of the ship, but where there was corrosion that had caused small holes to appear –

in the sheet metal of ventilators, for example – we had covered the holes with Elastoplast and then painted them over!

All the lifeboat equipment was carefully checked out, overhauled by the third mate during his watch below, and then, with the assistance of an apprentice, the lifeboats were painted inside and out – all four of them.

Some of the safety equipment, such as the distress rockets, were renewed every couple of years, to ensure that they would work in emergency.

Hamburg was a pleasant surprise. We were moored to dolphins (mooring piles), and four floating suckers came alongside to suck out the grain and pour it into barges – they discharged the lot in two days!

We were not paid off in Hamburg because we had then to sail back down the English Channel to Falmouth, where the *Bradburn* dry-docked and underwent her surveys.

I remember the bosun, the one who had found his wife in Australia, took all his 'pay-off' – quite a substantial sum – to the nearest bar and told the bar maid to let him know when it was finished. It lasted the month or so spent in dry dock, and then he was ready for sea again; and I was ready for my leave, after spending more than a year on the *Bradburn*!

It was not unusual at this time for seafarers to 'blow' all their pay-off in one 'glorious' booze-up, during the course of which they were often renowned for their generosity. Those were the days when many seafarers, particularly the seamen, were often recruited from orphanages or Sea Schools, which attracted young men who had no future elsewhere. For this category of seafarer, who might have no parents or come from a broken home, the discipline required by the nature of the work involved at sea was very beneficial. It was not the type of discipline encountered in the armed forces, but the discipline of watch-keeping, twenty-four hours per day, seven days per week, was considerable.

Any disruptive influence would soon be sorted out by their own shipmates. For example, one had to learn to be quiet sharing a cabin with someone who may be asleep after late night watches, and one rapidly learnt to be safety-conscious when most of the work was carried out on ships rolling and pitching in bad weather.

Once a young deck boy had grown up through the system, he might well have had only limited time on leave to meet someone who he would like to marry. Accordingly, many of the seafarers of that time spent their leave in a Sailors' Home, or just 'blew' their pay-off and found another ship.

Going on leave from Falmouth by train, changing at four stations, was a bit of a hassle. Although I did not have much gear – one suitcase – I had bought a carpet for my parents in India, which, although well sewn in burlap, was heavy and bulky, not easy to move from one train to another; but I always tried to buy something worthwhile, and in this case, it took nearly all my savings for the long trip on the *Bradburn*.

Although my parents had refused to take any money from me because they knew I earned so little, I was conscious of the fact that they were hard up with a big mortgage on a small private hotel. Anyway, it was one of the ways I could repay them, because they didn't take any money when I was on leave either. As another way of repaying them, which was both helpful and must have saved them a lot of money, I painted the outside of their three-story private hotel twice, because climbing up ladders and working from heights was no problem for me.

Twenty

IT WAS WITH SOME misgivings that I rejoined the *Orient City* at Falmouth, in October 1951. After all, I had written in to Head Office complaining about the poor state of the accommodation, and so I felt that I would not be in the company's good books, for one thing; and I was not looking forward to another trip in such archaic conditions. But there again, I needed to complete the requisite sea time, so I kept quiet and caught the train to Falmouth – or rather trains – changing at Preston, Crewe, Bristol and Exeter, with a fairly long walk to the dry dock at the far end of Falmouth harbour.

Imagine my surprise and delight to find that the accommodation had been completely renewed and that, on this, the last ship of my apprenticeship, I would be Senior Apprentice. The others were 'Christmas' Harry, Neal Jones, and Peter Becket.

As Senior Apprentice, I made sure that our cabins and mess room were kept spick and span, scrubbed decks, polished woodwork and plenty of brightness on the brass portholes.

We sailed from Falmouth on 9th October 1951, bound for Philadelphia, to load a full cargo of coal for Wakamatsu, in southern Japan, just across the Inland Sea from Moji.

The passage across the western ocean was rough, making it difficult to dismantle the shifting boards and feeders, but we had stowed and secured everything by the time we landed in Philadelphia, making sure that there would be no delay.

What an eye-opener! The speed of loading, compared to ports at that time in the UK, was amazing. We were all finished within two days. With the assistance of the pilot and two tugs, we cleared the berth and headed back out into the Atlantic, this time southbound against the fast-flowing Gulf Stream, and then across the Caribbean Sea, through the Panama Canal to the Pacific.

We called at Honolulu in the Hawaiian Islands for fuel oil bunkers, halfway across the Pacific Ocean. Our planned quick in-and-out for bunkers at Honolulu was not to be. The chief engineer had noted a small steam leak in one of the two Scotch boilers, so he called in a surveyor from Lloyd's. I don't know if the chief had realised what the repercussions of his action would be, because the surveyor, being a man of professional integrity, insisted on both boilers being blown down and a thorough internal inspection made.

The upshot of the surveyor's inspection was that he determined the steelwork of the boilers were weakened by caustic embrittlement, caused by the chief using too much caustic in the boiler water.

Lloyd's Register were completely unswerving in their conclusion that the *Orient City* was unfit to steam at full power until the boilers were renewed. We were in the middle of nowhere, really, with absolutely no chance of finding boilers to fit exactly in Hawaii, and with the prospect of us having to charter an ocean-going tug to tow us back to the USA or UK after we had discharged our cargo in Japan. The surveyor gave the ship a dispensation to make the passage to Japan at reduced boiler pressure, which meant in effect, greatly reduced speed.

In addition to both the main boilers, we had a smaller, 'donkey' boiler, which we also used, the totality of which gave us about half speed, until we reached our discharge port of Wakamatsu.

The approaches to Wakamatsu are up a winding river with plenty of small craft clogging the waterway. I was on the fo'c's'le head with the mate, Chippy, bosun and three sailors, ready to make fast to the mooring buoys. We were low in the water, being fully laden, and could not see further ahead than the next bend in the river, but as we approached the bend, the Captain shouted something through the hand-held megaphone from the bridge.

'What was that?' the mate asked me. I didn't know, so the mate cupped his ear with his hand – no VHF or mobile radios in those days – and the Captain responded, '*Drop the anchor!*'

The mate looked at me in disbelief. 'He said, drop the anchor!'

'*Which one?*' The mate roared back, but already it was too late. There was a shout from the bosun, a barge being pushed by a tug appeared round the bend in midstream, and we had been looking aft to the bridge and could not see it.

'Let go the anchor!' roared the mate.

Chippy walloped the brake with his hammer and one of the anchors roared out of the hawse pipe in a cloud of rust-coloured dust.

'Hold on!' yelled the mate, but obviously too late. You cannot stop a ship like a car, even one going as slow as ours, and we collided with the fully laden barge which, with the tug pushing from the other side, collapsed under the combined pressure and immediately started to sink.

In retrospect it was quite comical, really. The barge skipper jumped into a small sampan which he was towing and then immediately started to collect the washing off the line strung from the barge's little wheelhouse, whilst his wife stood helpless on deck, clutching a baby as the barge sank beneath her! We were hastily throwing heaving lines down to them, but by this time, two sampans put out from the riverside to rescue them, leaving the tug to drag the rapidly disappearing barge to the side of the river.

We immediately weighed anchor and the pilot manoeuvred us to our buoys off Wakamatsu, where we discharged all our cargo. What we did not know then was that the exact position where we had dropped our anchor was the charted position of the power cable joining one side of Wakamatsu to the other – we had blacked out the whole of the town!

This voyage was turning out to be disastrous, and we were all glad to see the last of the coal discharged into barges, before we moved across the strait to the southern tip of Honshu, to tie up alongside the shipyard at Shimonoseki... where we were to remain for 4½ months!

The decision had to be made about where the boilers could be renewed, as they were beyond repair. If we had to go back to UK it would have meant being towed halfway round the world, which would have cost a fortune, but as luck would have it, three new boilers were found in Nagoya and they were the right size for our ship. No doubt we had to pay extra to get them, because they were meant for a new ship being built in Japan, but, especially at that time, everything in Japan was cheap.

We knew that we were in for major engineering works which would involve taking away the engine-room skylight, all the steam pipes and ladders in the stokehold; also, we would need domestic steam to see us through the colder, winter months, twenty-four hours per day. This was resolved by hiring a donkey boiler from the Japanese, placing it on the afterdeck and connecting it to the domestic steam system. Two Japanese were on shifts stoking it with coke.

One more major decision had to be made: what to do with the crew? There were few planes flying internationally to the Far East then, which meant that it would have been very costly to fly the crew to and from the UK so they stayed on board.

We now knew that we were in for a long haul, four months' work we were told, so we had to learn to cope with a most unusual situation. Sailors are used to being at sea and then spending a comparatively short time ashore, normally never spending a single night on board ship, unless we were on watch. But how to do that for four months, and where would we get the money we needed? It needed ingenuity – but we did it!

We all went our different ways. The bosun, for example, found some obliging lady who looked after him for a few months, because the crew had taken a dislike to him and so beat him up regularly – yes, they were a tough bunch. As we had no bosun, I was made Acting Bosun; fortunately, I had no trouble with the crew.

We very often found our way to a little bar-cum-dance place, a few minutes from the dock gates, called the *Shintenshi*. It was a very basic place with a little coal-burning stove in one corner for heating and also to warm a pot of green tea that the *Papasan* used to drink and offer us occasionally. Even though it was basic and cheap, we could never afford more than a couple of beers, so various ways were found of making money.

The apprentices took it in turns to be nightwatchman, and one morning, the nightwatchman noticed a mooring rope was missing. Nothing could be done about it, a ship is big and the nightwatchman cannot be everywhere. All we could do was notify the police, but the rope was never found, nor were the culprits.

On another morning, as the nightwatchman was filling up the saltwater sanitary tanks – simply by whistling down the open top of the engine skylight for the junior engineer to start the pump – water spurted out from everywhere! During the night apparently some impecunious sailor had removed all the brass fire hydrants, no doubt to sell them for scrap brass! On yet another occasion someone had unscrewed all the brass tops of the storm steps!

The whole thing came to a head when the Captain noticed several of the little local shops selling ship's blankets, and immediately ordered an inspection on board. To everyone's amazement, all the crew had the requisite number of two blankets per bunk. It was only some months later when I found out that the chief steward had been suborned into issuing extra blankets from his store.

The apprentices resorted to more legal ways of making money – legal, but extremely dangerous. After the discharge of our coal cargo at Wakamatsu, small deposits of coal were still reposing on the bottom flat surfaces of the deep H-section girders which strengthened the top of the cargo holds. I suppose that they must have been about forty feet above deck and only very narrow, with no hand-holds, yet we crawled along these beams, knocking off loose coal, down to the apprentice waiting below, who swept them up, bagged them and then we carried the coal ashore by the sackful to sell to the *Shintenshi* – two beers per sack!

The officers resorted to less risky ways of raising money. When they were short of cash, which was frequent, they would ask one of us to take some article of value to a local pawnshop we had discovered. A lady was the owner, and she would give a reasonable price for cameras, watches, etc., which were then retrieved the following month – at a substantial profit, of course.

There was yet another way of earning money which one of the officers, one apprentice and the deck boy discovered. Purely by accident I found out that the second mate was singing for his supper! I went into a rather gloomy 'nightclub', which I didn't normally frequent because I couldn't afford it, and who should I see singing on the stage but our second mate, who, as a Welshman, had a good singing voice, one which was obviously much appreciated by the audience.

The junior apprentice and deck boy had developed a dual act: the deck boy played the drums, and the junior apprentice played the piano – we were obviously a crew of many talents.

The dockyard was in an area that was out of bounds to the US servicemen who still occupied Japan, so we were treated rather specially by the locals – perhaps because we spent nearly all our money locally. One evening, with little money as usual, I decided to have a look inside a local amusement arcade. It was very basic, having only machines that flirted steel ball bearings when the handle was pulled, but the interest here was taking your 'winnings' – ball bearings – to the proprietor, who would then exchange them for cigarettes. We all smoked and as the shipboard bond was only opened by the Customs once per month, this was one way to obtain cigarettes at a low price – if you were lucky!

I became friendly with the proprietor who invited me to his home – very different from anything I had experienced in the UK. His wife did not go out to work but stayed at home looking after their little baby, cooking food, washing clothes etc., but the routine was the same in most Japanese households of that era. The man would come home, his wife bowing low to him at the door, where she changed his outdoor shoes for felt slippers. They would all then take a bath, the man first, then the children, then the wife, strictly in that order, and using the same water which had been heated by a charcoal burner under the stone bath. To keep the bath water clean, the bathers washed themselves down alongside the bath and they poured water over themselves to rinse off the soap before stepping into the bath for a final rinse-off; that way the bath water stayed reasonably clean.

During the course of my friendship with the family, I found out that as a matter of course, the man of the house stayed out every Thursday evening, spending it with Kimisan, one of the local *Pan Pan* girls, as they were known. It was a cultural shock to me because, in a way, I suppose I was rather prudish, not used to this sort of goings-on but in fact it was the norm. Actually, there was a street full of small 'houses of ill repute', we could call them; but in Japan at this time, such girls were not looked down upon, nor were such activities swept under the carpet. This only changed when the Olympic Games were held in Japan around 1980, when I read that all such establishments had been closed.

There were many strange incidents that happened during our enforced sojourn in Japan. I decided to take the ferry across from Shimonoseki to Moji, as I had been there before, and a repeat visit would at least take me to more familiar territory. On the bus to Shimonoseki, I sat next to a young lady who was cuddling a little puppy dog – a bit surprising on a bus, but she smiled at me, and as the puppy was wriggling, she popped a breast out of her dress and suckled the puppy! Frankly, I didn't know where to put myself, it was not the sort of happening that one would experience on a tram in Blackpool – that was certain!

One of the hostesses at the *Shintenshi* had fallen head over heels in love with our second steward; admittedly, even to a man he was good-looking, but perhaps what made him more desirable to a woman was that he showed little interest in them!

He wasn't a homosexual, but he had this addiction to alcohol, and any spare time or money were spent that way. But finally she waylaid him, after about two months, and she was on the dockside crying as we left… yes, she was pregnant!

As Acting Bosun, I couldn't take a hard line with the crew, but they seemed to work reasonably well and, in fact, the whole of the internal structure of the cargo holds was painted with bitumastic and the whole of the outside of the ship, the black topside, red boot-topping, and top of the red anti-fouling were chipped, red-leaded and painted, along with the names and draught marks in white. Had we been in a British yard, the unions would not have allowed the ship's crew to work at all.

Another ship came in for repairs near to us; she was the *Kola*, one of Jardine Matheson's. We were interested enough to have a look around and found out that she was short of a third mate. At this juncture in my life, perhaps having no confidence to be able to pass for my Certificate of Competency for Second Mate (Foreign Going), I asked the Captain if he would take me on as

Uncertificated Third Mate. He agreed, subject to owners' approval. The owners' representative was called Mr Jardine, so I suppose he was one of the owners' family; he met me on board and, in retrospect very sensibly advised me to complete my sea time and then take my examinations, and he would then offer me a second mate's job straight away! I have a lot to thank Mr Jardine for, because, as an uncertificated third mate, I might have drifted around the Far East for years without bettering myself.

We were glad, though, when the last piece of the engine room was put back in place, the decks cleared of all the shore-side mess, the 'donkey' boiler removed from the afterdeck, new boilers flashed up, pilot on board, tugs made fast – and slowly we pulled away from the dockyard quay; streamers were thrown and tears were shed by the girls on the quay, but now the crew had different thoughts. We were bound for British Columbia to load timber for the UK – we were homeward bound!

Twenty-one

HOW WE ENJOYED being back at sea again, on a ship cleaned of all the accumulated rubbish of 4½ months in port, freshly painted inside and out, and no holds to prepare as we were loading timber and not salt, grain or coal!

The bosun had turned up just before we sailed so I no longer had the responsibility of running the crew, turning my attention, perhaps belatedly, to my studies in my spare time.

The new boilers performed well, no problems whatsoever, and with a clean bottom, we made good speed, around ten knots, all the way to Chemainus in British Columbia, where we started to load our cargo of timber. We loaded at three different berths; the others were at Kowitchin Bay and Victoria, on Vancouver Island.

We were not directly involved in the loading; the stevedores knew their job and we left them to it; most of them were Indians. I remember watching some of them using sign language across the bottom cargo holds, to overcome the noise. This was an era when the native Indians were treated differently. Perhaps they were segregated ashore, I don't know, but I do know that they were not allowed into bars or to buy alcohol.

We were interested to see how tightly and how well they stowed the timber. They managed to fill every inch of space in the lower hold and the 'tween deck, and after battening down the cargo hatches, timber was stowed on deck from stem to stern, covering the whole deck right up to a height of around three metres. On top of the cargo, the stevedores built a walkway with rails either side, and then the whole of the deck cargo was lashed with chains, from one side to the other, tightened with bottle screws.

There are three main dangers with the carriage of timber on deck; one is that it can be washed overboard in stormy weather, and this is why we would tighten the bottle screws every day on passage.

Another danger was that with the consumption of fuel oil bunkers from the double bottom, the ship would become unstable and capsize; and the third danger was that if the wind blew mainly from one side, then this side of the deck cargo would gradually become soaked, causing the ship to list.

It was this third problem that we encountered on our passage to Manchester. The port side became heavier than the starboard and we arrived at Manchester Ship Canal locks with a port list!

Just before our arrival at Manchester, the mate instructed me to lower the forrard telescopic topmast. I thank him for this, because throughout my four years of apprenticeship it was the very first time anyone had bothered to train me to do anything. Of course, by this time, I was experienced in most shipboard activities, and the mate had seen that as senior apprentice, I ran the apprentices without any trouble; and indeed, during my spell as acting bosun there had not been any problems.

I won't go through the detailed technicalities of lowering a telescopic topmast here, but it does require a good level of seamanship and of course, no nerves, dangling in space in a bosun's chair!

As we entered the locks, the topmasts had been lowered (essential, as we had to pass under low bridges) but as we were listing, the steel side rubbed against the granite wall of the locks causing a shower of sparks to shoot out; but we passed through without incident, mooring alongside the railway line in Manchester, and started discharging.

We were signed off articles the next day; I was ordered by the Captain to stay on board until we finished discharging. I refused; I was my own man now, my Apprentice's Indentures were satisfactorily completed, I had been away for nine months and wanted to go home to start studying in the hope (but not the expectation) that I could eventually qualify as an officer. Difficult though it was, that was my objective, and I was determined to see it through.

Junior Officer

Twenty-two

AS SOON AS I arrived home, I registered with Fleetwood Navigation School. In order to advance my career, it was essential to pass all the Certificates of Competency, issued by the DTI – a government license; the first of these was for Second Mates (Foreign Going).

Captain MacFarlane, the principal of the Navigation School, put me on the right course, and straight away I started on the 'preliminaries'. First of all I wrote off for my Certificate of Service from Rearden Smiths; this to prove to the DTI (MOT as it then was) that I had served the requisite number of years and months actually at sea during my apprenticeship, and that my conduct had been satisfactory. Next I had to take another eyesight test, and then take a First Aid course, then a week's Lifeboat Course at Liverpool. The latter was issued after examination but passes were high, about 80 per cent.

Then it was down to the daily grind of studying, all day every day, including weekends, and some nights. The subject for this first Certificate, or 'Ticket', as it was termed by us, were Navigation, Chart Work, Ship Construction, Cargo Work, English, Knowledge of Principles and Mathematics, so there was much to learn. Of course, I had studied a lot at sea and pre-sea, so most of it was familiar but the examinations were of an extremely high standard. The passmark was 70%. There was no such thing as good, bad or indifferent. If we failed, or 'dipped', in one subject then we 'dipped' in the lot, and had to retake the examination at a later date.

In addition to the written work, we had to take a practical Signals test because we depended upon visual Morse signals, and flags between ships and often between ship and shore. Usually this test was taken more lightly than the written ones because it was a separate entity, and in consequence the failure rate was about 30%, perhaps due to the amount of coding and decoding of flag signals that were included.

The final part of the 'Ticket' was the most terrifying – the orals! I well remember a contemporary turning up, as we all did, in tie and suit, only to turn round and never come back. He just couldn't face it – he left the sea.

The orals were especially geared to testing the candidates' knowledge of the Rule of the Road, or as they were officially termed, 'Regulations for the Prevention of Collision at Sea'. There were thirty-two articles and we were expected to know them off by heart, as the examiner thrust different coloured lights at us demanding to know what it was, arc of visibility, range, etc. If one was too bad, whether through nervousness or not, that candidate would be told abruptly, 'Six months' sea time,' and he would have to serve at least another six months before coming back to go through the mill again.

Much to my surprise, I passed everything at the first attempt; having never passed an examination of any kind before, it was certainly a novel experience, and bolstered my self-confidence. Perhaps I had a future after all!

It had taken about five months to become certificated and, of course, I had spent some time considering in which direction my future lay – hoping that I would pass my 'Ticket'. A friend of mine, Barry Caley, was on leave at this time, and he was Third Mate in Clan Line, a prestigious Liner company; with his encouragement, I wrote to Clan Line, that I was sitting for my examinations and would like to serve with them as Fourth Mate, when I passed. To my delight, they accepted me, subject to my success in my 'Ticket'.

Fourth mate is a lowly starting point, but I needed that because of my 'chipping hammer' apprenticeship. My knowledge of practical navigation and bridge duties was virtually zero, as the only time I had worked on the bridge previously was to either steer the ship or scrub the deck! Now was the time to inform Clan Line of my success and wait for an appointment.

It was during this period, just after my twenty-second birthday that I met Dora, later to become my wife; we met briefly before I was appointed as Fourth Officer on the *Clan Shaw*, the newest ship in the Clan Line fleet, which I joined in Glasgow.

My uniform still looked smart because I had hardly worn it during my apprenticeship; all I had to do was change the two lapel tabs and have a thin gold band sewn on each cuff, and with a Clan Line badge on my cap, I was all set to take on the world!

The *Clan Shaw* was loading general cargo in Glasgow. It was my first experience of this sort of cargo, and it was really interesting to see the heavy lifts, especially being lifted up by our own heavy lift derricks, the locomotion carriages and engines being landed on to wooden rails at the bottom of the hold, and some on the specially strengthened deck. We also loaded boilers, machinery, chemicals and of course, whisky. The whisky was loaded into a special locker in the 'tween decks where it could be safely locked away, but the Glasgow stevedores knew a thing or two. By dropping a wooden case of whisky heavily on its corner, one or two of the bottles inside would break, whisky would dribble out of the case, and the stevedores holding enamel mugs underneath had their fill!

When all the cargo was stowed and lashed with wires, chains and bottle screws, we set sail for Cape Town. I was on watch with the chief officer, he must have been astonished by my lack of practical knowledge of normal bridge watch-keeping routines, just as I was astonished by some of the duties I was asked to perform. The *Clan Shaw* was a cargo/passenger ship with crew of eighty, and twelve passengers; we also had the luxury of an all-Indian crew, plenty of hands to do everything. We even had quartermasters, called 'seacunnies', whose job was to steer the ship and clean the wheelhouse – nothing else. One of the strange duties I had to perform was to go down the ladder to the Captain's deck below just before eight o'clock in the morning; there I would knock on his door and when he appeared, I had to say, 'Permission to make eight bells, sir?' He would reply, 'Carry on, Four O.' I would then go back up to the wheelhouse, pass on to the chief officer that permission to make eight bells had been granted, and then he would say to me, 'Carry on, Four O.' I would then turn to the seacunny on the wheel and order him, '*Maro* Seacunny,' he would then acknowledge, '*Atcha*, Sahib,' and 'make' or ring the bell eight times. I never did know what all that was about, and still don't for that matter.

But it was good in those days to have such big crews, there were always plenty of hands to do whatever work needed doing. *Colasses* were the sailors who were run by the Serang, or Bosun, and under him would be the *Burra Tindal* or Bosun's Mate, and under him the *Chota Tindal* or Junior Bosun's Mate, with the *Casab* as Storekeeper and the *Topas*, the lowest form of shipboard life, whose job was solely to sweep the scuppers and clean the toilets. Although the Indian crew were lowly paid, it was a steady income for them, and when they returned home, after twelve months, they were comparatively well off, because, apart from their pay they had other ways of making money. The most popular way was to buy clothing in Glasgow from church jumble sales and the like; they would then take these clothes ashore in Cape Town to sell at a profit to the Cape Coloureds. Of course this 'trade' would not be formally allowed by the Customs, so the crew could often be seen with strange clothes, like women's dresses being worn, sometimes one on top of the other and occasionally with hats on or wheeling second-hand bicycles, returning from the shore much slimmer but richer!

Shipboard life on board all British ships was well ordered; one instance was the flag ceremony. Every morning at exactly 0800 hours the country flag on the foremast, the house flag on the mainmast and the national flag over the stern would be raised together as the officer of the watch blew his whistle from the bridge. Similarly, at exactly sunset, the OOW would check the time by the bridge chronometer and blow his whistle precisely at sunset, calculated to the nearest second from that longitude. On the Clan liners, the serang would man the foremast, the burra tindal the mainmast and the chota tindal the ensign. In later years, it was obviously not cost-effective to use so many men to do 'unnecessary' work. Compare the crew of the *Clan Shaw* at eighty for a vessel of around 12,000 tons, with the crew of the *Globtik London*, at thirty-four for a vessel of nearly half a million tons!

Watch-keeping duties at sea were more or less standard on all British ships. The officer coming on watch would check the course being steered, check the position on the chart, and the officer he was relieving would point out the various lights of ships, if it was night-time, indicating which way they were heading and which could cause problems. He would also point out the shore lights, if it was night-time and near the coast, indicating which lights had the characteristics of those on the chart, e.g. 'Flashing twice every ten seconds,' or, as it was on the chart – 'fl 2 ev 10s'. He would also point out any potential dangers such as shallows or isolated rocks. The OOW would also read, and sign, the Master's Night Order Book; this supplemented any National or International Rules and Regulations, such as *The Regulations for the Prevention of Collision at Sea* issued by the United Nations offshoot, International Maritime Organisation, IMO, and it would also supplement any Company Standing Orders.

Once all these routine matters were carried out, the OOW would be on the bridge on his own, the lookout man being on the fo'c's'le head, ringing the bell when he saw a new light; but, as ships became bigger, so the lookout man would be placed on the bridge. If the OOW wanted the standby man to come to the bridge, he would blow a whistle, and if he wanted the standby man to read the log, which was trailed on a propeller over the stern, he blew the whistle twice. When the whistle was blown three times, it was for the apprentice on watch to come to the bridge.

It was pitch black at night, all the alleyway lights and official steaming lights were completely shaded so that they would not interfere with the vision of the OOW, and all the lights of the instruments on the bridge or in the chartroom were shaded and controlled by a dimmer switch, so that the only lights at night were from a very faint orange or green glow showing the gyro or magnetic compass heading or from the shaded light over the current chart in the chartroom.

The OOW would take visual bearings of lights about every half-hour to determine the vessel's position, which he would check with the depths of water using the echo sounder and, later on, with more sophisticated equipment, would check it with the radar. In dangerous waters the Master would also be on the bridge, as would the helmsman.

Apart from fixing the vessel's position by visual bearings, the OOW had also to calculate the compass error by taking bearings of heavenly bodies, stars, moon, sun, planets and working out the difference between what the bearing should be and what it actually was. This gave the gyro compass error, which, when compared with the magnetic compass, gave the magnetic compass error.

When out of sight of land, the ship's position was also determined by measuring the altitude of the sun and noting the exact time to the nearest second, in the daytime and in the evening, or early morning, taking the altitude of a number of stars or planets and calculating the position – this was only possible in the half-light of dawn or twilight because it was necessary, also, to be able to see the horizon.

Very often, if it was a clear ocean passage, the second mate would correct charts during his watch to introduce all the new corrections that were promulgated by the weekly *Notices to Mariners* issued to all British ships by the Hydrographic Office.

The routine work was quickly dealt with by the OOW and he would spend much of his watch pacing up and down, so that he was able to keep a sharp eye on all potential dangers, by day or night; it was lonely but one became used to it.

Over the years there were naturally improvements in many aspects of shipboard life and duties, as far as the OOW was concerned. It was a boon to be able to communicate to every part of the ship by telephone instead of the voice pipe, which had been used for small ships but which was useless as ships became bigger. Not only were there telephones to all parts of large vessels, but loudspeakers to the forrard and after mooring stations and, of course hand-held radio communications, which were intrinsically safe, to avoid the possibility of incendiary sparks causing explosion on tankers.

The introduction of VHF ship-to-ship radio was a boon. Gone were the days when the Aldis lamp was used, except, possibly to call up a ship 'VHF', and then the other ship would respond over the VHF radio on Channel 16.

Never once would any OOW leave the bridge whilst he was on watch unless he was relieved. This was standard internationally, and even prevailed when a ship was at anchor; but once alongside, the OOW would be in charge of the cargo loading and discharging.

After discharging all our cargo in the ports of Cape Town, Mossel Bay, East London, Port Elizabeth and Durban, we started to load for the homeward passage at the port of Beira, in what was then Portuguese East Africa. Copper was the main cargo, in heavy slabs, with a protrusion at each corner to facilitate handling. They were very heavy and when one was let slip on to the foot of one of the stevedores, it caused a major injury. As I was the OOW, he was carried to me and I had him laid on the bed in our little surgery. His foot was completely smashed, blood everywhere, bones protruding, a real mess. No worry for me, or so I thought, as we had a doctor on board!

I knew the doctor was in the saloon, having lunch with the chief engineer and passengers, regaling them with his tales of yore, when he had been one of the surgeons on Ernest Shackleton's expedition to the Antarctic. I knocked timorously on the door and said, 'Excuse me, sir, one of the stevedores has a serious injury to his foot.'

He glared at me, probably annoyed that his ability as a raconteur had been interrupted. 'You've got a First Aid Ticket, haven't you?' he bellowed, and then left me to it! No doubt he dealt with the expedition men more sympathetically!

I returned to the injured stevedore, cleaned and bandaged his damaged foot and sent him off to the local hospital; actually, the doctor would probably have done no more, because we had no sophisticated equipment on board.

Because we visited so many ports, and because the other officers knew their way around these ports, one was again hard up. Not only did I spend money in socialising but cigarettes had to be bought, and I repaid the money loaned by my mother to purchase a second-hand sextant, which I still have to this day. I had received a letter from Terry Dancy, telling me that he was now on tankers, earning twice what I was earning and also having longer spells of leave; that made me think. I realised now that there was no long-term future for me in Clan Line; I knew that promotion was slow and that there would be no chance to earn and save any substantial sums of money and perhaps, even then, I had thought of getting engaged. Whatever the reason, I had made the decision, and as we were heading back to Liverpool after having loaded our full cargo of copper, manganese, chrome ore, canned fruit and apples, I resolved to try for a change to a tanker company, now that I had had bridge experience; and especially so as the Captain had given me a very good report – a Watch-keeping Certificate had to be issued at the end of every voyage duly signed by the Master, with comments as to sobriety, ability, etc.

Twenty-three

I HAD NO IDEA to which company I should apply, so I asked the Officers' Union representative in Liverpool and he gave me the address of Athel Line Ltd.

Duly presenting myself at their office, I was received with open arms by their manager; after all, Clan Line was a prestigious company; accordingly, I signed off the *Clan Shaw* on 18th May and signed on the *Athel Queen* on the 21st May 1953, as Third Mate.

We sailed from Ellesmere Port, on the Manchester Ship Canal, on 22nd May 1953, bound for South East Asia. I knew nothing of tankers but was told by the mate that the pumpman would handle the cargo, not strictly true, but at least it gave me a little comfort!

Now I could stand my 8-12 watch on the bridge with confidence; I knew the practicalities of navigation and chart work by now – which was just as well because we had no modern aids to navigation! In fact, we had nothing more than Captain Cook had during his voyages of discovery – and probably less, because our compass was badly adjusted and was seriously affected by the induced magnetism of the steel hull.

We were on a Shell charter, carrying mainly crude oil between Miri, in what was then British North Borneo, and refineries in Singapore, Indonesia and Japan. It was useful experience, although my navigational capabilities were more than adequate, by the time we had navigated between all the narrow passages and straits of the East Indies and called at numerous ports and islands, all of us were on the top line navigational-wise.

As I indicated earlier, we had no modern aids to navigation. Like Captain James Cook we used the sextant and chronometer, our echo sounder did not work and, of course, we had no radar or satellite navigation. Apart from the sextant fixes, obtained only when there was no heavy cloud, we were dependant upon the magnetic compass, which, in turn, was dependent upon the accuracy of the deviation card; this showed what correction to apply to the compass whenever we changed heading; which we did with great frequency, because we had to navigate in and out of the numerous islands.

We became adept at quickly obtaining the compass error whenever we altered course and then carefully checking it thereafter. Actually, the Captain, 'Black Bob' Lonsdale, should have had the magnetic compass readjusted in Singapore because he obviously did not have the capability himself. This was understandable, really, because all the academic part of compass adjusting learnt ashore was not the same as doing the same thing on board ship. The whole subject of magnetism affecting shipboard compasses was an extremely complex subject, and as the *Athel Queen* was also navigating around an area of magnetic anomalies it was increasingly difficult to be certain of the course we were steering. In the days of Captain Cook, referred to earlier, his wooden-built ship would have had no adverse effect upon his magnetic compass, so that his only concern would have been the variation of magnetism from the earth's core – which was a known quantity.

Anyway, we managed and navigated safely throughout for nine months without any mishap.

When we went up the Palembang River to load at Pladju, in Java, it was narrow, with dense jungle either side, and when we had to anchor, waiting for a berth, swinging to the tide was quite hilarious; the river was so narrow that we ended up with the bow in the jungle as we swung round to the anchor. I can remember the mate on the fo'c's'le, standing by the anchor, with Chippy fighting his way through the jungle that engulfed the whole of the fo'c's'le head!

We loaded fuel oil at Pulo Bukom, an island off Singapore, where I bought a beautiful teak chest camphor lined with wood for my mother. It was expensive, but I felt that she deserved it; and I have it now, as it was passed on to me after her death.

The other thing that we took on board was water; it was time to top up the freshwater tanks before we set off for our discharge

port across Singapore Strait, Rhio Strait and then to Surabaya.

I had never been to Surabaya, so I took a few hours off to treat myself to a nice steak ashore and then back on board to take over my cargo watch at midnight. Halfway through the meal I started to feel ill, with violent stomach pains. Thinking that it was the food, I paid my bill and crawled out, helped by the small staff of the restaurant. I was helped into a pedicab and cycled to the dockside. By this time I was so ill I kept falling out of the pedicab.

Nobody spoke English but I eventually made them understand that I wanted a launch to take me back to my ship, moored to buoys in the harbour, and that I would pay them with cigarettes because, by this time, the driver of the pedicab had let me fall on to the quayside and then taken all my money. I was lying there completely helpless!

A launch took me back to the ship, but as I crawled up the gangway, I remember wondering what on earth the Captain was going to think of one of his officers crawling on board, looking for all the world as if I was in a drunken stupor, when in fact I had had no more than one beer!

I needn't have worried, because as soon as my head appeared above deck level I saw the pumpman, pale as death, completely prostrate on top of one of the tank valves, and then one of the two apprentices clutching hold of the ladder up to the officers' deck. In fact, the whole of the crew were affected, except the Captain and the chief engineer.

We were all really ill. The shore doctor was sent for and treatment given to all hands. It was apparently some virulent bug that we picked up with the water the day before, from the new supplies at Pulo Bukom. After three days of treatment and treating the water tanks with chlorine, we all recovered, more or less. It was some time later when I discovered why the Captain and chief engineer did not suffer the same as everyone else; I learned from the Captain's steward that the Captain was a secret drinker, and although he kept a 'dry' ship, he himself would drink quite heavily, especially during the tense period prior to entering port. The chief was allowed beer and had apparently drunk enough to ward off the worst of the affliction.

As we were almost on the equator much of the time, we experienced a lot of tropical storms – difficult to obtain sun sights, and difficult to check our compass error. One night whilst on watch there was a vivid flash of lightning which struck the electric cable leading to the clear view screen, and then the bolt of lightning leapt right across to the steel deck just in front of me; another couple of feet and I would have been killed instantly!

'Black Bob' ran a tight ship, it was his only way of keeping control because he obviously had no confidence in his own ability; accordingly, there was no alcohol allowed on board for anyone. Not that it mattered, because none of us were heavy drinkers and I was intent, anyway, on saving money. So, like the second mate, 'Titch' Elliot, seldom went ashore. At Christmas time, 'Black Bob' had observed that one of the stewards had had something to drink; he acted immediately, putting handcuffs on the steward and fastening him to the boat deck rails – shades of Captain Bligh!

Not content with that, he went round to every cabin on the ship to check if there was anyone drinking – there weren't. Next, he inspected the steward's cabin, taking one of the officers with him and found – not beer, but ladies' clothes in one of his drawers! The poor fellow was some kind of transvestite but he had done no harm to anyone. Eventually he was released from the rails because he wanted to go to the toilet. 'Do it over the side!' roared 'Black Bob'. 'I can't, I want to sit down!' the poor steward told him.

I do not know how 'Black Bob' ever qualified as a Master Mariner, because he was an ignorant man; I just presumed that they had 'fast-tracked' him during the war.

We headed back for Stanlow, in the Manchester Ship Canal, in January 1954, with a cargo of slack wax which needed keeping at a high temperature in the tanks, otherwise it would solidify. As we were passing through the Suez Canal, I thought I would write to the Liverpool office, assuring them that I had had so much experience in my nine months as third mate on the *Athel Queen*, that they should consider my promotion to second mate. Of course it was expecting a lot, but nothing ventured, nothing gained...

We arrived off the River Mersey to pick up the pilot in very poor visibility, which made our navigation difficult, but by proceeding cautiously, we made our rendezvous and the pilot guided us upriver to an anchorage, whilst we awaited a berth at Stanlow. I took the seamanlike precaution of checking if the vessel was dragging her anchor by lowering a hand lead over the side; to my horror, I noticed that it was rapidly leading ahead, indicating that we were in fact dragging, and quickly too. I called the pilot and 'Black Bob', who immediately controlled the situation and the pilot made a point of congratulating my alertness. This was duly noted by the Captain because next day, the manager came on board and confirmed my promotion to Second Mate: faint heart never won fair lady.

Twenty-four

I WAS HOME FOR only three weeks before signing on the *Athel Crest* in London, as Second Mate. She was one of the Athel Line's older tankers, specially built to carry molasses, which were loaded at various ports in the West Indies, mainly in Cuba or in Port Everglades, Florida, which we then brought back to various ports in the UK, such as London, Ipswich, Hull and Liverpool. There we discharged the molasses, which were used to make alcohol or, in some cases, animal feed.

The temperature at which we carried the molasses was quite critical; if it was too hot, cinders would form round the heating coils and insulate the rest of the molasses from the heat; too hot reduced the bacteriological action in the molasses and too cold meant that the molasses were so viscous that they could not pump. When each tank was drained as good as we could get it, we then introduced live steam through a valve in the deck that would clean all the molasses from the sides and off most of the bottom.

Navigating in and out of the bays and shallows around the eastern side of Cuba was not easy. Cuba, as we all know, is a very poor country, and this is reflected in the quality and quantity of their aids to navigation; their lights were often unreliable and, very often, their 'buoyed' channels were, for all practical purposes, non-existent. Very often the buoys marked on the chart did not exist or had been replaced by a floating plastic container 'anchored' to the bottom with a weighted line!

We always had to take a pilot, and this was sensible with the unreliability of any buoyed channel, but with the pilot's local knowledge, we could weave our way through the coral heads in the bays, easily seen with the water being so crystal clear.

The berths themselves were in a very dilapidated state, such that we were cautioned not to land too heavily when we came alongside – usually without the aid of tugs. By letting go the offside anchor, this acted as some sort of a brake as we moved gently alongside; not that it mattered, because we were invariably handed a bill for damage to the jetty!

At one particular port, I think it was Bufadero, the configuration of the bottom alongside was such that we could load only part cargo, and this with the bow elevated and the stern almost under water – it looked as though we were sinking!

We also loaded at a place called Jucaro, on the south coast; once again it was approached through a channel between the coral heads with buoys either out of position or non-existent, until we berthed, very gently, alongside a hulk, the *Jucaro*. If I remember rightly, she had been built around 1880 and her original iron hull had gradually been replaced by patches of steel plate welded over the holes! Nevertheless, the system worked, and we loaded a full cargo of molasses there for discharge at Port Everglades.

It was impressive entering the port of Havana, because there was a stone fort at the entrance, on the port side, built in the days of Captain Henry Morgan, the pirate, who later became Governor of Jamaica.

We loaded also at Neuvitas Bay, and I took the opportunity to go ashore and see how the molasses were produced.

All the sugar cane was chopped by hand, put into railway trucks and taken to the factory, where steel crushers squeezed all the juice out. Once the canes were completely dried and chopped fine, this residue was blown into boiler furnaces, where it was burnt and used as fuel to heat the boilers that provided steam for all the operations.

After the raw sugar crystals had been separated from the thick juice the remainder was molasses, a thick, dark, treacle-like substance, which was then stored in tanks ready for export to be used, ultimately, as cattle feed or to make alcohol.

My 2½ months on the *Athel Crest* was a learning curve for me. It was my introduction to the carriage of molasses, and also into the duties expected of the second mate, which, apart from keeping a watch every day, the 12-4, twice per day, meant correcting all of the two thousand or so charts we carried, plus maintaining the gyro. So, what with these duties, in addition to the standing by as we entered and left port, there was little time to feel homesick; or indeed, little chance to do anything but work!

The Captain of the *Athel Crest* was known as 'Ropey' Jones, for reasons which will not be given here; he was an easy-going Captain who, later on, I heard, had retired to Falmouth to run a boarding house. The mate, 'Winnie' Churchill, I was to meet later.

Athel Line was unusual in that it specialised in the carriage of molasses, which, because of their viscosity (measured in 'brix') and because of their sensitivity to heat, took extra care to ensure that they arrived at the discharge port in prime condition. What made the carriage of molasses really difficult was when a cargo of crude oil was carried, in between molasses cargoes, this entailed a complicated and dangerous procedure to clean the tanks, pumps and pipelines, after the crude oil was discharged, in order to ensure that the cargo surveyor would pass the tanks as suitable for the carriage of an edible product, such as molasses.

After the crude oil was discharged and the ship ballasted to a suitable, safe draft, the empty tanks had to be washed clean of any oily residue and then gas freed. During the time that I sailed in the Athel Line, we used a very basic way of carrying out this essential work. Usually the mate himself would work from first light until about eight p.m., down the tanks, usually with an apprentice at the top, hosing down the sides and strength members with a hand-held, high-pressure, saltwater hose. Often the water would be heated and the nozzle of the hose wrapped in burlap to stop it scalding hands and fingers. In cases where it was too difficult to wash the oil out cleanly, for example, if it was a crude oil residue with a high wax content, sometimes a steam hose would be inserted into a drum of caustic, and this was hung from the top until all the wax was removed. The mate himself would always have to wear a smoke helmet when down the tank; this was used as a sort of breathing apparatus as there was no such sophisticated equipment on board at the time. By opening the front of the mask, and by the apprentice at the top pumping some bellows with his foot, air was driven into the helmet and out of the front, allowing the mate to see what he was doing.

It was an antiquated system, and usually all those working in and around the tanks were full of gas before the day was out. The one perk looked forward to by the whole crew were the bottles of

rum given to them daily – supposedly to help cope with the gas. Frankly, it just knocked them out!

Once the tanks were considered clean enough, then long canvas wind chutes were lowered to the bottom to help drive any remaining gas out of the tank. It was all really dangerous, but accepted by all of us at that time, even though, on average, one or two men were killed down the tanks every year.

Later on, with the introduction of high-pressure 'Butterworth' hoses, which were lowered from the top and did not entail any hand-held washing, the situation improved, and that was the time when extra equipment, such as air-driven and water-driven ventilation fans were introduced. Of course, this was a time when tankers were getting bigger, and when there were increasing pressures to reduce pollution, so all tankers retained oily residues on board. Thereafter loading any new oil on top; but this presented problems for molasses carriers, and was one of the reasons the molasses were sometimes carried in chemical tankers.

Later on still, with the introduction of the really big giant tankers, not only did they have permanently fixed tank-washing machines in each tank, so that none of the officers or crew needed to go into the tank, but a system of crude oil washing was used, such that each tank was rinsed out with its own crude oil before it was completely empty, thus using the lighter fractions of the crude oil itself to completely clean every bit of oily residue from the tanks.

As I write, belatedly, most new tankers are built now with double hulls to help prevent pollution when in collision or grounding, and also to provide permanent clean ballast tanks which never need washing.

I joined the *Athel Monarch* in June 1954 at Glasgow, leaving at Amsterdam in October, serving as second mate, gaining more experience all the time, and now thinking more seriously about my next examination for First Mate (Foreign Going). It was time to study and a time to save money and leave for my planned studies ashore.

In October 1954 I flew with the crew from Amsterdam to Stansted before taking the train back to Blackpool, where I immediately enrolled at Fleetwood Navigation School to continue my studies. As for the Second Mate's 'Ticket', the standard was high; we all had to produce Watch Keeping Certificates, signed by every Master; there was the requisite eyesight test, a renewal of the First Aid Certificate and a two-week Radar Observers' Course, as we were now in the era of radar being widely used.

We still had to gain a pass mark of 70% for our written papers which were Navigation, Chart Work, Cargo Work, Stability, Electronics and Maintenance and Engineering, as well as taking another Signals and oral examination; fortunately I passed them all at the first attempt. Having the luxury of a little more time than usual at home, I was able to catch up on my love life, and Dora and I were engaged.

I joined the *Athel Duchess* at Hull in February 1955 and stayed on her as second mate until November 1955. We spent all of that time loading and discharging molasses from many out of the way places in Cuba, such as Bufadero, Neuvitas Bay, Pastallileo, Jucaro, and the larger ports such as Cienfuegos and Havana, sometimes shuttling back and forth to Port Everglades in Florida, where shore tanks were filled so that our larger capacity tankers could transport the molasses back across to the UK, or sometimes Rouen or Dunkirk.

Sailing up the River Seine to Rouen was a memorable experience. We picked up the pilot at Le Havre then motored steadily up the winding River Seine for about fifty miles, through such beautiful countryside, unspoilt by riverside development or any major industrial complexes, and with numerous quaint châteaux perched on hill tops along the way.

We reached the berth just outside Rouen in about five hours and made fast alongside very securely, because we knew from the Pilot Book and the pilot himself that we could expect a tidal bore of some significance twice per day. Once all the moorings were doubled up we actually had to standby fore and aft, with engines on stand-by, as the bore caused the ship to surge, quite drastically. Even though the moorings were taut, the kinetic energy developed by the surge was such that all the moorings had to be tightened again to avoid the cargo's flexible pipelines from being damaged, as they were connected to the shore.

I was the second mate on cargo watch from 4 p.m. until 8 a.m. the next morning, when I saw a young lady hovering around in the vicinity of the gangway that first evening. I was busy with my cargo duties. We didn't have any gangway watch because, given the size of crews, we could not spare the manpower; but in any case, there was no danger to the ship carrying molasses, and as the berth was in a remote location, little chance of thieves boarding.

I was busy through the night but next morning, when the crew were being called, at about six thirty, there was the young lady again, but this time walking down the gangway *off* the ship, swinging her handbag as she teetered down in her high heels; it was later that day that the news went around the ship that as we were in a remote location, and as the crew had had to stay on board, she had 'entertained' the whole crew!

With money and leave saved I left the *Athel Duchess* in Avonmouth in November 1955 – this time not to study for examinations but to get married!

Twenty-five

DORA AND I WERE married on 10th December 1955, and after a week's honeymoon in Paris, I received instructions to join the *Athel Templar* on New Year's Eve, at Saltend Jetty, Hull.

The thought of leaving a brand new wife behind was not the way I wanted marriage to be, but in 1955 junior officers were not allowed to take their wives with them. Just on the off chance, I phoned Athel Line and, after pleading with various managers and superintendents, was given permission to take my wife across from Hull to Vegesack, Germany, where we were to dry dock; but on the understanding that she would not be allowed to stay on board after that. This was a big concession, and both Dora and I were overjoyed.

We joined the *Athel Templar* late at night. There was a howling gale whipping the spray from the River Humber all the way along the length of Saltend Jetty, which was about a mile long! We fought our way to the end, lugging heavy suitcases, being buffeted by the wind – and there was the *Athel Templar* discharging her cargo of molasses, but being smothered with heavy spray. We boarded and were welcomed by 'Titch' Elliot, formerly second mate of the *Athel Queen* and now promoted to Mate.

It was a rough passage across the North Sea to Vegesack, so Dora was not feeling very hungry! Although dry docks are dirty, uncomfortable and often cold places, with frequent disconnections of electricity, fresh and sanitary water, and without steam heating, nevertheless we enjoyed our sojourn in Vegesack. I was busy in the daytime supervising repairs but each evening we would walk into the small town of Vegesack and call into a different restaurant and pub; but we also splashed out at a nightclub in nearby Bremen. As I was the senior officer left on board, both the Captain and mate going on leave, we were also invited out to dinner with the yard managers.

After three weeks in Vegesack, we sailed for Mauritius. It was sad to leave Dora behind, but there was no other option. She left to continue her work at the Ministry of Pensions and I resolved that, ultimately, I would leave the sea to try and live a more normal, married life. But how to achieve this?

I knew that I must pass my final examination, for Master Mariner, to give me future security and I also knew that by saving money I would have a better chance of changing directions in whatever the future held. I still had 1½ years of sea time to complete before becoming eligible to sit for my Master's 'Ticket'; and so I decided to take the bull by the horns and asked Athel Line if I could stay on board the *Athel Templar* for eighteen months to complete my sea time in the shortest possible time. Of course, by so doing, I could save up all my salary and accumulated leave pay, which, together with an allowance for study leave pay, would be a fairly substantial sum.

I was lucky, because the *Athel Templar* made several trips to Mauritius, Durban and the West Indies which ended up in the UK, so Dora was able to join the ship several times during this period.

Ships were not 'female friendly'; I remember that I used to stand guard whilst Dora had a shower, which was shared with the third mate. When she washed her hair, an ideal way to dry it was by standing on the desk in my cabin and holding her head near the hot air blowers. One day, I sent the third mate to collect something from my cabin and, observing Dora standing on my desk in the corner, he asked, 'Does he always make you stand in the corner?'

By now I had a lot of experience as second mate; I worked hard and conscientiously, which was my way, but also it helped to make the time pass more quickly.

In addition to my normal 12-4 watch-keeping duties, I studied every single day, morning and evening, determined to take as little time as possible over my future examination.

The 12-4 watch, or 'middle' nightwatch, was not everyone's cup of tea, but it was well established that the experienced second mate kept that watch whilst the Captain could sleep more easily. The 12-4 watch in the afternoon was often spent correcting charts as well as the normal watch-keeping duties of lookout, taking bearings, checking compass errors and filling in logbooks. Every morning after breakfast, the second mate would take a morning sight and relieve the third mate, who went down for breakfast; at lunchtime the second mate would have an early 'seven bells' lunch, at 11.20. The totality of the watch-keeping duties meant that the second mate worked nine hours every day, seven days per week, and often with extra hours when arriving at and leaving port. Working these rather long and unsocial hours was normal for us and still gave me plenty of time to study – I never went ashore, though, for one and a half years!

We loaded alcohol in bulk at Durban, South Africa; this did not create any problems, but the carriage of it did! We found out that the crew had been collecting mugs full as it dripped out of the valves and flanges in the bottom of the pump room; we heard that, when mixed with two parts water, it tasted just like gin! Naturally this had to be controlled, so we locked the pump room and switched searchlights on the deck every night.

The one thing that helped me with my studies was that I had stopped smoking in December 1954, and so to keep my hands and mind occupied, I worked even harder – so that I had no spare time whatsoever.

The fact that we returned to the UK at fairly regular intervals had one happy result – Dora was expecting our first baby, which meant that I was even more anxious to leave the sea at this juncture. This feeling was strengthened at Christmas 1954, when some of the crew went berserk, after being allowed beer by the Captain, resulting in one junior engineer having his finger nearly sliced off by the cook and the officers' steward being lost overboard. We never did find out what happened to the officers' steward; the police boarded in the UK and took statements, but nothing tangible came of it, although he had been known to talk about suicide. At the end of April 1957, I paid off the *Athel Templar* to be with my wife and to study, finally, to become a Master Mariner.

Dora had located a small flat near to the tram stop, not far from where she lived. It was ideal. Every morning I took a tram to

Fleetwood and was always first in the door when Captain MacFarlane opened up. I never wasted a minute all day, even at coffee and lunch breaks, but the result of all this industriousness, combined with my study time at sea, meant that I passed my Master Mariner's (Foreign Going) Certificate after only two months, instead of the more usual nine months.

The curriculum was somewhat different, naturally; written examinations included Navigation, Magnetism, Engineering, Ship Master's Business, Ship Stability and Electronics, with the usual Signals and oral examinations and preliminary courses, of two weeks, for Ship Captain's Medical Certificate and a Radar Simulator Course.

Now I had achieved my short-term objectives. I was a fully qualified Master Mariner. This was my security, and also both Dora and I had saved up every penny we earned, so that this could help in some way to find employment ashore. But what was a Master Mariner qualified to do ashore?

The Shop

Thirty-six

IT WAS NOT EASY to find work ashore, despite having such a good qualification and nine years' work experience. All the marine-related jobs, such as pilots, were long gone; for example, my mentor and principal of Fleetwood Navigation School, Captain MacFarlane, had put the names of his twin sons down as Liverpool pilots at birth! The British Merchant Navy was still the biggest in the world and so there were no shortages of experienced mariners to fill any vacancy that occurred. There was another option, I could carry on studying for another two years – without pay – to try for my Extra Master's Certificate, which was more academic and lead more naturally to the *possibility* of a position as college lecturer, but even then, the salary was poor and it would mean spending all our hard-earned savings. In the end, I decided that the best way forward was to invest in a small business and try to build it up. I followed this route by popping into small shops in the neighbourhood and weighing up the qualities of the owners of the most successful; my conclusion was that, with all due respect to those owners, I could do at least as well, and so I started looking seriously through an agent who specialised in the sale of small businesses. By that time, I had also reasoned that it would be best to sell food, mainly because everyone had to eat!

With a sheath of papers in hand, I visited several shops and decided that one in Cleveleys, named 'Handy Stores', more nearly filled the bill than the others – or, more correctly, was within my price range.

Dora was in hospital having our first baby when I decided that we should go ahead with the purchase – subject to Dora's approval when she came out of hospital. The upshot was that we purchased this small corner shop, near the seafront, within 100 metres of a caravan site and surrounded by small houses, some of which were boarding houses.

In fairness to the estate agent, who was an honourable man, he felt sorry for us when he realised that, after paying for the property, goodwill and stock, we would have no capital left and he did advise me that he would not purchase such a business without at least a float of £200 (probably around £7,000 today) but despite his advice, I decided to go ahead anyway, having a lot of confidence in my own ability and a great deal of determination. I also had the fallback of my Master's 'Ticket', because Athel Line had noted that if I decided to return to the sea life, I should contact them again, and I did have a good reputation in the company.

After checking over the stock, we opened our shop on a Monday in September 1957; we had no knowledge or experience of how to run a small general store, and we had only enough change, £5, to put into the wooden drawer we used as a till.

That first day we took around £15, not a lot certainly, but an encouragement because it was the quietest day of the week and towards the end of the holiday season. We sold anything and everything in the beginning: buckets and spades, and postcards from a stand outside the shop; sweets – weighed out of jars; chocolates, biscuits – weighed out of tins; ice cream, gas mantles for the caravans, collar studs, cotton of every hue, tinned food, bird seed, cigarettes, matches etc., etc.

We earned enough that week to pay for replacement stock from local wholesalers, giving us a profit margin of around 12.5%; but to achieve this we opened from eight in the morning until eight at night, seven days per week. It was not easy, but we were young and strong and fully committed, and that was not easy with a six-week-old baby, needing frequent feeding and changing. I well remember Dora coming to help me in the shop during busy periods, in the middle of feeding the baby, whom she put on the settee, quickly buttoning her overall and dashing into the shop, returning to find the baby – our eldest daughter, Anne – fast asleep.

We had been in the shop for only about three weeks when I caught Asian flu. I was really ill, and with my susceptibility to chest infections and asthma, had to spend a few days in bed; thankfully Dora managed, with help from my cousin, Neville.

It was just at this time that many of the traditional holidaymakers started to spend their holidays at Butlins or Pontins holiday camps, and some of the more adventurous were taking coach holidays on the near continent. This harmed Blackpool and Cleveleys, with a decrease in the prominence they had enjoyed for half a century; which meant, in effect, less business for us. Despite this, I managed to build up the business by knocking on doors of boarding houses and hotels during the bleak winter months, offering wholesale discounts; this initiative gave us some success, because it built up our turnover, enabling us to buy at better prices and thus give us better discounts.

We were helped to some extent by the Blackpool Illuminations restarting again after the war, and this extended the holiday season; but, at the same time, supermarkets started to open; small ones at first, but enough to take business away from the small shops. I found that I had to work harder and harder to increase the turnover so that the profit, at the year end, kept increasing. I managed to do this for five years.

It was obvious that increasing business meant we needed more space. We managed with only very basic furniture, no carpets, a painted table and chairs from my parents' garage, a bed given by a neighbour, a tea chest with an embroidered cloth as an 'occasional' table, and a settee bought from a neighbour for ten shillings. But we had managed for three years and now we had just enough money to improve our little shop, first knocking out the backs of the display windows to let in more light and a little more space, and then to have the wall knocked down from the shop into our back room/lounge. This was a major undertaking for us but was a big improvement.

We now lived upstairs on the first floor and in the two attic bedrooms, and furnished it with furniture bought wholesale from Manchester and delivered by our own van, which we were paying for out of our small profits. The inside of the shop was now twice its original area, and was fitted out as a small self-service store – the first in Cleveleys.

By the time we had increased our turnover and improved the shop, it was becoming increasingly apparent the big supermarket chains were threatening the very existence of small businesses. Virtually all the small shops in our vicinity had to close because they did not make enough profit. We were the sole survivors, but the work needed to keep increasing our turnover and profit was taking its toll. One day, with my now two little girls with me, I experienced a haemorrhage from my mouth, much to the distress of my eldest daughter, but she was somewhat mollified when I told her it was just my tooth bleeding. I drove quickly back to the shop to drop off the girls, then round to Doctor Schofield to ask for his help and advice.

'Don't worry Donald,' he said, 'go to bed for a day or two and then we will check you out, but it is probably due to your bronchitis and not tuberculosis or anything more serious.'

I didn't want to go to bed but, by this time, we had several staff working for us, and it was not such a major problem.

I checked with the specialist at the Health Centre, who assured me that I did not have tuberculosis or cancer. So, somewhat reassured, both Dora and I agreed that we had better sell our shop before it killed me.

Having always had a weakness in my chest with asthma, bronchitis and pneumonia, and a long spell in hospital when I was younger, it really was obvious that the conditions we were working in were not the best for my condition. For example, the Blackpool coast is famous for its breezes, and as our shop door opened on the corner, the wind whistled through the shop as we often opened our back door as well to stock up for our storerooms. There was virtually no heating in the shop, and I was going downhill fast, with one chest infection after another. We both decided that we should sell our shop and move to a warmer climate, perhaps Australia, to see if I could recover my health.

Businesses are easier to buy than to sell, but we did sell it by leaving a loan on the property as a second mortgage. In the meantime, we had applied to the Australian immigration authorities, so whilst we were awaiting their reply we moved in with Dora's mother and father at their little semi in Anchorsholme, Cleveleys.

We lived with Mum and Dad for five months, awaiting the reply from Australia, which, despite my letters, never came. In the meantime, I looked around for a job to stop our hard-earned cash from dwindling, but most local jobs on offer were not for me, I was told because I was too qualified! I did try one job in Lancaster with Curry's electrical goods, but realised after two days it was not for me.

Sensibly I had kept in touch with Athel Line and they welcomed me back with open arms. Accordingly, in May 1963 I joined the *Athel Sultan* in Amsterdam as Second Mate.

I didn't feel badly about it because I had been ashore for nearly six years, watching my two eldest daughters grow up; I had gained a lot of experience and we had increased our capital. During the months spent with Dora's parents, I had helped them a bit by sprucing up their property, and now I had to continue earning a living by returning to the sea, certainly not as healthy as when I left but much wiser and a little richer.

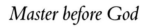

Master before God

Twenty-seven

I JOINED THE *Athel Sultan* in Avonmouth as Second Mate in May 1963, having taken the precaution of spending a couple of days at Fleetwood Navigation School to familiarise myself with all the usual duties of a watch-keeping officer. I was confident but a little disappointed that I was going back to sea after trying so hard to stay together with my family, but my health problems were the last straw, and I was more or less forced to seek alternative employment.

The Master of the *Athel Sultan* was none other than 'Titch' Elliot, and having sailed with him twice before, it was easy to fall in with his ways – he had been a good shipmate then, so a good start for me now. The only downside to my appointment was that the mate was not as qualified as I was and also a few years younger; I had, naturally, lost my position in the promotion ladder, but that could not be helped and I determined not to let it bother me.

On our way to the Far East, the fresh air and sunshine, together with a release from all financial worries, worked wonders. I was no longer gasping for breath and the haemorrhage from my chest had ceased. It seemed like a miracle to me, which helped to offset the separation from my family. Dora and I always kept in close touch by letter, both of us writing a couple of pages every day; not an ideal substitute for being together as a family, but it did help us to become the close family unit that we are to this day.

There was a big plus from my experiences owning a shop; it really did help me to relate more closely with the crew, having served their like for several years, I could empathise with most of their situations at home, and this did help in my bid for a 'fast track' promotion.

The only problem that arose to mar my return to seafaring was a demand from the purchaser of my business for a few hundred pounds that he maintained was due to him because of certain aspects of the business with which he disagreed; even though he had been given full access to the accounts and to my accountant. Our solicitor advised that, as the sum was small, we should pay it and have done with it. We complied with his recommendation – it was a mistake!

During the course of my voyage on the *Athel Sultan,* Dora sent me a letter from my solicitor advising that the purchaser was now asking for substantially more from us. I was enraged; the business was good and genuine, so I did then what I should have done in the first place. I instructed our solicitor to take counsel's opinion. Counsel wrote back that we had nothing to pay and that we should not have paid anything in the first place! This was a lesson well learned, I resolved never to take the easy way out if I was not happy with a particular situation; taking the harder route is very often easier in the end!

This incident apart, the family was in good shape. We had purchased a fairly new three-bedroomed bungalow, furnished it and bought a new little red Mini so that Dora could take the family around and visit her parents nearby. The bungalow was in a pleasant and safe neighbourhood, with a school nearby, which all helped to give stability to my family.

Being separated from the family, ironically, brought us closer together, and I know that Dora felt the same; it was for that reason she kept the following write-up entitled, 'Tanker Thoughts' which was always pinned up on a notice board at home.

Tanker Thoughts

No word, one can only hope that she will be there.
I have written. Four days, that's all we have.
The company must have told her by now.
Will she be there?
Maybe the kids are sick, or she can't get a babysitter.
Suddenly my mother-in-law is a wonderful person.
Seven days to go and we will be home.
There is still the ship to paint, but will she be there?
I can only hope.
Six days to go and the tension is mounting, will she come?

The ship is getting painted, but do you think she will come?
Five, four, three, two days to go, I am on tenterhooks.
Is she coming? I am making excuses, maybe the kids are sick,
maybe she can't get a babysitter, maybe my mother-in-law is sick.
No, she is never sick...
I seem to be smoking a lot these days.
One day to go, I hope she comes.
The ship is painted, all the paperwork is done, she must come,
like the daisy, she will, she won't, *she will*.
Docking, and there she is standing on the quay, smiling at me.
Suddenly the world is a wonderful place to live in.

I left the *Athel Sultan* at Cardiff in November 1963 and after a happy spell of leave reunited with my family, I was sent to Immingham to stand by the repairs of two of the company's vessels, the *Athel Prince* and the *Athel Mere*. It was a good time for me because I spent a month in Immingham but travelled back home by car every weekend, and had Christmas and New Year at home.

By the end of January 1964, work on the two vessels was nearing the end and the company decided that they were in need of another chief officer. Whether it was due to a good report from 'Titch' Elliot, or my previous record, or possibly my hard work in the shipyard, I don't know but I was promoted to Chief Officer of the *Athel Prince*.

Twenty-eight

IT WAS A DOUBLE-EDGED sword. On the one hand I was promoted, and on the other, I had learnt that we would probably be away for a long time, as the ship had a twelve months' time charter to the British Phosphate Commission in New Zealand, and that was as far away from the UK as one could get!

Anyway, it was a new challenge and another step up the ladder; I beavered away every day in Immingham Dry Dock, crawling over the whole ship, inspecting every nook and cranny so that I was completely au fait with every aspect of the *Athel Prince*, from truck to keel.

She was a bulk carrier of around 15,000 tons deadweight, so designed that she could carry dry cargo in bulk with minimum hold preparation – no feeders or shifting boards to rig if we carried grain. She was of a three-island design, with raised fo'c's'le and poop, with bridge and officers' accommodation amidships.

The new Master joined, Captain Stan Hill, a short square man who cautioned me immediately about being prepared for a long trip. Then I was able to brief him about the general condition of the ship.

We signed on Articles on 10th February 1964, having left home the previous weekend with heart-searching, tearful farewells. The next day we battened down the steel single-pull hatches and left the berth with the aid of tugs on a blustery, cloudy day; I was standing by on the fo'c's'le head, as is normal for the mate, bosun and carpenter, when entering or leaving port.

We were just entering the lock gates when the wind caught us. Flying light as we were, the tugs couldn't hold us, and the port bow slammed against the granite side of the lock gates. Whilst we were waiting for the locks to fill, I had a pressure hose sprayed on the dent in the ship's side, which was in the way of the riveted plate landing, but no water came through inside number one hold – thank goodness, as the indentation was low enough down to be below the waterline when we were fully laden.

Tugs let go, pilot departed, and out we sailed into the cold, dismal waters of the North Sea.

We were heading across the western ocean via the Windward Passage in the West Indies, to La Romana, a port on the south coast of the Dominican Republic, on the island of Hispaniola, where we were to load a full cargo of raw sugar.

It was a terrible passage. The weather was atrocious, and we took nearly three weeks for a passage which should have taken us seventeen days, hardly seeing the sun at all; but I remember obtaining a single position line from an early morning star sight. Being chief officer, or the mate, I was now on the 4-8 watch night and morning.

Despite the weather, all the holds had been cleaned out by the crew and then, with the help of ladders suitably lashed against the rolling, and long-handled rollers or 'man helpers', all the inside of the cargo holds had been painted silver. She looked in good shape, and I had no fears that the cargo surveyor would not pass the holds as fit for their sugar cargo.

There was one major problem on this passage; when the steel pontoon hatches were lifted it was discovered that the watertight rubber, strip around the sides of the hatches had become stuck fast to the hatch coaming, which had been newly spray-painted with epoxy paint in Immingham Dry Dock. Fortunately, we had enough rubber to renew all the seals, and this work was completed prior to our arrival at La Romana.

The surveyor duly passed all the holds. Loading by conveyor and chute was started immediately afterwards, the ship being moved up and down the quay by ship's moorings to fill each hatch in turn.

During our five days of loading, I again tested the indentation on the port bow with a pressure hose, but no water came through. I did, however, recommend to Captain Hill that we should call in the surveyor to check it out before we completed loading, but he did not think it was necessary. Maybe he thought that calling in the surveyor would delay the ship, but, whatever his reason, it turned out to be the wrong decision!

With time to spare during the loading of the sugar, I walked around the storage warehouse to examine the loading system. It was quite simple; dumper trucks tipped the sugar into a hopper where it was first weighed and then tipped onto the conveyor that ran out to the ship. The only fault in the system was that the man designated to tally all the sugar weighed in the hopper had a habit of nodding off to sleep – this had repercussions!

When we were loaded to the marks allowed us to navigate freely through the Panama Canal, I advised the shore stevedore, who insisted that there was more to come. Captain Hill advised that we should continue loading, perhaps thinking that, as a first-trip mate, I could be mistaken. In the end, we did finish loading – but were about 200 tons overloaded, according to me.

We arrived at Panama two days later to top up with bunkers and transit the canal and we were four inches down by the head on completion. It was not really what the pilot liked, but he accepted us without the need of a tug to help steer her through the canal, which would have been expensive for the owners.

At the second lot of locks, the draft had changed, we were now more than six inches by the head and it took a lot of persuading for the pilot to continue without a tug. The Captain was not very pleased with me either, perhaps in part blaming me for misreading the draft. Anyway we cleared the canal and proceeded on passage across the Pacific, directly to Auckland.

One of the many duties of the mate was to check all the tanks every day to make sure that there were no leaks anywhere. To assist with this, the ship's carpenter would sound the tanks first thing every morning and note the soundings on a blackboard in the wheelhouse. The mate would then fill in the logbook and include the soundings.

For the first two days out of the canal I had not seen Chippy actually taking the soundings of the forrard double-bottom tanks, and this was strange because being on watch, I would normally see everything. Yet he had noted on the blackboard 'MT' for every tank, indicating that they were dry. I asked him about this and he assured me that he had been sounding the tanks and the very next day he made a big 'play' of obviously sounding every tank and noted all of then on the blackboard as 'MT' – except, that is, number one double-bottom which he had noted as having about 2'8" in. I wasn't worried because this would be the size of the 'hatbox' or drain in the hold; but nevertheless I checked the drawing, and found that, according to the drawing, we had a couple of inches of water in the hold, which meant that the bottom of the cargo was wet also. I couldn't believe it – water in my very first cargo as mate!

I called Chippy so that we could re-check the sounding. He had given me incorrect information, it was in fact about ten feet – the number one hold was flooding, and we were going down by the head, which would slow the ship, damage the cargo and maybe even lead to damage, if we encountered heavy weather.

What the hell had caused the water to flood into the hold? Of course, I reported it to the Captain and he was not delighted, but he agreed with me that Chippy could not have been sounding the tank, and that it had probably flooded a couple of days earlier.

I examined the steam smothering system for leakage, and sign of water running back through the bilge. Accordingly, the only possible solution was that the heavy indentation, caused by landing heavily leaving Immingham, had started to leak into the hold.

It was not enough to inspect the void space between the ship's side and the steel plating lining the frames in the V-shaped hold, but by various means we were able to determine that the ship was leaking and that the water was finding its way into the hold.

By calculation, I had determined that there was no danger of us sinking, but it was not a happy situation: I had to stop the water flooding into the hold.

Eventually I found a solution. By drilling holes in the forrard bulkhead of number two port wing ballast tank, the water flooded out of the void space and was then pumped out daily by the engineers; but what about the water already soaked in our cargo of sugar?

I found a solution to that problem also, by crawling through number two double bottom – not pleasant if you are claustrophobic, and not really safe because the air was not too fresh; but at the forrard end, I remember seeing a flange protruding from number one 'hatbox' when I was inspecting the whole ship in dry dock. By opening the flange, a viscous splurge of molasses came pouring out into the double bottom. I scrambled out covered in the sticky mess but delighted to find a solution to the problem. All we had to do now was let saltwater run into the double bottom to thin the molasses and then pump it out. That way, we drained all the surplus water out of number one and kept it dry until we arrived in Auckland.

We enjoyed a pleasant week or so in Auckland letting the shore grabs discharge our cargo, and all of us had a spell ashore, as the 'wharfies' didn't usually work at weekends. This also gave me chance to meet up with my mother's sister, Auntie Audrey, and Uncle Norman, who kindly drove me round part of the North Island.

It was here that I first tasted red snapper, a fish caught locally. One of the sugar factory workers, a Dutchman who had migrated to New Zealand five years before, sat on the edge of the quay, fishing during his lunch break; I don't think that I have ever seen a happier man, sat there in the sun, eating his sandwich lunch and catching fresh fish for his dinner!

Because of the problem with the leaking number one hold, I had purposely left the discharge of the bottom part until the very last; it was late afternoon, and when the Captain saw that they were about to discharge that part, he immediately decided it was time to go ashore!

We hadn't long to wait before the foreman stevedore was knocking at my door. 'Chief, there's a problem with the cargo in number one, it's absolutely solid, the grabs won't touch it.' Surprise, surprise!

It is normal not to admit any liability in these cases so we called in an independent cargo surveyor, who took samples, and as the 'wharfies' were knocking off for the day, we left it until the next morning, when two things happened to surprise us. First, the sugar factory accepted the sugar because, as they said, it made no difference to their processing and, as I had always maintained, they actually received a couple of hundred tons of cargo more than they had paid for! It was a simple matter for them to hoist a mini dumper truck down into the bottom of the hold. This broke up the sugar and allowed the grab to discharge it. The second surprise was when the cargo surveyor reported that the sugar had been damaged by *fresh* water and not salt. This really knocked us out, and it was only when I had time to think about everything that I realised the fresh water must have flushed in first, when we were in the freshwater lakes of the Panama Canal – and this would have been the reason why we were tilting more and more by the head. Of course, if the Chippy had done his work more conscientiously, we would have known much sooner; but, as Shakespeare wrote, *'All's Well That Ends Well'*!

Twenty-nine

AFTER DISCHARGING OUR cargo of sugar we were on twelve months' charter to the British Phosphate Commission, so our next cargo was to be phosphate, loaded at the small island of Makatea, one of the Tuamotu Archipelago, about six days' steaming from Auckland.

The island was steep-to, as are all the islands in the South Pacific. We had to moor to four buoys, which were themselves moored somewhat precariously in the steep-sided depths of water, close enough to the coral beach so that the conveyor could carry the phosphate out to the chute and direct it into each hold in turn.

It was quite easy for the ship's staff. All the loading was done by the shore gang. All we had to do was make sure that all the derricks were topped upright to clear the hatch, and then open each hatch to let the phosphate pour in – if it rained it did not stop the operation.

There was one major problem with Makatea, because the buoys were moored on its very steep-sided depth of water, any undue pull on the buoys would mean that the ship would pull the buoys off the bottom and drift off the island and, in the process, probably damage the conveyor belt system. Accordingly, if the swell came up suddenly, all loading was stopped immediately, the chute withdrawn, the buoy moorings let go and the powerful mooring launches would then push the ship away from the island to drift in the ocean swell.

Twice, whilst we were on this run, we were pushed out unceremoniously from Makatea. It created problems for us because as the ship rolled, so we had difficulty stowing and securing the ten 20-ton derricks; it was a risky business handling them in the dark at night when such occurrences happened for us.

Normally, loading took only about twenty-four hours and then we headed back for New Zealand to discharge at various ports, the first of which was Dunedin.

On the way back to Dunedin we had an engine breakdown, not unusual as the *Athel Prince* was a motor ship that required more maintenance than steamships; but this presented a good opportunity to dump all our old wire runners overboard without the possibility of fouling the propeller and without polluting the seas, which were several miles deep. What I did not know was that old runners were in great demand in New Zealand for hauling logs that were felled in their forests. I was mortified, upon arrival in New Zealand, to be asked if we had any old wire runners; this was the first time in my years at sea that I had ever had the opportunity of a 'perk' and, unwittingly, I had blown the chance!

What did surprise me in Dunedin was that we were asked to work the cargo ourselves because there were not enough wharfies available. This really was something unusual because both the Australian and New Zealand wharfies were renowned for their militancy and I would have expected them to complain but, apparently, it was the custom in New Zealand, and readily accepted by the wharfies.

All the crew were eager to cooperate because they would be paid a comparatively high hourly rate on top of their shipboard pay; altogether, we needed twenty men, four to each hatch. The team of four was used by having two winch drivers, one hatchman who directed the winch drivers because they could not see down the hatch, and one man on shore who opened up the hopper to let the phosphate run down into the lorry which drove underneath.

It worked quite well for a time but number four hatch was a problem. The irascible and unreliable Chippy was the hatchman, and on the quayside operating the hopper was our Sparks. Due to Chippy's incompetence, the grab full of phosphate sometimes opened before it reached the hopper and this meant that Sparks had to shovel the phosphate into the lorry – very hard labour, and it resulted in much fist-shaking and cursing at each other until peace was restored by giving Chippy another job!

There was one very delightful outcome from all our efforts at discharging cargo. After the crew signed their chits and were paid by the British Phosphate Commission, I was handed two envelopes, one for me and one for the Captain; apparently, according to union rules, two 'spare hands' were required to stand by, and both the Captain and I were so designated! The BPC supervisor assured me that it was all perfectly proper and, indeed, we worked cargo afterwards at other ports, enabling me to send cash home for the family to spend.

Indian City. First trip apprentice in Sydney Harbour, 1948

The author and Chris Barlow (Junior and Senior
Apprentices, 1949)

Painting on leave, 1954

Senior Apprentice and Acting Bosun, 1951

Senior Apprentice, 1951

Clan Line, 1953

Clan Shaw, 1953

Athel Monarch, 1954

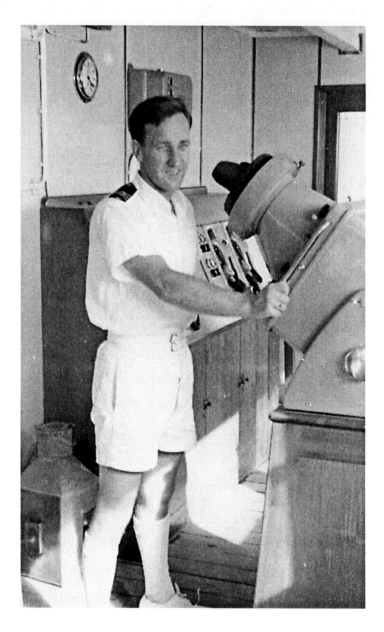

Athel Monarch. In the wheelhouse, 1954

Atheltemplar, 2nd Officer, 1955

Atheltemplar, 2nd Officer, 1955

Athel Duchess, 2nd Officer, 1955

Married to Dora, 1955

Wedding day, 1955

Athelprince leaving Dunedin, 1964

Athelprince at Lytteton. Discharging phosphate, 1964

Athelprince. Loading phosphate at Makatea Island, 1964

Athelprince, Chief Officer, 1964

Athelprince. Chief Officer with grass skirt, 1964

Athelprince, writing home, 1964

Shipping heavy seas in South Pacific – *Athelprince,* 1964

Shipping heavy seas in South Pacific – *Athelprince*, 1964

SA *Drakenstein*, 1970

SA *Drakenstein*, 1970

Buffet on board *Lankus*, 1970

Athelprince, Chief Officer, 1964

Athelking in Japan, 1965

Anco Queen. UK's first chemical tanker, 1967

Handing over *Gondwana,* South Africa's biggest ship,
with Sponsor, Mrs Thorpe, 1971

Handing over *Gondwana,* with Captain Thorpe,
Director, 1971

Gondwana. In a sea of gold, South Africa's largest vessel.

Gondwana, 1972

Gondwana, South Africa's biggest ship, 1972

Gondwana, South Africa's biggest ship, 1972

Gondwana. Taking helicopter spares
off Cape Town, 1972

Globtik, 1973

Globtik, 1973

Bunga Mawar. Malaysia's biggest vessel, 1974

Arya Pas, 1978

Arya Pas, 1978

Kurdistan, a tanker which broke in two off the coast of Newfoundland. I was Nautical Assessor for the British Government, 1979

Thirty

AFTER LOADING AGAIN at Makatea, our next discharge port was Bluff, right at the southern tip of New Zealand and close enough to the roaring forties to experience plenty of wet, windy weather. Once again we worked cargo, but I was surprised when I was told that we had to stop because of light rain. Actually the rain did no harm to the phosphate, but union rules dictated that all cargo work must cease when there were more than a certain number of spots of rain per minute; counted by a union representative who sat in a little cabin, or 'roost' as it was termed. Apparently he sat there all day just counting spots and when he said 'Stop!' all work had to stop.

Bluff was a pleasant little place, though, and the town was within walking distance, making it easy to go ashore for a bit of shopping, a drink or two and church services at the Methodist Church.

At that juncture, New Zealand had the same laws governing drinking as Australia: bars closed at 6 p.m.! This meant that workers rushed out of their workplaces and dived into the pubs at 5 p.m. to participate in, what was euphemistically termed 'the five o'clock swill'! Usually jugs of beer were lined up to be sold quickly to thirsty workers and then each jug would be filled up again by a pipe connected to the barrels of beer, opened by the barmaid or barman by a petrol-pump-type nozzle. There was beer everywhere. I heard that when the bar closed at six, the doors of clubs were opened.

Our second mate was well experienced in the trade out in New Zealand and Australia, and he assured me that it was the custom for Merchant Navy officers to dress up in full uniform and to parade with the Returned Services Association on ANZAC Day. I really thought he was pulling my leg because being in the Merchant Navy was vastly different to belonging to one of the armed services. By the time I had heard the same story from the

BPC supervisor and the mate of a Blue Star ship astern, I knew that it was no joke and, upon enquiring further, found that the Merchant Navy actually led the parade.

As this was Friday and the parade was scheduled for the next day, I put all the officers and apprentices on standby for the parade – in full uniform. I emphasise the 'full uniform' bit, because during working hours the engineers wore oily white boiler suits, the apprentices wore dungarees and the deck officers wore white boiler suits on cargo watch.

But Saturday came with little or no rain and every one of our officers turned out resplendent in his uniform; they were joined then by officers from the Blue Star ship astern, and then by the pipe band from nearby Invercargill and a contingent of war veterans. I still have a photograph of us all marching in step, leading the parade, from the town hall to the RSA memorial, where we stopped whilst a local priest conducted a service. Then we marched back to the town hall.

I knew nothing about these ANZAC day parades but found out later that it actually started at dawn with a parade of cars round the town, hooting horns and ensuring an early start to the day-long drinking session!

On our arrival back at the town hall, we were invited inside where every table was well supplied with free jugs of beer and lots of fresh Bluff oysters – a sailor's paradise!

Now I was a senior officer, and as second-in-command had to set an example, so the Captain and I left early after a couple of drinks and went back to our ship nearby. We had a coffee and a bit of a chat at the top of the gangway, when we heard an almighty noise emanating from the direction of the town hall. Then, round the corner of the warehouse on shore, marched the rest of the officers, mixed with members of the RSA and led by the second steward off the ship astern who was acting as drum major of the remnants of the pipe band – swinging a mop as mace!

'Pull up the gangway!' was the order from the streetwise Captain. Both of us heaved away energetically, then hid behind the deck house as the mob veered away from us and headed for the ship astern. We saw them march along the quay, up the swinging accommodation ladder, round the deckhouses and superstructure until they reached the Captain's deck... Whether he was delighted or not at the presence of a drunken mob at his door, we never found out!

Thirty-one

AFTER LOADING OUR next cargo we discharged it at Napier, in the North Island.

Napier was quite easy to approach but it was difficult to stay comfortably alongside due to the swell that rolled in whenever there was an easterly component to the wind. To help us stay alongside without damage to the ship, floating rafts were placed alongside to provide a buffer as the ship ranged with the swell. It was disconcerting sometimes to hear the ship thumping against the quayside throughout the night sounding as if we were sustaining heavy damage, but in fact, we were not.

The harbour master had a system of judging when the swell was too dangerous for us to remain alongside, and whenever this happened, the pilot would appear and tugs came alongside, without prior notice, to tow us out to the comparative safety outside the harbour. This happened to us only once. We were all turned in. It was a Saturday night when the pilot boarded, tugs hooted and the nightwatchman called us all to stand by. Although we hadn't detected any worsening of the thumping and bumping, the weather forecast available to the harbour master indicated that the situation would worsen very quickly.

We stood by fore and aft, letting go moorings, making fast tugs and manning the engine room to facilitate a quick departure, but it was not easy. As it was the weekend, there was no cargo being worked and no reason for the crew not to go ashore, and most of them had had a few drinks, so it was difficult to get them out of their bunks and to help with handling of moorings etc.

Once clear of the port, the tugs were let go and the pilot went with them, but we were out in the open sea; all our derricks were topped and promising to cause major damage as they flailed around in the swell, and as the wind was rising, it was unwise to leave all the hatches open as she was fully laden and quite low in the water. We worked through the early hours of the morning, battening down all the hatches with difficulty in the prevailing conditions, and one of the ordinary seamen lost a finger trapped in a wire. We succeeded, however, and managed to lower the derricks without major damage to anybody or anything.

My aunt and uncle motored down from Auckland, which was kind of them; I was able to host them to a lunch on board and then they took me back to their home in Auckland; it was a pleasant interlude to see so much of the New Zealand countryside and to sample Auntie Audrey's home cooking!

We used all our working hours in port to work over the side to ensure that, once we were homeward bound, all the rust would have been chipped off and all the topsides painted, but we did need cooperation from the crew. I had worked out a deal with the bosun when we first arrived on the New Zealand coast, anticipating that the crew would want to spend as much time ashore as possible and yet knowing that there was a lot of work to do, I agreed with him that when we were not required to work cargo, half the crew would work on deck, the other half could go ashore; that way I reasoned, would ensure maximum effort from those working – it was a mistake!

The first morning, I was on deck before seven to count heads as the crew turned to, but only one or two turned out; the rest were sleeping off the previous night's debauchery. That was the end of 'deals' with crew, as far as I was concerned; thereafter, I made certain that they worked 'bell to bell' with not a minute of time off for anything; if they did not comply, then they were punished by deducting several days' pay, duly noted in the official logbook. I realised that trying to be 'kind' and 'considerate' to the crew was not the way, especially on a long voyage. It was never appreciated, and in future I never gave any crew time off, but would be fair to them whenever they had to deal with personal problems at home.

I know that I earned the sobriquet of 'Adolf' on one ship and 'God' on another, but I like to believe that I also earned the respect of both officers and crew by being firm but fair.

Thirty-two

WE HAD DISCHARGED our last cargo at Mount Maunganui, Tauranga, in the North Island, and headed west to Phillips Bay in Australia where we were to load feed oats at Geelong. On passage we cleaned all the holds and were ready in all respects to load on arrival.

Loading was a simple operation, really. Each hatch was opened and the oats fed in by chutes, so that all the main holds and wing tank were filled to the very brim with the oats. These being a very light cargo, we needed to fill every corner to lift a full cargo.

It took us only four days to load and then, after this long trip away from family and home we were *homeward bound*!

We called at Fremantle en route to top up our bunkers and, of course, receive mail, and then headed across the Indian Ocean for Ras Hafun on the Horn of Africa before heading into the colder climate as we moved north through the Red Sea and Mediterranean to Europe.

On passage, during bad weather, I had decided to paint out the void space on top of the forepeak tank; to do this, Chippy had to open up the manhole to the void space, and as this required ventilating, I left it for twenty-four hours for the movement of the bow plates in the seaway to pump fresh air in and out due to the bow plates panting.

The next day we went to inspect the tanks. It was only a shallow space and I had no reason to suspect that it would not be properly ventilated but, as Chippy climbed down the ladder, he nearly fell back in the space, and I grabbed him. Despite his size and weight, I managed to pull his head through the manhole so that he started breathing again. I don't know from where I drew strength to lift him but it certainly saved his life. Although there did not appear to be much rust in the void space, it was obviously enough to consume all the oxygen, leaving just carbon dioxide. Anyway he fully recovered and we improved air ventilation procedures by inserting a pipe of compressed air before we entered.

We did have another incident that could have ended disastrously, but was completed safely in the end. I wanted to paint the after freshwater tank with epoxy paints before we filled it again. To do this I had it completely drained, hatch opened for two days and then inserted a compress air hose. In those ships we did not have any sophisticated testing equipment, so I entered the tank myself to ensure that all was safe.

Once I knew that all was in order, I instructed the bosun to send the crew in to paint the tank, two at a time and then change with two others every fifteen minutes. He did not follow my instructions precisely, so that when I checked on what was going on, I found that four men were down the tank and he was peering through the manhole, completely intoxicated, laughing his head off. I managed to extricate them all safely but that incident confirmed my previous experience of the bosun; he was worse than useless – he was dangerous.

It was part of my job to carry out inspections and repairs to tanks of various types and size, and one day the chief engineer asked if I would go down the forrard fuel tank with him to see if we could detect a leak, because there was water in the fuel oil when he transferred it to the aftermost bunker tanks.

The forrard fuel tank was a peculiar shape. It was entered through a manhole under the fo'c's'le head, and then an upper tank about two metres deep was crossed; and to reach the bottom section, we had to climb down a ladder inside a narrow, vertical tunnel, just wide enough to squeeze down. At the bottom of this was the lower part of the forrard fuel tank. That inspection was definitely not for claustrophobics, pitch black and full of gas as it was! Obviously we had to wear breathing apparatus and climbed down without much difficulty by the aid of torchlight. I had just reached the bottom and suddenly couldn't breathe – and if I took off my mask I would breathe in the gaseous atmosphere! I quickly moved towards the vertical exit tunnel, just as the chief descended, and at that moment, the bayonet fitting at the end of my airline dropped on my head! I galloped up the ladder, tearing off my mask at the top and just made it out of the manhole, gasping for breath. Apparently, somehow, the chief had disconnected my air line inadvertently, but it certainly gave me a moment of panic as I fought for breath. Afterwards we had a good laugh about it, because he didn't know why I suddenly shot up the ladder as he came down; anyway we were able to reorganise ourselves and determine that there was no leak in the tank.

The chief also featured in an unusual incident as we crossed the Indian Ocean. I was on the bridge, near the end of my watch at night, the sky was clear of clouds, just myriads of stars reflecting from the calm sea, when, all of a sudden, a brilliant light illuminated everything, such that I could see the shadow of the chief engineer cast on to the forrard bulkhead of his accommodation as he enjoyed the cool of the evening, leaning on the rails.

The ball of light travelled horizontally from east to west, just above the horizon. I didn't know what it was; there was no 'Notice to Mariners' concerning firing of rockets in that particular area; so I reported it to the Admiralty Hydrographic Office, where such incidents are recorded, but I heard nothing more from them; after due thought, I put it down to a meteorite of some size, passing through the earth's atmosphere.

We were to discharge our full cargo at Hamburg, which, like Rotterdam, was very efficient, with floating suckers to suck out the oats and pour them into barges alongside for onward transportation through the rivers and canals of Germany.

Athel Prince was to undergo annual dry-docking and also a major alteration to her structure. Upon completion of discharge, we sailed round to Copenhagen, where she was going to be lengthened, or 'jumboised', by cutting her in two, drawing the two ends apart when she was refloated, and then inserting another hold. Apparently this jumboising would increase cargo capacity by 20% without a big reduction in speed.

This was my first trip as mate and I know that Captain Stan Hill had given me a very good report to the owners. Not only that, he was a decent man to serve under. He was supportive when needed, yet left me alone when he was not needed; and unlike many Captains of the day, he did not drown himself in booze but kept alert day and night, setting a good example to the officers and crew.

The Athel Line superintendent was on board as soon as we arrived at Copenhagen. 'I want you to work by the ship during this major refit,' he said.

Now by this time we had progressed enough to have shore telephone on board, so I pointed to it, as it was in my office, and asked him would he phone my wife and children to the effect that after being away thirteen months, I was now expected to stand by for another month! He got the message, and within a couple of days I flew home via Manchester Airport, where all the family were waiting excitedly to meet me. It was an experience I vowed never to repeat; being away from the family for thirteen and a half months was asking too much, but I had been prepared to take on a long trip because somehow or other I had to make up for the lost promotion, due to my six years ashore when we bought the shop.

After being away for thirteen and a half months, I was not estranged from my wife and family. I think that the years I had spent ashore when we bought the shop had helped a great deal in this regard. I can still remember the first day at home, when my two eldest daughters sat so close to me at mealtimes; Dora thought she was in isolation!

Whilst away I had never failed to write, from every port, individual letters to my wife and children. In fact Dora and I wrote something every day, which built up to a lot of letters each port.

Having kept in touch by letter, I knew, more or less, everything that was happening at home and I was determined not to disrupt the daily lives of my children, never letting them miss school nor Sunday school, and only taking holidays during school holidays – with the notable exception of a five-week spell in Japan, of which more, later.

Leave was also the time designated for repairs to property and major gardening works; this kept me fit and busy, and at the same time, kept operating costs to a minimum. We never had any real worries by now, with a good salary coming in every month, money invested, and both Dora and I working together on an agreed expenditure. This all helped to ensure family stability and gave us the means to live in reasonable comfort and to educate our children properly. Later on, we had a third child, and all three have been a credit to us.

Thirty-three

I HAD HAD A happy leave with the family, so I was excited by my next appointment, as Mate of the *Athel King*. She was the Athel Line's flagship, their newest and by far the biggest, at 60,000 tons deadweight. Most of the other ships in the fleet were around 12,000 tons deadweight, so it was a big leap forrard to a ship with five times their capacity; in fact, she was deemed to be so big at that juncture, that most of the Masters refused to sail on her, considering that she was too big and that they would rather see the rest of their working life out on ships with which they were comfortable.

I flew out to Cairo, staying overnight in a fourth-rate hotel booked for me by the agent. It was very hot in July and the hotel was very time-worn and shabby. That night just after I turned in with some illumination from the street light shining through the open window, I could see numerous little black bedbugs crawling on the pillow near my face. I leapt up, threw all the bedding into the bathroom and spent the rest of the night sat upright in a chair.

Sleep was not possible. Because of the heat, the local youths were playing football just outside the window, near the street light. Hardly had their exuberant noise died down when the local mosque started calling the faithful to prayer: '*Allah akbar!*' was the cry, by loudspeaker, right across from my open window. The next morning could not come quickly enough for me and I stood nearby to meet the agent in the foyer at around eight a.m. He then drove me to Port Tewfik on the Suez Canal, where I was to join the *Athel King* with the relief pilot as she transitted the canal.

It was a pleasant relief to board such a clean and cool ship; she was fully air-conditioned, and being on her maiden voyage was spotlessly clean.

I was overjoyed to meet Henry Marshman who was the mate. We had served together when he was third mate on the *Athel Templar,* and I knew him to be a really good shipmate – bright, intelligent and always cheerful; so I was not surprised to see him now as a senior chief officer in Athel Line. Of course, he had passed me on the promotion ladder during my six years ashore, but I did not resent it at all.

Henry was most helpful. He briefed me on every aspect of the cargo handling – she was a bulk crude carrier – and also briefed me on handling the crew, as this was the first all-Chinese crew with whom I had sailed.

The *Athel King* had loaded in the Gulf and was now on her way to Milford Haven, which gave me about ten days with Henry's help to really learn the ropes so that I was completely on top of everything.

I had made the mistake of encouraging Dora and my two daughters to visit the ship at Milford Haven. I hadn't realised that, in those days, it was about an eight-hour drive from Blackpool, and as she was expecting our third child it really was too much for her. Because the *Athel King* was new and efficient, she only needed one day in port, so the family had to return the next day. This was too much for Dora and this led to her having difficulties during her third pregnancy.

Completely unaware of the health problems at home, I sailed again for the Persian Gulf, to load for discharge in Japan. I had no trouble with all the usual operations of tank cleaning, ballast changing and then loading. The only problem I did have was trying to communicate with the crew, not that it was really necessary as all orders were given through the number one bosun. I wrote down as many Chinese words and characters as I could so that I could give essential orders in Chinese, only to realise that the Chinese could not even understand each other, as they spoke different dialects: Cantonese, Hokkien, Hainanese, Mandarin, etc.! So I did what I should have done in the first place, communicate only with the No. 1. This was the normal way and gave him 'face', which is of major importance to the Chinese.

I spent seven months on the *Athel King*, before flying home from Augusta, Sicily, looking forward, as always, to seeing the family and the newest addition, Christine, who had been born three months previously.

Thirty-four

BY NOW I WAS gaining a good reputation in the company and was a little disappointed to be appointed to the *Athel Mere,* which was the smallest ship in the company and one of the oldest; but I found out that this was for a short time, only three months, and after I was offered the position of Mate on the *Anco Queen.* She was a joint venture between Athel Line and Anco, which was the first purposely designed chemical tanker under the British Flag. Formerly the *Anco Queen* had been a product carrier then redesigned so that she could carry up to thirty-two different products/chemicals.

I joined at Freeport, Texas, and it was with great pleasure that I met up with Henry Marshman again. He was the mate, or more correctly, chief officer, as the *Anco Queen* carried four deck officers to help with the work load inherent in loading, discharging and preparing tanks for the very many different cargoes.

It was not easy. Athel Line had no previous experience of carrying so many different chemicals and products and depended heavily on the ship's staff, particularly the chief officer, to actually make sure that all the different chemicals, solvents etc. were loaded in the correct type of tanks, because different tanks had different coatings and loading the wrong produce in a particular tank could dissolve the coating. Additionally, some of the lube oil additives, for example, were carcinogenic. Others had no tolerance for water, so could be allowed to breathe on passage but only by drawing air through desiccators.

I can remember carrying styrene monomer, methyl ethyl ketone (MEK), dioctyl phthalate (DOP), toluene, lube oil additives and xylene; and whenever such cargoes as acetone cyanohydrins were carried, it was a case of wearing over-pressure suits to load. The whole business was dangerous and difficult; inhaling vapours from the tanks could cause cumulative health problems, and furthermore, loading different parcels in staggered tanks caused many fractures to appear.

I remember that Henry was discharging the last of a parcel of aviation methanol, and there was difficulty pumping out the last few feet; the only way to inspect the valve was to go in the tank in over-pressure suits because the tank was full of gas; the valve had fractured so we managed to tape over the crack sufficiently well to discharge the residue. This was one example of many, indicating that life-threatening incidents were common.

I mentioned acetone cyanohydrins; this was so dangerous that one drop could be lethal, yet it was carried in bulk. All crew were evacuated during loading through an aluminium pipeline that was lowered down through a manhole to the bottom of the tank. When the tank was full, the chief officer would stand by in his over-pressure suit, lifting the aluminium pipe out of the tank, the drippings from the pipe covering him from head to foot. The tank was then battened down and the deck thoroughly washed with a hosepipe and the chief officer, himself, would stand under a fire hydrant to rinse off his over-pressure suit.

Regardless of the dangers and difficulties of the job, I resolved to carry out all my work professionally and to learn as much as possible at the same time. There was plenty of literature on board to be studied before every different grade was loaded. Some of the chemicals seemed to be too unsafe to handle, but nevertheless we managed to clean all thirty-two tanks from their previous cargo, ventilate them, clean and dry all the pipelines and valves and have them all inspected and passed by shore surveyors.

We loaded our various cargoes in New York, Jacksonville, Freeport, Baton Rouge, Avondale and San Francisco, taking the ship right down to her marks so that she could take a full cargo to discharge at Yokohama, Manila, Saigon and Singapore.

The serious and demanding business of juggling thirty-two grades of chemicals, lube oils and solvents meant that shore leave was out of the question, but by the time we had completed loading all cargo at San Francisco, it was a great relief to head out into the Pacific to discharge our first parcel at Yokohama.

One of the first things that I had promised to do – when I had the chance – was to clean the *Anco Queen* of rats and cockroaches! Unusually, for a tanker, she had more than her share, and especially so as she was a chemical tanker; the sort of vessel which both species would have been reluctant to join!

I first tackled the rats. These seemed mainly to be more numerous around the refrigerating machinery, possibly because there were always drops of moisture around to drink. I put rat poison in every storeroom but in particular the refrigerator plant room – it killed them all. Next the cockroaches; these were the bane of my life, more numerous in the after accommodation because of the storerooms, saloon, mess room, etc. being in that area. I just could not stand cockroaches dropping down from the deck head in the saloon as I ate my food, or crawling across the tablecloth, fighting for the bread with us. No, I was determined to kill them all!

All the insulation for the ship's side protecting the refrigeration was stripped off and dumped overboard, every cabin was cleared of clothing and sprayed, every storeroom and mess room, all at the same time. This treatment was repeated every week for a month and this effectively eliminated the menace; later in the voyage the odd one appeared, but our determined approach had done the trick!

One other incident on this passage still stands out in my mind. I was sat in my cabin when I had a phone call from the second mate on the bridge.

'Sir, there is a fire under the fo'c's'le.'

Immediately, I was amazed that he had not pressed the fire alarm, because this is what we are trained to do, so I told him not very politely to press it. I dashed up to the fo'c's'le to see clouds of smoke pouring out from where I knew that the emergency compressor was working.

It was obvious that the smoke was coming from the compressor because had it been from any other source we would probably have been blown to kingdom come! We had used the fo'c's'le to store drums of MEK which we had drained out of the pipeline, to use later in our rather complicated tank cleaning methods. If the heat reached those drums, I shuddered to think what would be the outcome!

I donned the breathing apparatus and went charging under the fo'c's'le through the dense smoke, and almost immediately was choking – there was no air in the tanks! I had breathed in more than my share of smoke by the time I reached the deck again, retching over the rail; thankfully our tough bosun had followed me, and when he appraised the situation helped me to stop the compressor before it caused a major incident.

Of course it was risky storing forty-gallon drums of MEK in that space but, frankly, the whole business of carrying chemicals in bulk was fraught with danger, and with its cumulative adverse effects on one's health was not to be recommended.

We discharged our cargo of toluene in Yokohama and then set course to Manila in the Philippines. Here we were anchored in Manila Bay to discharge lube oils and lube oil additives into barges. We had to survey each barge in turn to ensure that the cargo carried such a great distance was not contaminated on the last phase of its journey.

The one thing that I did not like about Manila at this juncture was that there was a great deal of banditry and danger to life and limb by a group of thugs, called locally, 'huqs'. They were so dangerous that we had armed guards on board to protect us from armed groups who might board at any time. This was not scare mongering; only the week before, the chief officer of a Norwegian ship had had his arm chopped off by one of the huqs as he tried to stop their thieving activities.

Our next discharge port was Batangas, also in the Philippines, before we crossed the South China Sea to discharge the last of our cargo at Saigon.

As a married man with a family I was certainly not keen to visit Saigon, in the middle of the Vietnam War, and frankly I was annoyed that we, as mere seamen, and non-combatants, were expected to go there, but we had no choice. We had signed on for two years as usual, so we had to go where we were directed. There was only one small consolation: we would receive double pay for operating in a war zone.

We took a pilot at the entrance to the Mekong River and a helicopter was up above to keep its eye on us and, hopefully, to ensure a safe passage. The jungle on both sides of the river had been defoliated to deprive the Vietcong of hiding places close to the river.

There were no incidents marring our progress to the refinery situated just south of Saigon; we tied up and then awaited all the usual officials before I could liaise with the shore cargo superintendent. I was more than a little perturbed when he advised me to post lookouts to spot floating mines!

I told him that it was completely without purpose, because if we saw a floating mine heading for our ship there was no way we could vacate the berth in under about forty minutes! He shrugged and pointed to the wreck of a tanker grounded on the opposite bank. 'She was the last ship on this berth,' he told me, pointedly.

Well, I could do nothing but discharge as quickly as possible, knowing that as each tank was emptied, the gas inside would cause a very nasty explosion if something were to ignite it. The very first night was more than a little disconcerting; helicopters suddenly appeared on the other side of the refinery perimeter fence; their searchlights were switched on and then we could hear and see the flashes from small arms fire. Very definitely it was not a healthy spot to remain, and we were all glad to complete the discharge of all our remaining cargo within three days, and leave behind the warlike activities of Vietnam, for the protagonists to resolve the best way they could!

Our next port was Singapore for routine dry-docking to clean and paint the bottom and fulfil all the requirements of the Classification Society. It was not a demanding time for me, so I was able to enjoy a spot of shore leave with the Master, Captain Billson. We were having a quiet drink at the Tanglin Club when, out of the corner of my eye I noticed a familiar face. It was, I thought, 'Bill' Bailey, senior apprentice from the *Bradburn*, some fifteen years previously. Just to test that my eyes were not deceiving me, I said loudly to Captain Billson, 'When I was in Smith's of Cardiff…'

Immediately 'Bill' Bailey spun round and greeted me effusively with instant recognition; he was then a Singapore pilot, living there with his wife. It was a pleasant interlude; 'Bill' took me back to his apartment and we chatted away for a couple of hours.

Next stop, Durban! We completed our dry-docking and headed for Durban, where Athel Line had contracted to have the topsides sandblasted and coated with epoxy 'Anco Blue' paint, as it was cheaper than having the same work done in Singapore.

We were three weeks in Durban. The sandblasting and painting took longer than anticipated. The contractors were obviously inexperienced in this type of work and one wondered at Athel Line's judgement in having the work done by an amateurish company who had previously only sandblasted swimming pools, but that sort of decision was out of my hands.

I did have time to go ashore in Durban – and I made good use of it!

The premier shipping company in South Africa was the South African Marine Corporation; not only was it number one in South Africa, but it had gained a good reputation internationally, and, as it was still expanding, I thought this might be an opportunity to determine if there was any possibility of early promotion to Master in such a company. Although their head office was in Cape Town, they had a very substantial office in Durban, so I phoned their office and arranged to meet their marine superintendent the following day.

It should be pointed out that it was not easy at that particular time to change companies. One had to sign a two-year contract, which was standard throughout the British Merchant Navy, and if that contract expired during a voyage, which it normally did, then there was no chance to look around for another company. Whilst the contract system was good in one way, as it did give a limited amount of security, on the other hand, it was weighted very much in favour of the shipowners, who could relinquish the services of any officer, any time they wished, by just waiting for a contract to expire.

Anyway, I was now in a good position to change companies; I knew my contract would expire by the time we returned to the UK, and I also knew that because of the six years ashore, my chances of promotion had slipped, even though I had served as mate on both of Athel Line's Commodore ships, because I was still only halfway up the promotion ladder.

Safmarine welcomed me with open arms. It was a time when because of the political situation, sanctions against South Africa seemed possible, as they were against Rhodesia currently. Accordingly, Safmarine decided to buy five tankers to add to their liner fleet. There was little tanker expertise within Safmarine, so to start up something so new to them must have been very difficult and would, inevitably, mean that many of the officers and masters they recruited would be found to be unacceptable for long-term employment and/or promotion.

Because Safmarine could see me in action so to speak, they were of the opinion that by joining them as Chief Officer, I would be given a command within two years. My judgement was that Safmarine was the company for me and I signed a contract, then and there to become effective as soon as my present contract with Athel Line expired during my forthcoming leave.

We completed the sandblasting, then loaded a full cargo of molasses and set sail for the UK. It was fine weather most of the way, so I was able to ensure that the *Anco Queen* was looking at her very best by the time she arrived in Liverpool to discharge her first molasses cargo successfully, in March 1967.

My relief officer boarded in Liverpool, but because of the complexity of carrying chemical cargoes, I had to stay on board until we had completed loading all the many different parcels of chemicals and solvents in the USA. Our first port was New York, and on the passage across from Liverpool, all the tanks had to be cleaned to a high standard for acceptance by the cargo surveyors, most of whom were very strict in the USA.

The crew were new to the ship and none of them had experience of carrying these sorts of cargoes, so the work of preparing the tanks was slower than normal. For one thing, I always ensured the highest standards of safety, and for another it was a case of 'on the job training'! I remember writing a booklet and giving a copy to each of the apprentices and sailors to explain what we were doing, why we were doing it and the way it was being done.

We headed all the way down the East Coast of the United States: New York, Baltimore, Jacksonville and Avondale on the Mississippi, loading various grades of chemicals, solvents and lube oils. After loading at Avondale, we went further upriver to Baton Rouge, changing pilots on the way. I was busy on deck. We always had to be moving ballast either from one tank to another, or if it was clean ballast, pumping it overboard; and, at the same time, we were cleaning the last of the cargo tanks of saltwater by using fresh water to rinse them and then to dry them completely using pressurised water or fans driven by compressed air. It was a very complex business and as we were moving through the night, it was quite eerie to listen to the different sounds of air-driven and water-driven fans, plus the whine of air-driven hoists lifting the dregs from the tanks and, in the background, the thumping of cargo pumps being driven to cleanse the pumps themselves and associated pipelines of any unwanted residues. When all was clean, steam would be injected into pipelines to give them a final clean-out, and what with steam, water and air blasting out everywhere in the darkness of the night, and knowing that all had to be ready for the cargo surveyor at our next loading port of Baton Rouge, where we were to load seven grades of lube, some of it very high grade, it was a very challenging experience.

Through the darkness, just before the change of pilot, I was called to the bridge by the second mate to sign the chit for the pilot before he left.

'Where's the Captain?' I asked, and the second mate pointed to the chartroom where I found the Captain flaked out – too drunk even to sign the pilot's chit! I was really pressurised with the very great demands of my work, and furious that I had to take on this extra responsibility, not merely to sign a chit but to be responsible for the navigation of the ship, up a winding river in pitch darkness. Throughout this book, I have referred to the problems of excessive alcohol, but they pale into insignificance if one compares them to the total effect on the ship if the Master himself is the culprit. It angers me to this very day that I felt compelled to cover up for some of these Masters in the interests of getting the job done and the safety of the ship.

From the Mississippi, we loaded at Freeport on the Houston

Ship Channel, and once the last cargo was loaded successfully, I took my plane ticket from the agent and flew directly to Manchester Airport, where my wife was waiting to greet me. From there I posted my letter of resignation to Athel Line, before proceeding home to Cleveleys, where we now lived.

Thirty-five

I JOINED THE *Allamanda* as Chief Officer at New York in July 1967. New York was always an impressive city, even prior to the World Trade Centre being built, with its skyscrapers and Statue of Liberty, but my eyes were only for the *Allamanda*, discharging at the power station in the East River.

She was not very impressive, but the marine superintendent who escorted me on board was friendly and made me feel as though I belonged to Safmarine and had a future with them.

From the gangway we saw a steward walking along the flying bridge.

'How are you now, Hendricks?' called the superintendent.

'I'm fine now, sir, thank you,' replied the steward, fingering an eight-inch long scar down his cheek.

'What on earth has happened to his face?' I asked.

'Oh, he had an argument with one of the crew and it ended in a knife fight,' was his response.

This was my introduction to a Cape Coloured crew; it was not an auspicious beginning!

The superintendent introduced me to the Captain, and then I went down to the chief officer's cabin to meet the mate, a certain Mr Thomas. He was obviously the worse for drink, so I didn't waste much time with his ramblings, but encouraged him to leave as soon as possible and helped him down the gangway as quickly as I could!

The *Allamanda* did not operate very well. She had constant engine problems, and although they were always repaired eventually, overall, her performance was poor.

Once I had settled down to the actual running of the crew, I found that the Cape Coloured crew were hard-working and gave no trouble – except when they had had too much to drink! Anyway, I quickly found out that they were not too difficult to manage; but certainly one had to keep a tight rein on them, otherwise they would quickly get out of hand.

We had loaded and discharged a couple of fuel oil cargoes successfully and then in the winter of 1967, loaded a cargo of heavy fuel oil in Trinidad. There was no problem at first, but as we sailed, the chief engineer advised me that he had difficulty giving me steam to heat the cargo. We were heading north for New York and in the first few days were in the warm water of the Gulf Stream, which helped to keep the heavy fuel oil warm enough to be able to pump it; but nearing New York the temperature dropped and by the time we arrived at the power station in the East River, the fuel oil was too thick to pump.

The chief did the best he could by trying to give us enough steam to drive the pumps, and enough to heat the cargo, but gradually as the cargo became more viscous, the discharge rate was abysmal and was accompanied by a dense black cloud of smoke from the funnel. Predictably, it was only a matter of time before the coast guard boarded to complain about the smoke. Of course, I apologised, phoned the chief and told him to shut the boilers immediately, and then offered the coast guard officer a cup of coffee. By the time he had finished the smoke had disappeared and he left the *Allamanda*, satisfied.

As soon as the coast guard officer had disappeared I phoned the chief. 'Okay, Chief, give us steam again,' was my instruction to him. Sure enough, within minutes we had steam but, alas, accompanied by clouds of smoke, if anything worse than before. Sure enough, the same coast guard officer was back in minutes wanting to know what was going on. I apologised profusely, phoned the chief to shut down everything and after much head-shaking, the coast guard officer retreated once more.

Knowing I was skating on thin ice, I told the chief to give us steam but the result was the same; steam enough to run one of the three pumps and billowing clouds of dense black smoke! This time, though, there was no compromise with the coast guard. He strode purposefully into my office and despite my pleading and apologies turned a deaf ear. 'Look, Chief,' he said, 'that smoke is so dense it has halted the traffic on the Brooklyn Bridge!'

When he told me that I knew the argument was lost, and told the chief to shut down everything.

We had no power to do anything until the two forced draught

fans for the boilers were repaired; accordingly, we were towed, without engine power, across to the East Side and lay there ignominiously whilst essential repairs were carried out.

It was snowing and, of course, cold. I still tried to discharge small amounts of cargo into a barge alongside whenever I was given steam, and I can remember swinging valves on deck in a swirling snowstorm as the marine superintendent boarded; he must have been encouraged by the fact that we were trying everything we possibly could to discharge our cargo, because I heard later on that he had sent in a good report about me to the Head Office and, as this was my first ship in Safmarine, it was helpful for my future career prospects.

Thirty-six

AFTER A WELCOME spell of leave following six months on the *Allamanda* I joined the *Thorland* at Ras Tanura, in Saudi Arabia. It was a relief to join such a clean, well-ordered ship with a peaceful crew; this time they were Pakistanis, and, for a change, everything worked!

We loaded crude oil in the Persian Gulf for discharge in Europe, taking the long route round Africa, as the Suez Canal was closed due to hostilities between the Israelis and Arabs. It was a long way round but we did have the advantage of being able to take mail, stores, and spares by launch as we passed Cape Town.

Another bonus for these long passages was that the maintenance of the ship was facilitated, ensuring that she was kept in top-notch order.

After discharging our cargo of crude oil in Rotterdam, we headed back towards Cape Town for the annual dry-docking; this meant that not only would all the tanks have to be cleaned but would also have to be completely gas-freed to allow hot work to be carried out on board. In 1968, there were no really sophisticated ways of tank cleaning, we used 'Butterworth' machines, a sort of high-pressure nozzle which rotates in the vertical as well as the horizontal planes.

It required a lot of high-pressure sea water, steam for the pumps and, later on, steam for hot water to make the final wash and change the ballast from dirty dock water to clean salt water.

When all this work was completed we used compressed air-driven fans and chutes to ventilate the tanks, then we dug out any waxy, rusty residue from the tank bottom.

It was dirty work, and entailed working long hours and, in fact, was quite dangerous. One particular tank was difficult to gas-free, yet we still had to dig out the residue, which in turn released more gas. The only way I could carry out this work satisfactorily was to lead the crew into the tank, fill up rubber buckets in the gassy tank and have these hauled up. We could only stay down the tank a few minutes at a time, so there was an almost continuous changeover of workforce but, eventually the tank was clean and gas-free in time for the whole ship to be spotless and tidy on our arrival at Cape Town.

Again, Safmarine was impressed with what they were able to see of my work and this helped my future prospects in the company.

The Captain of the *Thorland*, who shall be nameless, had been my chief officer on the *Athel Crest;* and now, as Captain, he had regrettably taken to the bottle to hide from the real world. He didn't exactly cover himself with glory during our stay in Cape Town, and on the way to the Gulf, on our next voyage, he fell off the bar stool and injured himself.

I ordered the chief steward to take away all his alcoholic drinks and not to replenish them. The Captain stayed in his cabin for the rest of the time I was on board; I kept him informed of everything that was going on but conned the ship in and out of port and ran the ship to ensure our safety, until I went on leave from Kharg Island in 1968.

It is a moot point as to whether one should cover up for the Master if he is drunk and incapable, or whether one should report him to Head Office; I could not bring myself to completely destroy his career so chose not to do the latter.

The business of excessive drinking on board ships has given me cause for concern many times. I remember very clearly, during my apprenticeship with Smith's of Cardiff, all the ships were 'dry' and there was absolutely no problem whatsoever with officers or crew.

On the *Clan Shaw*, there had to be a bar on board because she was a cargo/passenger ship, but this was mainly used by the chief engineer and the doctor, who quite happily regaled the passengers with their stories whilst drinking excessively, but as neither of them had many duties to carry out, it made no difference to the running of the ship.

During my years as junior and senior officer, it was only when there was free access to alcohol that problems developed with the crew and this was exacerbated when the shipping companies took the view that one way to keep people at sea was to let the officers and crew have a bar. Of course, many liked the idea, believing that people working ashore could have a drink when they were not working – so why not us? The facts did not justify that type of thinking, because it was often the case that men were not fit to take over their watch, and that was really dangerous.

It was regrettable that, out of the twenty-three Masters under whom I sailed, and the three that I sailed with as supernumerary/pilot, there were twenty-five per cent who were alcoholics and certainly not fit to do their job. Of course, there are reasons for this: the loneliness, the stress, and the ready availability of alcoholic drinks, because the Master would invariably have a locker full of wines and spirits with which to entertain port officials – all free!

It is sad that so many succumbed to the temptation, because they were in a position of authority and should have set an example to the officers and crews under their command, instead of taking themselves away in isolation waiting for their leave to come so they could enjoy the more relaxed atmosphere and lesser responsibilities of home life.

Not that I am against social drinking. We all enjoy wine with our meals and 'sundowners' in sunny Cyprus, but I never could tolerate the lack of professionalism shown by some of my peers. It was quite different, for example, from the offshore oil industry, which forbids any alcohol on the rigs and platforms.

Despite a 'drunk in charge' Captain, the *Thorland* voyage was behind me, and now it was time to fly home from Kharg Island in the Persian Gulf to rejoin the family for Christmas at home.

Thirty-seven

MY INSTRUCTIONS TO join the *Marland* at Umm Said on the peninsula of Qatar in the Persian Gulf arrived in March 1969. By this time I had been assured by all three of Safmarine main offices at Cape Town, Durban, and New York, that I was next in line for promotion to Master.

I boarded the *Marland* at night; it was not well lit and did not look in very good shape. The mate gave me details of all the problems – and there were many – which surprised me, really, because she had just come out of dry dock in Cape Town. The following day the mate left and I was even more disconsolate when I saw the general appearance of the *Marland*. Captain Barnes welcomed me on board and then left me to get on with my work, which suited me fine. I always supported the Master, as his second-in-command, but would make all the decisions regarding operational and maintenance matters and handling the cargo, naturally keeping him informed.

I realised then there was only one way to quickly get the *Marland* up to scratch, and that was by lots of hard work and plenty of overtime. I gave the bosun a breakdown of what I expected to achieve, and pressurised both him and the crew from day one. It was the only way; she was in such a bad state. Not that the crew objected; tankers were not 'fun' ships and the chance to earn extra money by lots of overtime was always welcome, because that money could then be spent when they went on leave.

I found out that none of the four lifeboat launching mechanisms worked properly; as this was a priority, I set one squad and myself to resolve this problem; the rest of the crew were cleaning and painting the whole ship from truck to keel.

After the first month the overtime sheets were passed to the Master for co-signature and then sent to Head Office. It wasn't long before we had a radio message telling us to cut down on the overtime! I promised the Captain I would reduce it, and I did, by a fraction! More radio messages, more recriminations from Head Office and Captain Barnes, but I did not reduce the overtime for four months. However, by this time the *Marland* was operating properly and looking like a new ship!

We were ordered to load a full cargo of crude oil at Mamanol, in Colombia. Our charterers, Shell, had cautioned us about the dangerous activities of some of the gangs there, but I was not really prepared for the first night, as we lay at anchor awaiting a berth.

It was dark, and even with the deck lights on, the after accommodation was not well lit. I was standing outside my office, and noticed some sort of shadowy movements around the poop and in the water. At that moment the chief came walking along the flying bridge toward me. 'What's going on, Chief?' I asked him.

'I wouldn't go down there, mate, the crew have broached the paint store and are selling it to some dangerous-looking characters in canoes, they have also been at the booze, or maybe it's drugs, but the situation is too dodgy for me. I'm keeping out of the way.'

Such was his response, but I was determined that there were not going to be any 'no go' areas on any of my ships, and went rushing down aft to see what was going on.

The poop was in darkness but I made out the shadowy forms who, seeing my white uniform in the dark, dived into their accommodation whilst the canoes, into which they were lowering drums of paint, paddled away silently into the darkness. It was a dangerous situation, but I found out that by taking positive action worse disasters were averted. The poop paint store was re-secured, but I estimated that about half the stock had already disappeared.

When we went alongside the following day, we were given the 'protection' of an armed customs officer, and I gave the three deck officers specific instructions to call me if any illegal activity was detected. It was.

In the early hours of the morning, my phone rang; it was the second mate. 'I can see some movement on the fo'c's'le head,' was the message.

I joined him on deck, armed with an iron wheel key, called the customs officer and crept up the foredeck. As we rushed on to the fo'c's'le head, there was a splash as someone dived over the side. This prompted the customs officer to fire his revolver in the general direction of the swimmer, but I suspect that it was his intention to miss because we saw the swimmer disappear into the darkness.

We discovered that the thief had crawled up the anchor cable, and despite the pressurised salt water rushing down the hawse pipe, had managed to crawl up, then heave back the heavy steel plate cover, and was in the process of lowering one of our mooring ropes into a waiting boat when he was stopped. Of course Colombia was desperately poor and extremely dangerous, I was glad to complete our loading and get out of Mamanol.

We discharged in Hamburg in July 1969. The Captain had told me that he would be visiting the doctor there because he kept getting pains across his shoulders. I was pleased that he was doing something about it because he had not looked well for a few weeks.

We left Hamburg and I was on the bridge in the usual murky North Sea weather when Captain Barnes came up to see what was going on; it was then that I asked him what the doctor had said, only to be told that he had not had the time to see him. I was angry because he was obviously not well, and it had been an extra problem for me worrying about his state of health. I told Captain Barnes that I had been worrying about him for some time and was disappointed he had not seen a doctor. He almost immediately replied, 'If you are worried, mate, it's time I was leaving, because I really don't feel well.'

Striking whilst the iron was hot, I sent for the chief steward to help him pack Captain Barnes' clothes. I also sent for the Radio officer to contact the pilot boat at Dover to arrange to land Captain Barnes as we passed by the next morning.

All went as planned. Captain Barnes left, looking not very well, and I sent a message to the owners to the effect that I had assumed acting command until we arrived at Cape Town, in a couple of weeks' time.

The passage down to Cape Town was fine, no bad weather and a chance to give the ship a final spit and polish before our arrival off the Cape; but there was one comparatively major problem with one of the engineers.

Shortly after I had assumed command I was entering the saloon for my evening meal, passing close to the bar where several of the officers were having a drink before dinner, when I heard some derogatory remark from one of the engineers, which I believe I was meant to hear. I sat down at the table, with the chief engineer already there and told him that I wanted to see both him and his third engineer the following morning, sharply, at 8 a.m.

The next morning, I sat behind my office desk whilst before me were assembled the third engineer, chief engineer and chief officer, all resplendent in uniform; and, open before me, I had the official logbook.

The third engineer was looking a little pale. He had not had much sleep, being on the 12-4 watch, and was perhaps feeling the effects of drinking too much the night before. Without preamble, I told the Third that I had heard him make a derogatory remark the night before and I had entered that, formally, in the official logbook and now I was giving him the chance to either repeat it or to give his reason. He had nothing to say, as was usually the case when such matters were put formally to the perpetrators. I told him that the following entry would be put in the logbook – 'He had nothing to say' – and then told him that the matter would be conveyed to Head Office in Cape Town, and that he would be replaced on arrival.

Whilst this may seem to be making a mountain out of a molehill, I had found out that letting even the slightest matter slide could lead to major problems later on and, in this case, it did the trick. Just before our arrival at Cape Town, the chief came to see me and advised that our troublemaking Third, for such he was, had pleaded with him to let him stay on board. The chief also assured me that he was a reformed character and that he, the chief, would stand surety for his future good behaviour. I did not immediately relent, but told him that I would discuss the matter with the personnel manager in Cape Town before making any decision.

This, amongst other matters, was discussed with the personnel manager in Cape Town, and he agreed with me that we could keep the Third on board with the chief guaranteeing his future conduct.

'About time someone pulled that Third down a peg or two,' was the comment from the manager, which proved what I had learned over the years, that taking the easy way out is the hardest in the end, and I never hesitated to deal harshly with anyone who really deserved it.

The officials from Safmarine came swarming on board, confirming my official appointment as Master immediately, and congratulating me on the appearance of the vessel.

'Now we can see how all the overtime has been used,' was the comment of Captain Bluett, the marine manager.

Sadly, just after we left Cape Town, we heard that Captain Barnes had died in Dover hospital.

Now that I was Captain I was determined to take an active interest in everything on board, and when the chief advised me that they needed time to shut down one of the boilers to effect a repair, I was naturally interested in having a look at the problem. We waited until the boiler had cooled down slightly before squeezing through the tiny manhole to inspect the water tubes. It was hot! I have no idea how hot, but searing is the adjective that comes to mind. Whether it was the heat or the gaseous atmosphere, or perhaps the generally poor condition of my lungs I don't know – but I couldn't breathe.

I managed to wriggle backwards and out through the manhole on to the steel platform outside; my lungs just would not operate. Without dramatising the event, I was dying.

My parlous situation must have speeded up my perceptions and responses, because I threw my body against the upper handrail of the platform, this pressed against my chest and expelled the air. Immediately I turned over on my back, placing my open mouth under the wide ventilator shaft that forced fresh air into the engine room; this re-inflated my chest. I then flipped over to expel the air again and repeated the process several times until I was able to breathe normally again. Not a situation I want to repeat, and with a family at home, it was, in retrospect, an unnecessary risk.

Another incident occurred on the *Marland* that has stuck in my mind. We loaded a cargo of crude oil in the port of Durban and amongst the correspondence from Head Office was a letter requesting that I consider taking on board a new cadet. Now this was unusual; normally the Head Office would just advise crew changes – not ask for my consideration! I investigated further by telephone and found out that the cadet in question had never been to sea, nor had he had any nautical training; in fact he was working in an accountant's office, but apparently had convinced someone in Head Office that the sea was his real vocation, and they were really putting pressure on me to accept him. I presume that his family was well connected. Anyway I indicated that it should not be a major problem, and that he would not receive any preferential treatment, which was accepted; but as an afterthought, I was told that he was twenty-two years of age – far too old to start a sea career, where the preferred age was sixteen. Anyway I was persuaded and left it at that.

Our cadet joined just before sailing. He was overweight but full of enthusiasm and assured me that he would be the best cadet in the world and would never let me down, etc. So I signed him on.

During our passage back to the Persian Gulf, I checked the bond accounts of all the officers, as a routine, and noticed his was far higher than one would expect of a cadet. I sent for him. After I had explained that cadets are supposed to set a good example etc., and that heavy drinking was not considered the thing to do, he promised me on his knees almost that he would stop altogether – and he did.

A few days later we were in the stifling heat of the Persian Gulf in midsummer and our cadet was so anxious to prove his worth that he was like perpetual motion, sweat pouring off him as he rushed his heavy frame around the decks. I sent for him again and told him that he was likely to suffer from heat exhaustion the way he was acting, and that could mean hospitalisation, which could cost the owners a considerable sum if I had to deviate the ship and land him. He understood and, in fact, acted in a more reasonable manner for a while.

When we were fully loaded we headed back to Durban, but

once we had left the Persian Gulf and the Gulf of Oman and rounded Ras al Hadd, entering the Arabian Sea, we met the full force of the south-west monsoon, head-on. In August/September, the monsoon often reaches force 9 on the Beaufort scale, which is a storm force gale. There was no way round it; we just had to plough through it, with heavy seas pouring constantly over the decks of our fully laden tanker.

For three days I never left the bridge, until we were far enough south for the wind and sea to abate somewhat. Then I went below to enjoy one of the Captain's perks – a good hot bath, to relax me before my longed-for sleep in bed – without worrying about the safety of the ship.

A knock came at the door. I was irritated by this because no one just comes knocking at my door without good reason. Pulling on my bathrobe, I wrenched open the cabin door, and there was our erstwhile cadet.

'I want to resign, sir,' he said.

'What the hell is all this about?' I asked him irritably.

'I can't do what you do sir,' he said.

'Can't do what I do? You've only been on board about two weeks, how the hell do you expect to be able to do my job?'

'I want to leave in Durban, sir.'

There was nothing I could do to make him change his mind or reconsider; apparently he had been terrified during the bad weather.

The last I remember seeing of him was when we arrived at Durban. Normally, before any ship's business can be carried out, we have to have clearance from Port Health, Customs and Immigration, but as these officials were boarding our cadet was pushing them to one side in his haste to get down the gangway and darted across the quay out of the docks, and as far as I know he's still heading across Africa!

Thirty-eight

I REALLY ENJOYED MY leave after seven months on the *Marland*. I had been confirmed in my command by Safmarine, and was able to slacken the purse strings a little, bringing my wife and three daughters a good present each and having more holidays.

My next appointment was to command the *Lankus*. She was unaffectionately known as 'the Rattling Monster', partly because she was Safmarine's biggest ship at that time, at 86,000 tons deadweight.

Joining at Cape Town was again a bonus for me because it gave me a chance to keep in personal touch with Head Office for a couple of days, before I joined the *Lankus* by launch.

As Master, my accommodation was immediately behind the wheelhouse; it was quite small and not as opulent as that on the *Marland* which was not only fairly large but was completely lined with solid teak; but the *Lankus* had obviously been built at a keen price – there were no frills, and yes, she did rattle and shake quite a lot. This was exacerbated by the fact that my accommodation was so high up and because she was much longer than any other vessel on which I had served so far.

I learnt that the chief engineer was none other than Brian Freeman, with whom I had sailed in Athel Line. He was quite a character, six feet six inches tall and hefty with it; I used to tell him to sit down when he came to see me because he gave me an inferiority complex standing there like a colossus!

He was a character, not only because of his size but also partly because he was Jewish, and this was unusual because I have never met any serving seafarer, before or since, who was of the Jewish faith.

It was some time before I found out more about his background, because he was a modest man; apparently, when he was serving his apprenticeship as an engineer in Liverpool, he was the reserve goalkeeper for Everton Football Team, also he was the

Junior AA high-jump champion for England, as well as the Junior AA heavyweight boxing champion for England. During our conversations he told me that he had difficulty keeping out of trouble because, for example, if he went for a drink, inevitably someone, after a couple of drinks to give him Dutch courage, would become aggressive towards him, and he was a mild-tempered man, frustrated at having to deal with such situations.

We had carried out two routine voyages from the Gulf to Europe via the Cape, as the Suez Canal was still closed when we were heading north towards the Gulf again, after having had our usual very brief stop-off in Cape Town for stores, crew changes etc., by their efficient launch service. I was sat at my office that was directly abaft (behind) the chartroom; from this vantage point I was always very close to everything that happened on the bridge and could hear the radio officer as he sent and received his messages in Morse, because, generally, if I concentrated, I could pick up the gist of what was 'in the air'. It was 11.30 on the 9th June 1970 when I knew that something was wrong; as Master I was attuned to anything and everything on board, and especially radio messages!

It was only moments later when the Sparks came in with a distress message. I hurriedly glanced at it and immediately dashed into the chart room to plot the position, because I knew that we were not far away. As we had received the message from a vessel called *Bjorn Ravne* there was no undue concern about any personal involvement, but by the position I plotted on the chart, the vessel in distress was more or less on our course line, only about fifteen hours away at our present speed.

The next message really knocked me for six, and I have a copy of it:

FOLLOWING RECEIVED FROM SDVA = SOS FROM TANKER *THORLAND* PANAMA POSITION 0334S 4715E EXPLODED ON FIRE STOP STANDING BY ALL SHIPS CONTROLLED BY SDVA

It was the *Thorland* – my last ship!

Of course I immediately advised Safmarine in Cape Town and gave our ETA.

In the meantime, we received a message telling us that fifty-two survivors had been picked up but that nine were missing. All the messages to and from were relayed to our Head Office.

I then contacted the rescuing vessel asking that the senior surviving officer contact me by radio telephone, as we were then in range. Within an hour or so I was pleased to receive a call from the Master, who had survived, and he advised that he was returning to the *Thorland* with a salvage tug to see if there were any survivors left on board, as he thought there was a remote chance of the second officer's survival in the midships accommodation.

We would reach the last known position of the *Thorland* before the salvage tug and I had advised Safmarine that we would look for survivors and try to have a line on board the *Thorland* before the tug arrived, in case we could claim any right to salvage later on.

As we would arrive in the vicinity of the distress when it was still dark, I had instructed the chief officer to prepare the Suez Canal searchlight, which was connected permanently in the bow of this ship; this exercise nearly ended in disaster because the heavy steel plate covering the searchlight aperture had been lifted by several of the crew and then it landed on the carpenter's thighs when it slipped out of their grasp. He was unconscious for a while but, happily, no serious damage was done, we just laid him up in our hospital on board for a few days; the last thing I wanted to do was kill any of my own crew in an attempt to save life on the *Thorland*.

We had difficulty locating the *Thorland*, even though we had obtained a stellar position the night before, and even though we had radar. We did pick up the echo of a vessel on the radar but, by plotting its movements, were able to determine that she was moving in a north-westerly direction at two knots. We presumed that this was another vessel trying to salvage the *Thorland* but keeping radar silence.

As dawn approached, we decided to close in on the unidentified echo. At first sight through the binoculars, she seemed to slowly move in a north-westerly heading, and as we could see the smoke puffing out of her funnel she was obviously a motor ship, not a steam turbine like the *Thorland*.

Handing over *Globtik London* – biggest ship in the world
– with Ravi Tikoo, owner, and my wife, Dora, 1973

Handing over *Globtik London,* with owner, Ravi Tikoo,
1973

Globtik London, world's biggest ship in 1973

Globtik London, world's biggest ship in 1973

Morland, Master, 1969

Marland, My first command, 1969

Shipping seas, *Thorland,* 1968

Fore-deck of *Thorland,* 1968

It was a little while before I realised that the tanker we identified at a distance as a motor tanker was no such thing; we realised that the smoke puffing out of the funnel was not from the main engine at all but was from the emergency generator, which I recalled from my service on board as being very efficient. It would automatically cut in if there was a power failure.

We closed with the *Thorland* and then realised why she had apparently been moving ahead slowly under power; the explosion had blown up the whole of the afterdeck, which had curled up, like opening a tin of sardines. Then this huge, heavy length of steel had landed on top of the midships accommodation, and had then effectively been a kind of sail, with the south-east trade wind blowing her steadily along.

As the Master had indicated to me that there might still be someone alive on board, I approached very close to the *Thorland*, sounding the ship's siren to give encouragement to anyone left on board, and slowly circled the wreck.

Now there was no smoke nor flame from the vessel, just an eerie silence as we slowly circled her but, having received the information that there could be someone trapped on board, we just had to find out and I decided to send away a lifeboat.

It is not easy to lower a ship's lifeboat in a seaway because, for one thing, one's own ship rolls and the lifeboat is jerking up and down, as well as swinging out and then back to land heavily against the ship's side. Once landing on top of the waves, it is essential to let go the lifeboat falls simultaneously, otherwise the whole boat will be tipped into the sea. I had to make the decision as to whether or not to lower the boat, and decided that with a good crew it should be safe enough.

The lifeboat was launched and then came the problem of boarding the *Thorland*; she was also rolling, with empty lifeboat falls flailing around, and it was with some difficulty that we now managed to board.

The *Thorland* was inspected as thoroughly as practicable, but with the gas escaping out of the open tanks, it was becoming quite dangerous. The chief officer had closed the tank lids on the foredeck and all the accommodation had been checked for survivors. As can be imagined, on a ship that had been partially destroyed by explosion, rolling in a seaway, lots of eerie sounds were emanating from the wreck as the torn plates moved and open doors in the accommodation swung as she rolled.

The first crew reported back, all of them rather pale and distressed, but this did not stop a second lifeboat crew from volunteering to make fast a light line to the stern, to prove our possession if Head Office gave approval to salvage her.

The second boat crew also did a fine job but just as the line to the stern was being made fast, we received a message from Safmarine not to attempt to salvage her. When the lifeboat crew returned safely on board, they reported that two bodies had been located on board. Our second officer had located the body of his counterpart, squashed by the ripped open steel afterdeck landing heavily on to the wheelhouse.

We continued our voyage to the Persian Gulf, loading at Ras Tanura in Saudi Arabia; the chief had closed down one of the three generators for overhaul, when, unluckily, one of the other two broke down; this meant that we could not proceed on passage after loading, with only one generator functioning, and although Brian Freeman was trying his best, it could not be fixed in five minutes. This situation was in the month of June with the air and sea temperatures sky-high in the Gulf, yet not enough spare power to operate the air conditioning. We had to leave the berth when we completed loading but could only proceed at slow speed, unable to generate our own fresh water now, as well as being without air conditioning. There was no way that we could make it to the cooler waters of the Arabian Sea and I resolved to anchor off Bahrain, an island nearby, and then order fresh water to be sent out by barge; we were too big to go very close through the shallow water surrounding Bahrain.

I did not make this decision lightly because the deviation and delay would be costly to the shipowner, but it was essential to give the engineers chance to repair one of the generators.

We had been anchored only for a couple of hours when Brian came up out of the engine room to see me. He looked dreadful, white as a sheet and obviously completely exhausted. He briefed me on the situation in the engine room, which, without the powerful electric ventilation fans working, was absolute hell. Brian, at this time, was in tears – and he was no wimp. He needed help!

'Everyone stop work,' I ordered, 'and sleep until morning.' I also called the chief steward to issue salt tablets, and enjoined Brian to take his immediately. This he did, and it perked him up somewhat.

There was only emergency lighting and little chance of sleep because of the heat and high humidity in our steel box, designed for use of air conditioning and without fans or other ventilation. Unbeknown to Brian, I sent a message off to Head Office, apprising them of the situation and suggesting that under the circumstances, in order to boost morale, they send a radio message immediately, direct to the chief (they would normally only communicate through the Master), saying that they appreciated the engineers' efforts, and that they had the full support of Head Office.

The next morning, Brian came up waving the radio message he had received from Head Office, absolutely thrilled that they had been so understanding, and as the engineers were all somewhat refreshed by their rest and salt tablets, we were off on our passage out of the Gulf within twelve hours, the water barge topping up our water supply whilst they worked below.

I have never met Brian since leaving the *Lankus*. He told me that he planned to set up a stud farm in the Isle of Man to breed horses. I hope he succeeded.

Thirty-nine

THE *THORLAND* INCIDENT was distressing, no doubt about that; it highlighted to me the dangers inherent in the carriage of oil and the operation of oil tankers. Most of the dangers were well known, and were drummed into us on the courses we attended concerning tanker safety, but so many tankers were lost through explosions that changes in design were already underway.

My next ship was a complete change; I was given command of the SA *Drakenstein*, one of Safmarine's cargo liners, trading between the UK and South Africa. Apparently, I was given this spell on the *Drakenstein* as a sort of 'rest and recuperation' trip after the somewhat traumatic events surrounding the *Thorland* incident.

I joined her in Cape Town in September 1970, and had only half an hour with her Master to hand over the various documents and brief me on the ship. One thing he did tell me was that the third officer had just returned to the sea after two years at university, which he had left without gaining any degree; he also advised me that the young officer had already been to the doctor with flu-like symptoms, and that the doctor had told the Master he strongly suspected the third officer was a codeine addict!

That first night, the previous Captain having left, I walked around the deck to familiarise myself with the ship, but as she was still working cargo, was surprised to find that the duty officer, our young third officer, was not around. I knocked and opened his cabin door; he was sat, pale-faced, staring into space with the porthole open, allowing the cold air to blow on him. He was startled and made some excuse about not feeling well, and then stumbled out to carry out his duties on deck. *Must watch this guy*, I thought.

The next morning we sailed for our next discharge port, just along the south coast, at Port Elizabeth. As we moved off the berth with the aid of tugs and a blustery westerly wind blowing, I noticed that the gyro compass was not working; quickly I switched on the light for the helmsman to see the magnetic compass and contacted the second officer to check the gyro; by now I was experienced enough to check such things as magnetic compass lights, so I knew that we could cope with this emergency.

As we moved across the harbour and let go the tugs, the second officer reported that the radar was not working; this was a bit of a problem because there was a haze practically covering the coastline which made visual bearings difficult; I called Sparks to have a look at the radar just as the pilot was leaving.

We were now heading out of the breakwaters; I instructed the third officer to take visual bearings with the magnetic compass on the upper navigating bridge (Monkey Island), and whilst we were threading our way through the ships anchored outside the harbour, wanted to plot our position frequently because of the indifferent visibility; but no sign of life from the young officer on the Monkey Island!

In the end, I had to take bearings myself and fix the vessel's position, knowing by now that the third officer's days might be numbered on board the *Drakenstein*.

By this time the second officer had fixed the gyro and, a little later, Sparks had fixed the radar; the situation was calming down rapidly.

As we rounded the Cape, the wind and sea had shifted and we took some heavy water on the foredeck, on which were a couple of containers, one containing N. Butyl Per Carbonate. I didn't know much about the contents but I did know that if the temperature rose above -10°C it would polymerise, and that would be nasty! I shone the Aldis lamp on to the fore-deck and saw that the sea had already damaged the refrigerating plant cover, and sent the mate to investigate. Fortunately, all was well and the plant was still fully operational.

As the third officer came on the bridge that night to take over the eight to twelve watch, he dropped a cigarette packet out of his pocket on to the deck and out of it rolled two white tablets! Time, I thought, to take some action. Down I went off the bridge, calling the mate to go with me and inspect our third officer's cabin. The drawer under his bed was filled to the top with proprietary drugs – every one containing codeine! It was obvious that such a man could not be left on the bridge alone, and the following morning, I contacted the agent at Port Elizabeth telling him to arrange for a doctor to check up on our man; in the meantime, I called Safmarine and advised them that the officer would be leaving and that we would sail short-handed until a replacement was found.

The doctor at Port Elizabeth could not certify that the third officer was a drug addict but he recommended that he go to hospital 'for observation'. That was good enough for me; we had enough problems without them being compounded with a drug-addicted officer on watch!

The next port was East London. As we turned to enter the port and pick up the pilot, we were temporarily rolling heavily as the sea and swell came on the beam before we gained the shelter of the breakwater. As the mate left the fo'c's'le head, after completion of mooring and letting go the tug, he checked the N. Butyl Per Carbonate – its temperature had shot up.

I gave orders fast and furiously. 'Call the agents!' 'Call the fire brigade!' 'Call the refrigeration engineers!' 'Call the electrician!' 'Advise Head Office!' and so on – expecting any minute that there would be a major conflagration. Fortunately, the man who had caused it – our own electrician – located the problem almost immediately. He had been working in the mast house the day before and had plugged in the electric cable through the open door instead of through the special opening provided; the result was that the heavy steel door had slammed shut when she rolled heavily, severing the electric cable. Everyone stood down, emergency over and peace reigned… for a while.

On our way round to our next port, Durban, some of the crew had been drinking, and, we suspected, smoking 'dagga' and were getting decidedly difficult to handle. One of the sailors was strapped into a stretcher because he was threatening to jump overboard, and at some risk we managed to confiscate some of the beer the crew had smuggled on board.

We had been in Durban for only a few hours when there was a fight between two of the crew, resulting in one being severely wounded with stab wounds, and his attacker fleeing the ship before he could be dealt with.

Time to call in the police! They did respond, insofar as they came on board, but they did not catch the attacker and when I suggested that they should put the man in jail if they caught him, I was told that the case would probably not stand up in court! So much for the much published activities of the police throwing people in jail and beating them up. One of the policemen came to me afterwards and said, 'Captain, I wouldn't have your job for anything!' Thanks...

We had another little problem with the N. Butyl Per Carbonate; a heavy-lift floating crane had come alongside with the aid of a tug and lifted off the container. We were delighted to disconnect the electric power and wave goodbye to it as it crossed the harbour towards the railway truck, where it landed the container. A few minutes later, a harassed stevedore was knocking on my door, asking if we could take the container back as the dock gates were locked and as it was Saturday, would not be open until Monday.

'Sorry,' I said, 'better hurry up and find the key.'

They did, in fact, find someone to open the gate, and were able to connect up to electric power again shortly afterwards.

I did two round trips between the UK and South Africa on the *Drakenstein*. Returning to Liverpool, I was greeted by the news that there were strikes of dockers throughout the UK but that at Liverpool the strikes were spasmodic. On the instructions from our London office, I arranged a shipboard cocktail party, not for the shippers or consignees, as we often did, but this time for the head stevedores and their wives; and we also surreptitiously supplied a few cases of beer to crane drivers and the like. It was a great success; usually in the UK we tend to forget the people in the 'front line', so to speak, who really make everything happen. But because in this case we had made every effort to show our appreciation of their work, not only did the stevedores enjoy the perk, they made sure that we continued working cargo through a very difficult period.

There were two unscheduled happenings at the party; one concerned a lady and her attractive daughter. Naturally, as host, I ensured that they were well supplied with snacks and drinks, as well as making them welcome on my ship; they responded with smiles and appreciative small talk, but as the saloon and bar area was crowded with about seventy people, I did not really take much notice of them. However I did find out later that the 'attractive girl' had somehow insinuated herself into the cocktail party but spent most of the time with the crew down below, ensuring that they shared our enjoyment – to their entire satisfaction and her enrichment!

The other incident concerning this cocktail party happened at the beginning because, although I wanted it to be a success as part of my duties, I also invited my mother and father-in-law down from Blackpool to join in and then to stay the night in the owner's suite; as father-in-law had lost a leg in the First World War, I did not want him driving back late at night in his hand-operated Mini. Whilst I was ensuring that all preparations were properly in hand, one of the stewards came to see me with the news that my in-laws were having some problem with their car on a bridge across the docks. I went to see what the trouble was and found that father-in-law had driven his little Mini down the centre of the swing bridge, right over the centre steel strength girder, which had had the effect of lifting the Mini's tyres off the bridge itself – so that they spun round, as the car was suspended and could not move!

It was a bit of a nuisance at the time because I had to send a number of crew down to lift the Mini up bodily and put it back on the bridge, but we have often laughed about it since.

On our return to Cape Town, it was nearing Christmas and as some of the crew were due to leave, we changed them; what I did not know about Cape Coloureds was that none of them would leave home willingly just before Christmas, so that it was only after we left Cape Town I started to find out that virtually all the crew replacements were 'bad hats'; some, I was told, had just been released from jail.

They really did cause a lot of trouble. They managed to get

hold of alcohol in some form, as well as dagga or other drugs, and were troublesome right from the start. As we were discharging at the usual South African ports of Cape Town, Port Elizabeth, East London, and Durban, I phoned the personnel department, telling them in no uncertain terms what I thought of my new crew and that I wanted them replaced as soon as possible; they promised to do this but could not replace any before arrival at Durban, and then only one or two; the rest upon our return to Cape Town.

It was not a pleasant situation; I knew that the Cape Coloured crew could be violent and dangerous, just as I knew that without the stimulation of alcohol and drugs they could be very good; but with a chief officer under me who had no idea how to run the crew, the situation was getting rapidly out of hand. As the mate had virtually washed his hands of the crew, I took it upon myself to deal with them the best way I could. It would not be easy, we had no police or army on board, nor did we carry guns, but I had determined in my first command, that there would be no no-go areas on my ships; so I took the bull by the horns and went down to the crew quarters alone, without any real plan of action, but with a great deal of determination. Of course, it was dangerous and, some would say, foolhardy, but I believe that going in alone turned out to be the best way. Had I taken in a group of aggressive officers and tried to restrain drunken crew, their response would have been extremely violent; but, on my own, not being of great stature, I posed no physical threat.

Purposely I strode through the crew quarters; mostly they stared in astonishment, some laughed nervously, some dashed into their cabins and peeped behind half-closed doors; but the man I sought – named Sharkey, if my memory serves me right – was in the engine crew side, and I saw him standing in the alleyway, naked as the day he was born, beer in one hand, 'cigarette' in the other. He moved quickly to his cabin when he saw me and I followed him but, to his surprise, instead of the haranguing he was expecting, I sat down on his chair, whilst he pulled on some shorts, and started talking to him. I even accepted a can of beer from him, and after about ten minutes calmed him down sufficiently to be able to tell him that I had had a lot of reports about him and that as he was a natural leader, I was promoting him immediately to Number One in the engine crew. I think he was bemused, befuddled, astonished, or taken unawares to such an extent that he accepted his 'promotion' gratefully. What this pseudo-promotion did was to buy time until replacements could be found for other violent crew members, and thereafter we had no problems.

We had an unusual chief engineer on the *Drakenstein*, he had also sailed with me on the *Marland*. I did sympathise with him somewhat on the *Marland*, because he had told Safmarine that he had no experience on tankers, so preferred cargo ships; also he had had only a few months' experience with steam engines, just enough to help him pass his steam endorsement to his Chief Engineer's ticket; in the event Safmarine had appointed him to the *Marland* – a tanker, and a steam turbine one at that! So, yes, he was a little disconcerted from day one and always seemed to have a lot about which to complain, especially with regard to the workload on his engineers, maintaining that it was too much to expect from anyone to be 'operators', carry out routine preventative maintenance and also repairs. He wouldn't listen when I pointed out that this was the lot of marine engineers; I think the fact that he had worked ashore in a power plant may have had something to do with it.

There were several other things about him that were unusual. The main one was his appearance. He looked a little mongoloid, with close-cropped hair and a slight squint in his eye. I never remember him being able to solve an engineering problem; it was either the second engineer or the shore gang that did, and really he lived on another planet. In fact, we sailed together when the first man landed on the moon, and he could never overcome his feelings regarding the amount of money spent on this odyssey, when there were so many starving and deprived people in the world who could have benefited from the money. I used to argue that the space project provided employment and, also, there were some useful spin-offs in technology and medicine, but we never agreed.

It was some time before I gradually came to know him well enough for him to tell me all about his background. He was an orphan, brought up in Dr Barnardo's homes, where there was a very disciplined regime, with barely enough to eat to satisfy growing boys' appetites. That was the reason, he averred, that he always cleared his plate, and he maintained that, given a challenge, he could eat more than any one person on earth – judging by his waistline, he was probably right!

During our conversations over the months, when he was not proclaiming that his engineers were underpaid and overworked, he used to tell me about his life in Dr Barnardo's. Of course it was disciplined in those days but they were healthy, and the home helped them to find work, hence the chief being found work as an apprentice engineer in a Merseyside shipyard; but the one thing that he could never get over was the fact that he had been 'birched' at Dr Barnardo's for some trivial misdemeanour, or so he maintained. It came up in conversation time and time again.

When he finished his apprenticeship, he went to sea as a junior engineer and, as is normal, was given all the dirty and menial engineering work in the engine room. Working in the bilge beneath the pipes, he looked up to see the godlike figure of the second engineer, resplendent in his clean white boiler suit, and he said to his workmate, 'How do I get to be like him?'

He was told that he had to learn everything in the two tomes of *Reed's Marine Engineering*. So he told me then that, after ascertaining that that was so, he learned every word in these massive volumes, to the extent that he could recall and recite every sentence, on every page, word perfect. Eventually, he sat for his Second's ticket, and although the examiner told him that he was a useless engineer, he had to pass him because he had all the answers – word perfect!

This was, in fact, true. He had a photographic memory: he tried to put this to good use when he observed a programme called *The $64,000 Question*, where people were paid what was then a huge amount of money to answer questions correctly. He resolved, therefore, to learn every fact and statistic about sport! Believe me, he knew everything about sport, football, horse racing, boxing; I tested him often and he would always come up with right answers, going back fifty years or more. People's names, times and events all were grist to the mill, but yet, sadly, he never put this to good use. I guess he was just a born loser, but a decent family man, for all that.

Because he was unusual and, as a chief engineer, useless, I always tried my best to motivate him to spend more time taking care of the ship's and owner's interests and less time on his past life. I took care of him, really, perhaps because I was a little sorry for him. During my second round trip on the *Drakenstein* we were approaching Cape Town in poor visibility, through a crowded anchorage; naturally I was on the bridge, when I received a phone call from the mate: 'Will you come and have a look at the chief, he's in a bad way.'

'What's the matter with him?'

'He's sat on the deck in the middle of your day room crying his eyes out, saying, "Everyone is too good to me".'

'Leave him where he is until we are alongside,' I instructed the mate.

By the time we were moored alongside and all the officials seen to, I had time to bring up the matter of the chief with the personnel manager. As there was no valid reason to replace him and as replacements were hard to find anyway, I told him that we would not sail until the chief had seen a psychiatrist! That did the trick and the next morning the chief went to the hospital to see the psychiatrist.

But life was not that easy. The chief came back averring that they tried to make out he was 'nuts', but he told them a thing or two, trying to convince them that it was *they,* not *he,* who should be seeing a psychiatrist!

Anyway, we continued the voyage with him on board. No doubt he has long since retired in the bosom of his family because he really did care for his wife and two children.

My spell on the *Drakenstein* was certainly interesting and eventful, but definitely not the sort of break envisaged by Head Office!

Forty

IT HAD BEEN CONFIRMED that I was to be Master of Safmarine's new building Very Large Crude Carrier (VLCC), the *Gondwana*; accordingly they were giving me a short spell on a BP VLCC *British Inventor*, as supernumerary.

I joined the *British Inventor* in the Persian Gulf in June 1971.

As I was supernumerary, I had no official status on board, so I kept very much to myself, either reading and studying drawings and documents concerning shipboard operations, or visiting different parts of the ship; drawing on the Master's and officers' knowledge of VLCC operations. They were all very cooperative, as one would expect from BP staff; I was also fortunate in spending some time with one of their technical experts, Percy Parmenter, who was experimenting with various aspects of tank cleaning, including crude oil washing; he was most helpful and informative, which, at this stage in my career, I greatly appreciated because BP, in my opinion, were ahead of all other companies with regard to safe tanker operations.

On passage from the Gulf, I was amazed to learn that the Master, Captain Alan Hole, who was Commodore of the BP fleet, despite all his wide and varied experiences, had never once in his whole career transited the Malacca and Singapore Straits. Gradually, I put the idea to him that perhaps I could help in some way during the transit, and he readily accepted. Of course, I was supernumerary. I had no official status, but by keeping in the background, mainly supervising the spot-on navigation required by such a deep-draft vessel with only a few feet under the keel clearance at various points in the transit, I was able to assist.

At one stage, as we turned round Raffles Light into the Singapore Straits, we encountered torrential tropical rain, which obliterated the echoes on the radar. I was quickly able to feed the course to the Master; it was a tense situation, with rocks and ships all round us. It was a difficult passage, but I saw the stress on Alan

Hole, who had not looked at all well after eighteen hours on his feet; his pallid face reflecting the results of this stressful passage. Subsequently, Alan thanked me for my assistance but, sadly, I learnt that he had to retire early due to bad health.

After this useful spell on the *British Inventor*, I was to have a short voyage on the *Lankus* again, before finally joining the *Gondwana* in Japan.

I flew to Cape Town in July 1971. It was a cold, wet day when I arrived, shivering, at the airport. The taxi dropped me at the dock gates, some way from the dry dock where the *Lankus* lay.

I had to walk in the rain carrying my fairly heavy suitcase on board, and made my way up to my cabin on the top deck. There was no electricity and no heating on board; it was an era when little thought was given to the welfare of ship's officers and crew, especially in dry dock, when the supply of such things as electricity, steam, fresh water and sanitary water were often disrupted, and sometimes discontinued altogether, with a distant, usually dirty, toilet on shore.

On this occasion most of the officers were still on board and in bed with flu, I was told; but as I had to report to Head Office immediately I could not meet any of them. By the time I had made my way back to the office I was soaking wet and after a rather short meeting, I was soaked again on my way back to the ship and into my cold, dark cabin.

When I had had a good look at the bedridden officers, and also experienced myself the conditions on board, I returned to Head Office the following morning presenting a very strong case to improve the conditions on board immediately, or put everyone ashore in a hotel. It had the desired effect. By the end of the day, the services were back, but by this time I was not feeling too good. Getting soaking wet three times, being tired and cold into the bargain, and my close proximity to my flu-stricken officers, all took their toll – I was really ill. I never have had time off all my years at sea and with my impending appointment to the *Gondwana* did not want to succumb this time; but I was too ill and was hospitalised.

What kind of pneumonia it was I do not know, but I was so weak after my eight days in hospital without eating that I could barely walk. The ward sister said to me, 'You will be needing to go home for two or three months' rest after this.' I remember telling her, 'My doctor will be recommending a long sea voyage!'

No doubt I could have been repatriated, but I did not want to be seen as too sick to do my work, so I bluffed my way through the next few days, pretending to be full of life when managers and superintendents boarded but, in reality, I was not fit enough even to be out of bed.

We went round the coast from Cape Town to Durban to top up with main engine lube oil, which the chief insisted was necessary; actually, the chief was quite a character, a down-to-earth 'Geordie' who had earned the sobriquet 'Black Bob', not because he was dirty or because of the colour of his skin, but because he was a 'hands-on' chief engineer, who preferred a boiler suit to a uniform and, like most of the engineers who hale from the north-east of England, he was well trained and good at his job.

On this short passage he had his wife with him. She was just the opposite of Bob, rather prim and proper, and very ladylike, as one would expect from someone brought up in East Africa with English parents. She told us a story, one mealtime, of how she had been sitting on the verandah of her house in Mombasa, facing the Indian Ocean, when a very bright light appeared travelling low over the horizon from east to west; when we pursued it further, we found out that it was the same bright light that I had seen some years previously when I was sailing as chief officer of the *Athel Prince* – quite a coincidence.

Bob then was in the mood for telling stories and told us how, when he was on leave in 'Geordieland', it was his habit to walk his dog to the local pub for an hour or two most nights, and that after satisfying his thirst, he always looked forward to something for supper when he returned home. Often he was disappointed, and complained to his wife, who was a little tearful about it, not perhaps being used to the way of a Geordie engineer when home on leave. On one particular night she had cooked a 'ready-to-eat' steak and kidney pie, which Bob duly ate. But, to his wife's disappointment, he did not enthuse about it, and when she asked him, 'Was it alright?' he said, 'Yes, but a bit chewy.' It was then she realised he had not only eaten the pie but also the plastic case in which it had been cooked!

We sailed for Dumai in Sumatra on 1st August 1971. I had neither barely the strength nor the breath to walk up and down the stairway to and from my cabin to the saloon, so I had one meal per day. How I managed to run that ship, I do not know. My breathing was dreadful; I was as weak as a kitten, yet I managed and dealt with a lot of problems during my spell on board.

On arrival at Dumai, I was appalled at the amount of dutiable goods that the shore officials were demanding – cigarettes and whisky, usually. In the end I called for the agent and gave him a typed message addressed to President Suharto, telling him that I would refuse to load my ship unless the officials ceased their unreasonable demands.

It did the trick. Probably the agent apprised everyone because demands ceased and we were able to load our cargo and set sail for Trinidad via the Cape.

We stopped off Cape Town for a couple of hours for spares and stores, and this gave the Head Office staff chance to look round the ship, which was greatly improved since they last saw her just six weeks before. They also confirmed that I would be relieved at the next port, and after a few days at home would fly out to Japan to stand by the new ship under construction – the *Gondwana*.

By the time we arrived at Trinidad, I was still feeling terribly ill; the doctor there could do nothing for me as I was leaving for the UK the next day.

I was so glad to be going home, this time not only to see the family, but also to have a thorough medical. As soon as I arrived home I went to bed and our local GP said that he would need to call in a specialist. The thoracic specialist gave me a thorough examination and prescribed lots of drugs, enjoining me to rest completely for about a month. He was more than a little displeased and frustrated when I told him that I was flying to Japan within a week. I would not have missed the chance to command South Africa's biggest ship for anything in the world!

Forty-one

I STILL FELT WEAK and unwell by the time I arrived in Japan; the long journey from Manchester to London to Tokyo to Küre, taking about thirty hours, had not helped, but after a night's sleep at the flat in Küre, on the Inland Sea near Hiroshima, I felt somewhat better, and joined all the other officers in the shipyard of IHI; most of them were standing by the slightly smaller sister ship, *Kulu*, which was shortly to carry out sea trials.

By the time the sea trials had taken place, I was ready then to start my daily inspections of the newly built *Gondwana*, and gradually, due perhaps to the medication received in England, I regained my health and strength. The fact that I exercised every day by clambering all over the huge hull of the *Gondwana* to carry out inspections must have helped, as did the diet we enjoyed in Japan: a lot of salads, fruit and vegetables and no stodge! It was good to feel so well again, at just the right time, enabling me to give of my very best to this exciting new facet of my life. By the time all the top brass came out for the naming ceremony at the end of October 1971, I was fit as a fiddle, and was able to expend plenty of energy as I covered every inch of the hull to ensure the very best quality of workmanship for the owners.

There was plenty of social life because we had every evening to ourselves as well as every Sunday and every alternative Saturday. I used to walk in the countryside outside of Küre, sometimes in the company with the chief engineer, Hans Belmer, and taking films on my now old-fashioned super eight movie camera, as well as photographs. I went also to visit Hiroshima and Miya Shima, as well as all the local places of interest.

In the evening, the Japanese used to like to meet us for a drink and entertainment in one of the little bars that were situated all around every town in Japan. Of course, the Japanese executives were well treated for entertainment of guests in those days, so that it was an important part of their own social lives – they seldom socialised outside with their wives, who seemed to spend most of their time in or around their house or doing shopping.

We were well treated in so far as we were all given an IHI flat and free transport to and from the shipyard, with a free lunch at the shipyard. Their lunch was invariably salad, rice and vegetables, with perhaps a little meat or fish and a piece of fruit; although it was served cold in a little lunch box, it was nutritious, and as it was free, there were never any complaints from the six of us standing by.

Generally I would just make myself some coffee and bread and jam for breakfast and buy a meal out at night, or sometimes cook something simple if I wanted to stay in, which I did quite often; just relaxing in the little square tub bath, with my feet up. As the flat was small, I was able to look into my bedroom and watch the sumo wrestling on local TV.

After a few weeks of our energetic inspections, we underwent sea trials. For this we lived aboard for about a week undergoing speed trials after dry-docking and repainting the bottom. During this period, as we were some distance away from Küre, the yard executives would take us out for a few drinks and a meal here and there and, as a special treat, took us to see the *Hai Dozo* show.

Well, I must be a prude, but frankly this show was disgusting. The Japanese really enjoyed it but I don't think any of the ship's officers did; I know that I walked out halfway through – discreetly – and waited outside until it finished. I think that this was a time when the Japanese themselves were becoming conscious of their image, internationally, because I remember one of the executives asking me after the show what I thought about it; he was already concerned about what foreigners thought about them.

We were given a quite good subsistence allowance by Safmarine and this, combined with the free lunches at the shipyard and lots of entertainment by the yard, meant that we all had extra to spend on gifts to take home after three months of standing by. It is not often that one can enjoy one's work to the extent that I was able on that occasion; feeling so fit and well, with all the status attached to commanding South Africa's biggest ship, and, indeed, one of the biggest in the world at that time; and knowing also that we were doing a first-class job for the owners, as well as setting a good example of conduct and professionalism in a foreign country.

There was only one thing that marred this halcyon period – my father died.

It was on 2nd January 1972 when I received the phone call from home; I didn't know what to do; we were due to sail on 8th January on our maiden voyage, but, with some determination, I was going to give it my best shot to be home for his funeral.

Getting from Küre to Tokyo was not easy. All the trains were booked, but by pressing on the agent I was able to book a train early the next morning and to connect to a flight that night from Tokyo via Moscow, returning three days later. It was difficult to arrange all the bookings, but I really pressurised the agent and he produced the goods; now I had to get permission from Head Office.

To this day I thank Captain Bluett, or 'Bluey' as he was known, the marine manager. It was he who had promoted me to Master, he who had promoted me to the *Gondwana*, and now he agreed to my going home – just before we were due to sail on our maiden voyage. Of course, I was able to guarantee that I would not let him down, and that I would definitely be back.

The journey home and back went without a hitch, so I was able to fulfil my bargain with Bluey.

We sailed on the 8th January 1972, slowly moving off the IHI builders' yard with the aid of four tugs; some of the staff and workers had come to wave us off, throwing streamers, all adding to the atmosphere; it was a very proud moment to be in command of such a fine ship. Safmarine had ensured that the quality of finish was first class and, more importantly, had included all the latest safety features, especially the inert gas system which, if operated properly, would ensure the safety of the vessel during tank cleaning, loading and discharge.

Being built to such a high standard, the Master's accommodation was luxurious, with a good-sized office, day room, bedroom and bathroom, plus quite a large room used to receive visiting officials.

On top of my accommodation was the wheelhouse,

chartroom, and radio room and, on top of that was the upper navigating bridge, or 'Monkey Island'. This I used to use as my 'jogging track' for half an hour every afternoon, from side to side forty metres each way, in an effort to 'fight the flab' and keep myself in reasonably good condition to be able to clamber all over this huge vessel; I also used the six flights of stairs for the same reason, ignoring the lift. Some of the other officers and crew would walk, or jog, round the main deck, covering about a third of a mile each time round. It is easy on these long, ocean passages to become slothful, which does not set a good example to the crew, and this was one of the reasons why I always expended some energy in the fitness routine, whilst at the same time I was keeping a high profile, which is something I did on all the ships I commanded.

The passage from Japan to the Gulf was without incident; we operated smoothly from day one, loading our full cargo of crude oil at Ras Tanura in Saudi Arabia, for discharge at Rotterdam; we were still taking the long route round Africa, as the Suez Canal was closed.

We had held all our routine emergency drills as soon as we left Japan, such as fire drill, boat drill, and tank rescue, but on this passage I thought that we should do something more about our emergency steering system.

We had electrically operated steering gear by hand and automatic. We also had hydraulic emergency steering but when I inspected the steering engine more thoroughly, because of its huge size, I reasoned that it would take a few seconds for anyone to climb on top of it and to operate the hand emergency steering; accordingly, I instructed the mate to have a ladder built to facilitate the changeover on top of the steering engine.

By the time we had safely rounded the Cape and were heading up the English Channel towards Rotterdam, I had no thought in my mind about emergency steering; it was the *Gondwana*'s first cargo, everything had gone in a really smooth way, which, of course, was what one would expect.

We were not even disturbed too much by the bad weather we encountered later on in the North Atlantic. The swell was so huge that a similar sized loaded VLCC heading north was hidden in the trough completely; at times even the top of her mast disappeared, and she would be about 70 metres from truck to keel. Regardless of the enormous size of the swell waves, as we were not heading into them, it didn't cause us any concern but just amazement that vessels of our size could virtually disappear from view.

I knew that we were about the deepest draught ship to enter Rotterdam at this juncture, but with a pilot on board and two tugs made fast to the bow, I had no misgivings as we moved slowly through the entrance channel towards Europort.

'Port a bit,' ordered the pilot; she did not respond.

'Port more.' Still no movement.

'Hard a port!' Nothing happened.

These VLCCs, especially when fully laden, do not respond immediately to the rudder – it's not like a car's steering wheel – but when they do swing, they take some stopping. However, in this case nothing happened; I had noticed that the rudder indicator did not move. Quickly I put the steering gear into hand electric – nothing happened – I immediately phoned the chief officer, 'Paddy' Ramsden: 'Get down to the steering flat *now* and put her in emergency steering!'

By this time we had swung outside the dredged channel; even with both tugs pulling their hardest, we just dragged them with us. It seemed an age before Paddy phoned me from the steering flat telling me that he was ready. 'Hard a port!' was shouted down to him and believe it or not, we slowly swung back into the channel. We continued using this clumsy system all the way to the berth. Clumsy, yes, but it worked, and the pilot told me that he was surprised that we had not grounded outside the dredged channel because there was not supposed to be enough water there. Had we grounded at high water, which it was, we would probably have broken our back as the tide fell, polluting the whole port of Rotterdam and probably setting the whole place on fire!

Whether the making of that ladder to the top of the steering engine to facilitate quicker access had played a part, I do not know, but I was relieved beyond belief that our maiden voyage had not ended in disaster!

After loading our second cargo of crude oil in the Persian Gulf (sometimes called 'Arabian Gulf' depending upon the current political situation), we were heading south through the Mozambique Channel; I was sat in my office, typing the monthly portage bill (wages) and doing the normal paperwork expected of the Master, when I heard the Merchant Navy Programme on the radio – the Master had the privilege of a short wave radio that I kept tuned in to the BBC World Service; I listened to this programme every week, but on this occasion, my ears pricked up, as they were interviewing a shipowner, a Mr Ravi Tikkoo, who had signed a contract to build two giant tankers in Japan and they would be the biggest ships in the world – twice the size of the *Gondwana*.

He was asked about the captains of his ships and he told them that he had not yet recruited anyone, but he would be British, early forties, with VLCC experience and a good record… he could be talking about me! I thought.

There was no real dilemma. I knew that to be the Captain of the biggest ship in the world was something that I could not resist, if I was given the chance; not only would it be the culmination of my many years at sea, but I thought that ultimately there could be some commercial advantage; precisely what, I was not sure.

With the confidential cooperation of Sparks I was able to find the cable address of Globtik and sent a message outlining my background, and adding that I would write more formally on our arrival in Europe. I did however ask that they do not contact my previous companies for references until/if we came to some agreement.

Of course I had mixed feelings. Safmarine were an excellent company and there were many fine executives and sea staff whom it had been my privilege to meet and work with; additionally, they had given me my first command, and now I was Master of South Africa's biggest and newest ship, it didn't seem the right thing to do to leave just like that. But on the other hand, I had fulfilled my contract obligations, helped in some way to stabilise their new tanker operations, put a lot of effort into training officers, cadets, and crew, so I thought that it was not improper to leave, providing that I gave them the requisite two months' notice as required by my contract.

We discharged part cargo at Rotterdam and then the rest was discharged at London, and from there I went on leave, accepting on offer from Globtik Tankers to take control of their new vessel *Globtik London,* then under construction, and to run the marine side of their office in the meantime.

During this spell on leave, I took the family on holiday, including my recently widowed mother, down to Falmouth and then on to Westward Ho! As we were passing near to Appledore, I decided to try and locate Captain 'Ginger' Harris, the Master of my first ship to sea, the *Indian City*, as he lived in Appledore. To my delight, I was able to contact him by his son, Vernon Harris, who was a local pilot and with whom I had also sailed. 'Ginger' Harris was delighted to see me and perhaps a little proud that one of 'his boys' had made good and was now Captain of one of the new giant tankers – twenty-five times bigger than the *Indian City*. He offered us afternoon tea, and we sat on the edge of the lawn at his pleasant house, overlooking the sea; we reminisced for an hour or two and he well remembered the time when the *Indian City* had to weigh anchor off Margherita di Savoia and 'dodge' offshore for two or three days.

Forty-two

IT WAS A NEW experience to be working from Head Office. At this juncture in the development of Globtik Tankers, there was only a small staff at their Head Office in Park Lane, none of whom were marine-orientated.

During this period I stayed at the Merchant Navy Hotel, walking every day up the Bayswater Road to Park Lane and then working all day in the Globtik office, and as I had each weekend at home, it was really very pleasant.

As the first giant tanker, *Globtik Tokyo,* was being built at the same IHI yard as the *Gondwana*, it was thought appropriate that I fly to Japan to attend the sea trials and report back to Mr Tikkoo on my return; this went more or less smoothly.

In the meantime, apparently Mr Tikkoo was in the throes of finalising details of the enormous loans he would need from the banks, so I was designated to recruit the rest of the officers for the *Globtik Tokyo*, in order that he could produce a list of the officers joining to the banks. This was accomplished without much trouble, except for one of the applicants, a certain Mr Thomas! The florid-faced Mr Thomas had applied for a position as Chief Officer. He had lots of experience and seemed to be just the sort of man we were looking for. He sat down before me in my office and started detailing his background and experience, but I stopped him almost straight away.

'Mr Thomas,' I said, 'we have met. You were the chief officer of the *Allamanda*; I was your relief, but you would not remember.'

He looked sheepishly at me, knowing full well that he had been drunk at the time, but also realising that there was no way that anyone with a known heavy drinking record would be recruited. He didn't say anything, just picked up his papers and left slowly, closing the door behind him.

One day there was some unusual activity at the office and by the end of the day, we had all been asked if any strangers had been seen or any telephone engineers. Apparently, what had happened was that a telephone engineer had presented himself to 'repair' the phones; this was casually mentioned to Mr Tikkoo himself, who immediately ordered an inspection of all the phones, as there was nothing wrong with them. What had happened, I was told later, was that Mr Onassis had threatened the bank, telling them that if they loaned the money to Mr Tikkoo he would withdraw his support from the bank; they still loaned the money. Apparently, the telephones in the office had been 'bugged' – whether on Mr Onassis' orders or not, I never found out.

I was a great admirer of Mr Tikkoo; I had heard that he had managed to raise all the money for the building of these two great tankers without using any money of his own! Of course he had connections in the banking world through his family, but he personally had managed to close the deal, and this included a five-year time charter to Tokyo Tankers, of such a quality as to virtually ensure that the tankers would operate at great profit – which they did.

As the staff at Head Office were recruited, so I found time to attend some of the courses available at the time to ensure that I was right up to date on all aspects of tanker safety, radar simulator, ship board management, ship captain's medical, etc., thus ensuring that I could concentrate more on the day-to-day aspects of commanding these giant tankers.

The *Globtik London*, slightly bigger than the *Globtik Tokyo*, was under construction at IHI, Küre; this gave me the opportunity to take over command of the *Globtik Tokyo* at Kharg Island in the Persian Gulf in May 1973.

By this time, Globtik had a personnel officer and an office manager, and they sent out replacements for the chief officer and chief steward. When I first saw the chief officer designate, I was appalled; he was certainly not the type of officer I would have recruited. He was fat and obviously unfit; he looked as though he had a drink problem, and according to his Discharge Book had previously sailed as Master. I had a word with him, encouraging him as much as I could, assuring him he would receive all the help he might need. What had happened in the world? Here I was, Master of the biggest ship in the world, trying to train someone, my second-in-command, to do a job which he should know inside out!

Despite my efforts with the chief officer during the ballast passage from Japan back to the Persian Gulf, I knew that he had been drinking heavily, so I called him up and gave him chance to resign – there was no way that I could leave the handling of the complex cargo and inert gas systems in the hands of someone drunk and incapable. He gave me a letter of resignation and I oversaw the loading of the cargo myself. At times we loaded at 40,000 tons per hour, and one had to be really 'on the ball' to ensure complete safety and to avoid serious damage to the ship's structure due to improper distribution of weights in the tanks.

On the return journey to Japan, we had a little problem concerning the chief steward. The acting chief officer's wife, an ex-Royal Navy nurse, was looking after the routine medical treatment on board. She knocked on my door one morning, standing to attention, and addressing me as 'sir', as was her way due to her naval training.

'Please come and look at the chief steward, sir, he is seriously ill.'

We both went down the stairs and entered the chief steward's cabin, and I was shocked by the sight of him; sitting bolt upright in his chair, staring, white-faced, with blood running out of his mouth and down his shirt. Frankly, I thought at first that he had had a burst aorta or something equally desperate, but when we carried him across to the settee and laid him down, he was still breathing and when he moved his mouth, we noticed that he had bitten his tongue – he had had an epileptic fit!

He came round alright, but then I realised some of his strange behaviour over the past month or so after he had joined was not due to excessive drinking, as I suspected, but was due to him passing out at inopportune moments.

Regrettably, I had to ask for his resignation; I know this passed his problem on to someone else, but on these big ships we were often too far away from medical treatment to deviate for a doctor – at great cost to the owner or charterer.

Actually, I did have one other serious illness on board. One of the officer's wives was laid low with some illness or other that I could not diagnose. We were passing close to Singapore, but did not want to delay the ship by calling in for a doctor, so I just gave her a good dose of broad-spectrum antibiotics – and she got better!

Prior to the giant Globtik tankers entering service, the Japanese ULCCs (Ultra Large Crude Carriers) en route from Japan to the Gulf would stop if they arrived at the entrance to Singapore Strait at night, and then proceed only during daylight hours. I think that they were surprised that we would pass through at night because the Straits of Singapore and Malacca are very busy shipping routes.

I believed that it was always best to proceed through these congested waters at full speed, but taking all seamanlike precautions to fix the vessel's position constantly and with great accuracy. By maintaining full speed, one did have the advantage of greater manoeuvrability, and moreover one passed through the danger area more quickly! The fact that our position was constantly fixed meant that during periods of very heavy rainstorms, which obliterated many radar echoes, one could still proceed with a reasonable degree of safety.

At loaded draught, it was impossible to pass through these straits as our draught, on tropical marks, was around ninety-four feet, so we had to take the longer route back through the Lombok Strait and the Philippine Islands, out into the Pacific and up to Japan. We had no difficulties in navigation through these areas; after all, we did have the latest equipment, some of it in duplicate; for example, we had two radars, two gyroscopic compasses and two echo sounders, which could also measure lateral speed for better control of berthing. Given our size, the jetty could easily be destroyed if berthing was not carried out very slowly and parallel to the jetty.

One became used to the bulk of these giant vessels mainly because, at sea, there was nothing with which to compare them, but during a transit through the Singapore Strait, one was only too aware of their size in relation to the numerous other ships of all types which one had to approach very closely at times... it reminded me of a child playing with toy boats in a bathtub! Although I write about this transit in a jocular vein, it was far from easy and, as Master, I was always on the bridge for twenty-four hours until we had passed through the whole of the Singapore Strait and the shallowest part of the Malacca Strait.

A night-time passage was naturally more difficult, with different lights all round, indicating whether that ship was large or small, or towing or being towed and, also, by the colours of the lights one could determine their aspect and by radar plotting, calculate their speed etc. Singapore is one of the busiest ports in the world, if not *the* busiest, so that the lights of vessels moving, or at anchor, with flashing or fixed shore lights intermingled, presented a challenge to any ship's Master, and even more so on such large vessels with restricted manoeuvrability.

There were lighter moments on passage. As I understood my role as Master of these giant ships, it was not just to ensure that they travelled from A to B safely, but also to keep the crew as happy and as contented as they could be away from home. There was no 'fun' or excitement or event interest, except mail at each port. The remote location of oil terminals in the Gulf ensured that no one ever went ashore there, and very quick turnrounds and remoteness of the terminals in South Japan at Küre ensured that hardly anyone ever had the opportunity to go ashore.

By arranging social events on board, one was able, to a limited extent, to give the officers and crew a little relaxation. One such event was a darts match between the officers and crew; naturally I allowed my name to be one of the team. Actually, I was busy on the bridge when someone came up to remind me that there was a darts match in progress and that I was to play shortly. As there was a break in the navigational requirements, I went down into the crew's crowded mess room to do my bit.

Apparently by some skulduggery, it had been 'arranged' for me to play the pump man, who was reputedly the best player on the ship. Without any formality, we each threw a dart at the bull. I was nearer, so started off. First dart hit treble 7; I was aiming for adjacent treble 19; second dart entered treble 7; again I was aiming for treble 19; third dart I aimed directly at treble 7 – and it went right in! I had won without the pump man playing, because of our rule 'Three in a bed wins'. Amidst a stunned silence, I thanked them all profusely and marched back up to the bridge. I believe that my memory will long live with that crew – even if it is only for playing darts!

It should be mentioned that shipowners were also concerned about morale on board ships, and Mr Tikkoo was no exception. He ensured that the feeding rate for his ships was kept at a high level and, accordingly, we were able to enjoy really good food and lots of it; for example, every breakfast would offer a choice of cereals and a cooked breakfast, such as bacon, eggs and sausage, with toast, marmalade and coffee. Lunch might offer soup, roast, two vegetables and potatoes, cheese and biscuits, and coffee; dinner would be salad or soup, a main course that might be curry and rice or steak and chips, followed by a dessert such as apple pie or rice pudding and coffee. All the watch-keepers had a sandwich to eat through their night watches as well as tea, coffee or cocoa to drink; in the early morning at about six thirty, the chief officer on watch would be taken toast and coffee by the officers' steward. What with the good food, plus the ready availability of cheap beer, it was no wonder that most of the officers and crew put on weight – and this was one of the reasons why I used to skip lunches and jog up and down the Monkey Island in the afternoons.

One thing that did disturb me was that the first three cargoes had taken up to fifty hours to discharge, whereas the builders' plan of discharge had estimated that it should take thirty-two hours. This was a serious business, because time is money to ships, as in most businesses, and in our case it was a heck of a lot of money. I knew that, ultimately, the builders, being thorough, would be liaising with Tokyo Tankers, the charterers, and would be more than a little concerned. I took the opportunity on my first round trip in command to spend hours making flow charts, cargo calculations, stress calculations etc., so that I had all the discharging at my fingertips, but, before I could put it into practice, I received a message from the builders, indicating that they were sending a team down to go through the discharge procedure with us. We were still under guarantee, so they had every right to ensure that all was well; but I did not like the idea of anyone interfering with the way I ran the ship. I decided that the best way was to invite their team on board *as observers*!

As the acting chief officer was not yet up to the mark, after conning the ship into Kagoshima Bay, and seeing her securely berthed alongside, I hastily dealt with all the paperwork and dashed down to the cargo room to greet the team of Japanese, who sat all round the room. I had posted flow charts round the room, and this kept the Japanese busy, furiously copying them down into their little books, and as soon as we were given the okay from the shore cargo superintendent, I started up the pumps.

The cargo control room was equipped with all the latest devices to facilitate the remote handling of all the cargo; there were remote controls for all four cargo pumps – each one of which could discharge at about 6,000 tonnes per hour, plus another ballast pump and a small stripping pump; two of the cargo pumps had also self-stripping devices. These remote controls were needed because of the enormous size of these vessels. For example it was at least 40 metres down to the bottom of the pump room, so it was certainly not practicable to keep running up and down every few minutes.

There were many controls, dials, gauges etc. in the control room. All the cargo tanks, twenty-three of them, could be operated from there, as well as the inert gas system which used flue gases from the boilers, after washing and cooling, to reduce the oxygen content in the tanks, thus virtually eliminating chances of explosion. The draught and trim of the vessel could be monitored all the time, as well as the amount of list.

We also had the added sophistication of a computerised stress calculator to ensure that loading of cargo and/or ballast did not place undue longitudinal stress on the vessel, which could cause her to break in two.

Whilst alongside, it was necessary to ensure that all the moorings were kept taut, otherwise any movement of the vessel would generate tremendous kinetic energy and cause moorings to part, cargo hoses to be ripped off and even, in extreme cases, destroy the jetty, because these vessels, together with the weight of their cargo, could not easily be stopped once there was any movement.

To facilitate the mooring and controlling the vessel's movement alongside there were two huge windlasses on the fo'c's'le head, each with a 29-ton anchor which also had drums with thick hawsers for mooring; and in addition, there were another nine self-tensioning mooring winches on the main deck with remote controls. These hawsers were so thick and heavy that they were kept stowed on the mooring winches to reduce manpower requirements.

The importance of the mooring requirements cannot be overstated. For example, should a strong wind develop, the windage of these ships was huge, bearing in mind that there could be a least 35 metres out of the water along all 379 metres of her length, plus the seven decks of her accommodation.

I worked right through the discharge, which took less than the builders' estimate, showing them that we were not incompetent and proving that my professionalism was at least as good as any in the world.

I went on leave from Küre, the oil terminal in Kagoshima Bay, in September 1973, looking forward, as always, to a spell of home leave. But in the meantime, I had to call at the Head Office in London, as Mr Tikkoo wanted to have a meeting with me.

Forty-three

MR TIKKOO CAME straight to the point when we met in his office. He reconfirmed my appointment to command the *Globtik London*, but I would have to go out to her almost immediately, because there were impending sea trials plus a lot of matters which would need attention prior to her sailing – not the least of which would be the various social activities already scheduled.

'But I haven't seen my wife for months!' I protested.

'Take your wife, Captain,' he said, soothingly.

'But what about my three children?'

'Take your children,' he added.

'But what about accommodation?' I asked.

'It will be provided,' he confirmed.

'But it is so expensive in Japan, how could I pay subsistence for all five of us?'

'How much do you want, Captain?' was his generous offer.

I named a reasonable rate, to which he readily agreed; so home I went rejoicing, knowing that next week we would all leave together to spend five weeks in Japan!

It was an exciting time for the family. The schools gave them enough homework to see them through the five weeks; new clothes were bought, and off we went together. We flew from Manchester to Moscow and then to Tokyo, where we stayed overnight before flying to Hiroshima and then by car to Küre.

The accommodation in Küre was a little cramped because Japanese flats and houses are smaller than what Europeans are used to, but nevertheless it was adequate, with two bedrooms, bathroom, a small cooking area and a small dining area.

The girls behaved admirably throughout. As I was out on the *Globtik London* most days, they were often taken out by our secretary, Hokie, who was a real godsend. Even at the formal functions the girls dressed themselves up properly and behaved like angels (which was not normal!); but for their ages – seven, twelve and fourteen – one could feel very proud of them.

There was a film crew taking films and recording everything for American TV; this team was headed by Karen Lerner, whose family name is often connected to American TV shows.

On the evening before we sailed, there was a final cocktail party, with lots of lovely food and drinks; but, as we were sailing at six the next morning, I had instructed my senior officers who were present to take it easy, and they did.

Not that their conduct was exemplary; when Karen Lerner was climbing up a spiral staircase to the room above – probably the bathroom – she was followed up by our first engineer and he, after a couple of drinks, could not take his eyes off the glamorous legs at his eye level, and he let his hand wander where it shouldn't have. There was a quiet but meaningful chat with Mr Tikkoo and I had the first engineer out of there in seconds!

That incident apart, all the officers behaved in an exemplary manner and everything was on the top line as we sailed out at six the following morning and, as the *Globtik London* was slightly bigger than the *Globtik Tokyo*, she was, in fact, the biggest ship in the world, and recorded as such in the *Guinness Book of Records*; she was three hundred and seventy-nine metres long and sixty-two metres wide, which facilitated my jogging across the Monkey Island – sixty-two metres each way. Some of the officers walked round the main deck – nearly a kilometre once round – and one or two of them preferred to cycle round. Yes, we did have bicycles!

We also had a tricycle, so that should the crew be working right up forrard sometimes two would sit in the little trailer whilst a third one pedalled; it always amused me to see them rushing from forrard for their smoko, with the ship being trimmed by the stern on light ship passages, they came hurtling down the deck at breakneck speed – not safe, really, but they did become quite skilled at manoeuvring the tricycle; they would then pedal back up hill after smoko, sometimes with drums of paint or equipment in the trailer.

Such was the ship's length, that I remember going up to the bridge and asking the chief officer where the crew were working, because I couldn't see them around the deck; he passed the binoculars to me. 'There they are, sir,' he said, pointing to the bow. They were too far distant to be seen by the naked eye as they worked around the gigantic windlasses!

The accommodation was luxurious – far too big, really, for one person. There was a large office, large day room, large double bedroom and bathroom, plus a separate saloon where shore officials were dealt with; the alleyways were exceptionally wide, which was a mixed blessing because they all had to be cleaned, and even on our maiden voyage, we never had more than thirty-seven total complement, which I understand was later reduced to twenty-seven!

I have always been against reducing crews, because the ships were just not designed for such small numbers, and with their enormous size, all work was physically demanding. We did have all remote controls for the cargo handling system, as well as all the engine room auxiliaries and main turbine, but sometimes they did not function correctly, and this took a lot of effort by the crew to cope with this sort of contingency. When one looks back at the standard-sized ship of yesteryear – about 10,000 tons, with a crew of forty-two and a speed of 10 knots – compare the productivity with a vessel of 500,000 tons, a speed of 16 knots and a crew of twenty-seven!

Times change, and we must change with them; but the numbers of officers and crew should be maintained at a level where the ship could be operated safely and efficiently and within the capability of the men on board who are called upon to operate the ship and carry out routine maintenance and repairs – not miracles!

It was certainly a proud moment in my life, to be in command of the biggest ship in the world; this was something to which I had never aspired. I'd never thought about it at all, but looking back on that period in my life, I had worked extremely hard for many years, always giving of my best to the shipowner and never going for the easy options. I had pushed myself to the limit at times, and had always been prepared to put myself to the test, confident in my own ability to overcome whatever difficulties I knew would lie ahead. I like to believe that, despite driving ambition, I had never neglected any of the men who served under me.

The passage to Kharg Island was perfect, as was the weather, together with the operation of the ship, plus the performances of the officers and crew. I had made arrangements to have a photographic developing and printing laboratory set up in a small storeroom, and this I used to take photographs of some of the personnel in various activities; and whenever anyone wanted a copy of the photographs, I made them one to send home to their nearest and dearest. A few of the crew were keen enough to learn the processing of photograph developing and printing, and this was exactly what I had hoped, because it all helped to boost morale.

I was disappointed that Mr Tikkoo had not contacted me because he had promised that he would review my salary; not that I was hoiding a pistol at his head, but I had put the matter to him in a proper manner. I reminded him by radio message and this elicited some response; perhaps he had seen the following article published in the *Daily Telegraph* on 4th November, but I swear that it was not prompted by me!

The man of the week for me is 42-year-old Captain Donald Hindle, who took over command of a £25-million asset – the super jumbo tanker *Globtik London*, at 483,939 tons, the biggest ship afloat – built of course in Japan and delivered five months ahead of schedule. British shipyard unions, please note.

Big? Well, it's as long as two Wembley Stadium football pitches and you could play 79 tennis games on its deck space, or for golfers, it is 74 yards longer than the record drive by Jack Nicklaus.

The ocean giant is owned by the company started by former Indian naval officer Mr Ravi Tikkoo who set up his now £100-million plus company but little more than five years ago.

But back to Captain Hindle, the former Blackpool Grammar School boy who with a crew of only 37 has the daunting task of bossing *Globtik London*.

Shipping friends tell me that Captain Hindle will be lucky if he is earning £7,000 a year to run this colossal asset.

And I say that if Captain Hindle was running another sort of business with a capital of £25 million he would be paid treble that pay packet with, of course, the Rolls thrown in as a fringe benefit.

But I imagine that, to Captain Hindle as he walks his lonely bridge, job satisfaction is more important than his pay packet.

A little disconsolate about my salary situation, I nevertheless looked forward again to my leave with the family. It was during this leave that I received a telephone call from the general manager of Malaysian International Shipping Corporation, from their Rotterdam office. He told me that I had been recommended to him by Athel Line as a suitable Captain to take command of their new Oil/Bulk/Ore (OBO) carrier, which, at around 160,000 tons would be their biggest ship. MISC were looking at my big ship experience, but also wanting my experience on chemical tankers, as they had a fleet of Palm Oil/Parcel tankers being built in Japan. There appeared to be a possibility that I could command their OBO, then their first new palm oil tanker and then be consultant in their Head Office at Kuala Lumpur.

It was an exciting prospect, really. The pay would be about the same as Globtik, but there did seem to be scope for some negotiations, and thereafter, chance of a job at their Head Office, in the warm climate of Malaysia. I was interested and negotiated a contract with them, but on the understanding that I would do one more trip with Globtik; not that I had to, because I had preferred not to be on long-term contract, but I felt that it would be unfair to let them down.

MISC sent me a contract; I then resigned from Globtik but offered to do one last voyage to give them the opportunity to find a suitable replacement.

I joined *Globtik Tokyo* at Küre in January 1974, loaded a full cargo at Kharg Island in the Gulf and returned to Küre in March 1974.

I was surprised to receive a letter from James Kagami, one of the directors of Tokyo Tankers, the charterers (I was also told that Tokyo Tankers had agreed to purchase the Globtik tankers after five years); he asked me to stop overnight in Tokyo on my way home and invited me out for dinner.

It was a pleasant evening in Tokyo, a really good dinner and a great deal of appreciation expressed by James Kagami for all I had done for the Globtik operation. They knew that I had helped to stabilise the shipboard operation and had established some precedents by loading to maximum draft for the first time, and by reducing the discharge time by around 30%; all of which was a tremendous saving for Tokyo Tankers. To my surprise, at the end of the meal, James gave me an envelope, an unsolicited payment for all that I had done for them. I was really overcome, because by then Tokyo Tankers knew that I had resigned from Globtik, and I remember all of their executives with great respect; and not only for their gift, but also for their professionalism and the way they showed their appreciation.

Forty-four

I JOINED THE *Bunga Mawar* (*bunga* is flower in Malay and *mawar* means rose) in the Persian Gulf, loading a full cargo of crude oil for Europe, around the Cape of Good Hope again as the Suez Canal was still closed. Having served as Master of much larger vessels, it was no problem for me, and as the officers and crew were all properly experienced and well behaved, it was really quite a peaceful voyage.

It had been confirmed that after a spell on board the *Bunga Mawar* I was to call at the Head Office in Kuala Lumpur, prior to joining their new building palm oil carrier *Bunga Sepang* in Japan; this would give me the opportunity to meet with the Head Office staff, and weigh up the possibility of working from Kuala Lumpur as my first permanent shore job – the aspiration of every seafarer. After my leave, following five months on the *Bunga Mawar*, I flew to Kuala Lumpur and met the senior executive of MISC. Although I liked Kuala Lumpur and Malaysia in general, the terms and conditions offered for an appointment ashore there were not attractive at all, so I quickly decided that I would not be working there, but, would consider my options after taking the *Bunga Sepang* out of the builders' yard in Japan in early 1975.

It was during this period that I learned of a new company being formed in Kuwait, the Arab Maritime Petroleum Transport Company (AMPTC); I read about it in the Lloyd's List and it sounded something special. Apparently, all the Arab countries were to invest substantial sums into a new company and then purchase a fleet of tankers, to be operated out of Kuwait. Ultimately, it was expected that the company would be run by Arab nationals, and that the tankers themselves would be manned by trained and experienced Arabs.

By ferreting around for information I found out that AMPTC would shortly be recruiting executives, and after further enquiries I located their current general manager, Commander Short, who would be in charge of the recruitment. I managed to send my CV to him and he responded, advising that, should I be considered, I must be available for interview in May 1975. This was a bit of a problem because I had signed a contract with MISC, but, out of the blue came the solution.

Although I had a contract with MISC, they had unilaterally changed some of the terms by not paying into the Merchant Navy Officers' Pension Fund, which had annoyed me intensely; accordingly, it gave me good reason to submit my resignation.

Before leaving MISC, I had a rather dramatic experience. We were en route from Japan to load palm oil in Bangkok, when the second mate, a Chinese called Oh Eng Ho (call me 'Jock') reported that one of the crew was sick. Normally the second mate dealt with routine sicknesses, such as earache, backache, etc.; but, in this case, the sailor in question had not responded to treatment, so I was called to have a look at him.

He was sick, no doubt about it. Not only was his pulse rate and temperature sky-high, but he looked sickly; thin, pallid face, bad teeth and now rattling noises from his chest. Although my medical training was limited to the Ship Captain's Medical Course, that, plus experience, plus the basic knowledge contained in the *Ship Captain's Medical Guide*, indicated very strongly that this man had a very serious case of pneumonia. I remember that when we left Japan, there was a lot of flu going around at the time, and as this man had just joined the ship there, it was probable that with his poor condition generally, he had caught a particularly bad dose of it.

I instructed 'Jock' to give him the recommended dose of antibiotics and then sent a message to the onshore medical team at Singapore, asking for advice. This was something I would not normally do, because all doctors will tell you the same thing – 'Proceed to the nearest port' – and that is exactly what happened in this case; but they did add, 'Continue your good treatment.'

The nearest port was Saigon – a war zone, so that was out of the question – but we were due in Bangkok anyway within about two days, so 'Jock' and I struggled to keep this man alive, but to no avail. In the end we tried mouth-to-mouth resuscitation, but it was hopeless; his lungs were full of water. We landed the body at

Bangkok and the doctor there conducted an autopsy, which confirmed that he had died of pneumonia.

Consultancy

Forty-five

I TOOK A CHANCE by leaving MISC, because if I had failed the interview with AMPTC I would have been without a job; but with my good record, no doubt, I would have been able to find one. In any event, I had a successful interview with AMPTC and was appointed as Marine Manager, in Kuwait, in the middle of 1975.

The fact that it was a shore appointment meant that certain luxuries were readily available, such as daily mail service, telephone contact available with home every day, and newspapers; no unsocial hours; no bad weather – offices do not roll around! There was the opportunity for family to come out once per year, the opportunity for me to go home twice per year, and, on top of that, a tax-free salary, much higher than I was paid as Master. In addition, I was given free furnished accommodation, a free car and free petrol, plus a generous settling in allowance.

Kuwait is a modern city, and although extremely hot, it is mainly dry and healthy. With plenty of modern shops around, buying food was no problem and there were lots of good restaurants. I joined the Sea Club and enjoyed dinghy sailing at weekends (Friday in Muslim countries).

The work was interesting; we were buying new ships all over the place and then arranging manning contracts to operate them, because we had not yet had time to train our own officers and crew.

As marine manager, I was called upon to take over a brand new ULCC, laid up in Norway because, at the time, freight rates had dropped alarmingly and it was more economic to lay up a new tanker than to operate it; hence AMPTC were able to purchase a number of new, or nearly new, tankers at about half price!

I was to proceed to Norway in company with one of the legal staff, a Palestinian called Mohammed; after our briefing by the

MD, we went through all the documents and procedures and flew out from Kuwait two days later.

Mohammed was a congenial companion; we chatted away and dozed en route, but as we neared Oslo, I became somewhat more serious, cautioning Mohammed about the women in Norway, whom I advised him, were very forward and even could go up to a complete stranger and kiss him in front of everyone – right out in the open! He took all this in, very seriously, as Arabs tend to be of a serious disposition, and so he kept very close to me as we arrived at Oslo Airport. We collected our cases and were checking out through Customs, and it was at this juncture that a rather attractive well-dressed lady approached me, threw her arms round me and kissed me right in front of everyone. Mohammed was wide-eyed with astonishment, and then realisation dawned, bringing a smile to his face when he knew that it was my wife, and that I had been ribbing him unmercifully on the flight!

The next morning we took a local flight with the shipowners to this new giant tanker we had just bought for AMPTC; although there were some matters raised by me that the documents had stated that we take over the ship 'in an ice-free fjord', in fact it was so covered in ice that we actually walked out to the ship!

The formalities were completed on board, after my inspection; documents were signed, flags changed at a small ceremony on the stern, a shake of hands, and then back to the warmth of our hotel in Oslo.

Of course, one knows that it is cold in Norway in winter, but to experience it first hand, especially after living in the heat of Kuwait, is something else; I remember that it gave an edge to our appetite, and I had two helpings of the delicious fresh fish – haddock, I believe – served for dinner.

We flew back to Kuwait the next morning, leaving Dora to make her way back home alone.

I had become friendly with the Vice Chairman of the Kuwait Oil Company; it was mutual respect really, because, at that juncture, he was the only Kuwaiti who had served his ten years on British ships and passed his Master Mariners' Certificate.

At that time, all the Arab countries wanted to expand their

shipping interests, and Captain Faisal, the Vice Chairman of KOC, was also interested. After discussing it with him, I suggested that it would be better to start a marine survey company first, which would give us a centre of expertise, and then, later on, when the freight rates improved, we could start a shipping fleet. This is what we did.

The survey company did well. We opened offices in Kuwait, Dammam and Dubai, and were appointed as the United States Salvage Association Surveyors for the whole of the Middle East, after successfully carrying out two major surveys for them, one concerning a ship on fire, the other a major engine breakdown.

It was about this time that I became aware that, if I were to sell my interests in the business, plus the money I had saved so far, I would then be able to invest in Lloyd's of London, as a name, which would, in effect, be my pension fund.

Accordingly, I sold my share to the Kuwaiti partners and invested in Lloyd's in 1978.

Forty-six

AS THE INVESTMENT in Lloyd's had taken most of my spare capital, it was necessary to continue earning something until such time as my income from Lloyd's would be adequate. I had heard that Arya National Shipping Line of Iran were looking for a consultant to work out of their office in Tehran, so I contacted them and was invited to their office.

Somehow or other, it did not feel right for me; but, as they had a cadet training ship available called the *Arya Nur*, I decided to accept an appointment as Master until such time as I could work my way into the consultancy field.

The *Arya Nur* was a fine ship, carrying mainly general cargo, but with some refrigerated cargo space and also heavy lift capability. It was a pleasant interlude to sail on her because it enabled my wife and youngest daughter to sail with me for part of the voyage, when we were discharging and loading along the eastern seaboard of the United States; it also gave me more opportunity to keep up with my activities in the Nautical Institute when we loaded and discharged, especially at UK ports.

I was actually a Founder Member of the Nautical Institute in January 1972. We had formed the Institute because we were all concerned that every aspect of our professional lives was controlled by either the government, education authorities, international bodies, etc., and we, the professional seafarers, had no say whatsoever in either operational or technical matters, not to mention national and international legislation and all aspects of training, both at sea and ashore. When we formed the Institute, we were very clear that we did not want to become involved in any matters concerning salary, leave and so on; those matters were better left to the various associations.

At first, the shipowners, government and unions/associations viewed us with great suspicion, but now, thirty years on, we are accepted, not only by our own government, but also internationally by the United Nations offshoot, the International Maritime Organisation (IMO), as well as educational and training bodies. Eventually I was proposed and accepted, as one of the first Fellows of the Institute, and am still a member of the Fellowship Committee.

I make particular mention of the Nautical Institute because, although my intentions for helping to get it off the ground were entirely altruistic, they were instrumental in helping me obtain my first purely consultancy work.

I was contacted by the Liberian Maritime Bureau in December 1977 and asked if I would be interested to be a Nautical Assessor for the investigation into the collision between the two sister ships *Venoil* and *Venpet*; apparently the Bureau had been given my name by the Nautical Institute. As I was looking for consultancy work and had deliberately kept my contracts with Arya to single voyage only, I could make myself available and immediately accepted.

The collision was one that should never have happened. These sister ships were on virtually reciprocal courses off the southern tip of Africa, in dense fog, with radar switched on, and yet they collided: how could it happen? There was much in the media about the two ships rendezvousing to exchange Christmas presents, as it occurred on the 15th December; but the truth would only be reached after a formal inquiry had ascertained all the facts.

The inquiry was to be held at Reston, Virginia, USA, and it was to be chaired by a Briton, the Rt Hon. Sir Gordon Wilmer, a former Appeal Court judge, with Dr Rocheforte Weeks as Deputy Chairman, Mr Wureh, Mr Lubin and myself as members, with a whole gathering of legal and other experts representing the various parties – the Liberian Government, owners, manning agent, the Masters of both vessels, and the charterer.

We sat for fourteen days and were able to determine, by examination of all the witnesses, exactly what had happened. These ships were two of the biggest in the world, at around 325,000 tons deadweight, and were carrying crude oil from Kharg Island in the Persian Gulf, round the Cape and up to Point Tupper in Nova Scotia.

The *Venoil* was fully laden, heading in a westerly direction; the *Venpet* was light and heading on an easterly course. Because of fog, the visibility was drastically reduced at times, so both vessels were operating their radars; but the Taiwanese officers on both vessels had never attended a Radar Observer's Course, nor a Radar Simulation Course. Accordingly, as they came close together, the movement of the 'spots', or 'echoes' detected on the radar screen were misinterpreted, which led to incorrect manoeuvres and, ultimately, to the collision.

There was damage to the starboard bow of the *Venoil,* whose protruding anchor ripped open the side of the *Venpet* and was ultimately found inside the tanks of the *Venoil.*

There were fires on both vessels. Flames reached up to three hundred feet in the air and sadly, two men were drowned as the crews of both vessels abandoned ship in their lifeboats.

The total pollution was around 10,000 tons, but most of the cargo was salvaged as the fires were eventually put out by salvage tugs with the help of the crew, who reboarded.

Both vessels were salvaged.

We did not find any evidence of arrangements for the sister ships to rendezvous, nor did we find any evidence of drunkenness or other impropriety on either vessel; what we did find was that the radar training of the Masters and officers was non-existent, and this was one of our major recommendations: that all Taiwanese deck officers should undergo proper radar training. This was implemented immediately. The second recommendation was that the ship routeing system off South Africa should be changed, and this was also introduced as quickly as possible after the inquiry had ended. It was also noted that the reason for the loss of two lives was associated with the type of lifeboat used, and this incident also highlighted the inadequacies of the present lifeboat launching system; this had been a pet project of mine since 1973, when I published a short paper regarding this problem, indicating that stern launching lifeboat systems were best for tankers and certain other types of vessels. Over the years, one has seen that the stern-launching system has gradually been introduced.

It had been a wonderful experience as far as I was concerned;

it was a prestigious inquiry because of the size of the vessels involved and because they were both sister ships. I hoped that it would lead to other inquiries and investigations, because I really enjoyed doing the work and, with all due modesty, thought that with all my training and experience, I was just made for that kind of work.

Arya were pleased to have me back, and in early 1978, I served for six months on the *Arya Pas*. I really enjoyed this time, carrying general cargo with lots of heavy lifts to make the work interesting. We took most of the machinery for a new steel works in Venezuela, right up the River Orinoco, which was both scenic and interesting professionally, with its winding course and fast-running current. We also loaded and discharged along the eastern seaboard of the USA, the UK and also in three ports in Iran.

Forty-seven

I WAS ON LEAVE when the Irish Department of Tourism and Transport contacted me in March 1979, asking if I would be willing to sit as Assessor to the Tribunal concerning the fire and explosion on board the MV *Betelgeuse*, on 6th January 1979, at Whiddy Island, Bantry Bay, Ireland. After ascertaining some of the salient points regarding the case and then the more personal ones regarding fees etc., I rapidly agreed. I was later told that I had been recommended to the Irish Government by the British DTI, as, up until that time, no major marine inquiry had ever been held in Ireland, whereas the British DTI had a wealth of experience in that area.

It was still three months before I actually would be working full time on the case, so I looked for work to fill in the time, and also to keep money coming in because I was certainly too young to retire and still had to look after my family.

I knew that Hammonds of Dover operated a professional deep sea pilots service for the English Channel and North Sea ports, and I thought that they would be in need of new pilots, with experience of handling the very big ships, and such was the case. I was advised that, if I were to obtain a Trinity House Deep Sea Pilot's License, they would use my services immediately.

I had kept up to date with everything possible during my career, so I had no hesitation in contacting Trinity House (I was already a Younger Brother of Trinity House by this time) and arranged for one of the Elder Brethren to examine me for my license the following week. By this time I had bought all the most up-to-date charts and knew every course, light characteristics and depths from the pilot station at Brixham to all the major ports in the North Sea; I passed the examination, and Hammonds immediately gave me my first ship to pilot.

Although I was not old – forty-eight by this time – climbing up and down the very high sides of these huge vessels is no joke, and bouncing about in a small pilot cutter is not fun either, but I wanted the experience because I knew that to be in demand for whatever the future might hold, I must be up to date and I must be fit. Standing on the bridge of a ship in dense fog for two days at a stretch ensured fitness!

Such was the system at Hammonds that one was self-employed as a pilot, taking turns as vessels were due, but, as in my case, given priority on the larger vessels. Although I had to desist from pilotage duties once the *Betelgeuse* case started, I had always fulfilled my obligations to Hammonds, as they had to me.

It is worthwhile noting here that I was only able to move from one company to another because I had built up a good reputation – I was in demand. That doesn't mean to say that it is easy to move from one company to another, nor from one kind of work to another, because one's professionalism is on the line all the time; one has to have confidence in one's own ability, as well as competence born of considerable experience; and to gain this experience, I found that all the difficult kind of work had to be readily accepted and not 'dodged'. For example, I readily accepted a long voyage on the *Athel Prince*, as mate, then the challenge of serving on a new and bigger ship, the *Athel King*, and jumped at the chance to serve as mate on Britain's first chemical tankers. Moving from Reardon Smith's to Clan Line, to Athel Line, to Safmarine, to Globtik, to MISC, to AMPTC, to Arya, to pilotage and consultancy was only possible if that reputation was kept intact throughout what were all new challenges. Had I not adhered to the highest standards of professionalism and conduct, I could have truncated my career; but I had this insatiable desire to succeed and supreme confidence in my own ability.

Subsequent to the inquiry, a report was written and, as I was involved in every aspect of this case, including writing parts of the report, it will be of interest to the reader just to quote the introduction to that report, which encapsulates, the whole disaster.

The MV *Betelgeuse* left Ras Tanura in the Persian Gulf on the 24th November 1978, bound for Leixoes, in Portugal. She was a large tanker (having a gross registered tonnage of 61,776) and was carrying a cargo of 75,000 metric tonnes (approximately) of Arabian Heavy crude and 40,000 metric tonnes (approximately) of Arabian Light crude. Originally the intention was to call first at Sines, which is south of Lisbon, to lighten ship but the weather was so bad that she could not enter the harbour. Her plans were further frustrated at Leixoes; a ship sank across the entrance of the harbour and she was prevented from calling there and discharging her cargo. She was then instructed to sail to Whiddy Island, which is situated in Bantry Bay, County Cork, and where an oil terminal is operated by Gulf Oil Terminals (Ireland) Ltd. She stopped in Vigo to change some of her crew, and sailed for Bantry on the 30th December. She encountered heavy weather in the Bay of Biscay and after reporting leakage of oil was instructed to head towards Brest and reduce speed. However, the origin of the leak was discovered and stopped, and the vessel proceeded on passage to Bantry, arriving in the Bay on the 4th January, 1979. She completed berthing at the offshore jetty (which is situated about 1,300 feet [396 metres] off Whiddy Island) at 20.00 hours on Saturday, 6th January.

Early in the morning of the 8th January, a disastrous fire occurred which enveloped a large section of the ship and the offshore jetty. The fire was accompanied by a number of explosions, one of which was a massive one. All the crew of the tanker, the wife of one member of the crew, two visitors on the tanker, the crew on the jetty and the ship's pilot (fifty persons in all) lost their lives. The vessel was rendered a total wreck and extensive damage was caused to the offshore jetty and its installations.

On the 9th January 1979, the Minister for Tourism and Transport appointed a surveyor in his Department to carry out an inquiry into the casualty under the provisions of section 465 of the Merchant Shipping Act, 1894. At the same time an inspector appointed by the Minister of Labour under the Factories Act, 1955, began an inquiry into the disaster. It was also announced that a public inquiry would be held into the disaster and subsequently it was stated that this would take the form of a Tribunal to be established under the provisions of the Tribunals of Inquiry (Evidence) Act, 1921 (hereinafter: 'the Act of 1921').

The first sitting was on 14th May 1979, in the West Lodge Hotel; on 26th August 1979, it was planned to hear all the evidence from local witnesses at Bantry, and we adjourned on the 15th June until part of the wreck was raised. It resumed for five days in October and then adjourned to Dublin where the public hearing lasted until 20th December, 1979.

The Irish DTT had provided me with a house and car, which ensured that I had the space and tranquillity required to spread out and read the thousands of pages of written testimony and inspect the very many drawings and calculations.

The Master of Trinity House had told me that the Irish were 'very capable people'. He had had a lot to do with Ireland, apparently, because of the role Trinity House played in maintaining all the lighthouses around the coast of Ireland. He was proved to be quite correct; I found all the Irish participants, whether legal or government employees, extremely conscientious and capable, as well as being by nature articulate!

The evidence heard from the staff employed by Gulf Oil Terminals (Ireland) Ltd. was at variance to that given by the very many witnesses, who were able to recollect and time the events leading up to the disaster with great accuracy. The totality of the evidence by independent eyewitnesses and by technical experts was such that, at the end of the twelve months examining all the evidence and writing the report, we were satisfied that we knew exactly what had caused the disaster, and were able to make appropriate recommendations to try to prevent such an accident ever happening again.

It was quite remarkable the number of people who were alert and awake at around thirty minutes after midnight on that fateful night. Naturally, there were staff on duty on Whiddy Island, itself but because of the differences between their version and that given by all the independent eyewitnesses, it was concluded by the Tribunal that some of the Gulf employees were not telling the truth.

Many witnesses saw the fire in its early stages and some heard 'rumblings' and other noises; very many of the witnesses checked the time by looking at clocks, watches or listening to the radio. One of them, who lived on a hillside that overlooked Whiddy Island, was a professional photographer, and he was able to photograph the whole scene.

The time of the start of the fire was given as 00.30 hours by the mass of evidence heard, including the witness of a nurse on duty, who had observed smoke from a window looking away from the disaster, indicating very clearly that the fire had been burning for some time when she actually saw the flames from the opposite side of the hospital at 00.40.

The precise timing of the commencement of the fire was of great importance because it was generally believed that, had everyone been alerted earlier, many, if not all those killed, could have been saved.

It was something of a 'whodunit' really, because there were no survivors on board the ship nor on the jetty, but we were able to piece together exactly how much cargo had been discharged, how much remained and how much intermediate ballast had been loaded, and from this information we could calculate exactly what were the still water bending moments due to all the weights (cargo and ballast) distributed along its approximately 260 metres in length; these calculations were made more accurate by measurements taken from the wasted longitudinal strength members taken from the wreck.

The calculations proved that the *Betelgeuse* broke in two due to wastage of longitudinal strength members and excessive stresses placed upon them by the improperly distributed combined weight of the cargo and ballast. The major share of the responsibility for the disaster lay on the management of Total, who owned the vessel, because they had not maintained her properly nor had they provided any adequate means to calculate the stresses. Had the *Betelgeuse* been equipped with an inert gas system (as were the *Venoil* and *Venpet*) then the disaster would have been of much smaller dimension.

There were many facets to the *Betelgeuse* disaster: the excessive wastage of longitudinal strength members, the improper distribution of weights, lack of supervision by the Gulf controller, the absence of a standby tug, and no escape craft at the jetty.

It is only when a disaster occurs that the causes of it are highlighted; what a formal inquiry does is to bring all these to the attention of the public and then make certain recommendations in order to minimise the chances of such a disaster recurring; in the case of the *Betelgeuse* disaster, there were a total of 45 recommendations, some of which have been introduced and others maybe in the future.

To be part of such a prestigious inquiry is both an honour and an education because, although one is appointed to give the benefit of one's experience and knowledge, the fact is that at this level, there are others of equal standing in different spheres of professionalism, and it is from these people that much can be gleaned. I was extremely fortunate to be working so closely with a man of such a calibre as the Hon. Mr Justice Declan Costello, a senior High Court judge, who headed the Tribunal; later, he was promoted to be President of the High Court.

Forty-eight

HAVING BEEN THE Nautical Assessor on two prestigious inquiries, I was beginning to wonder what I would do next when, out of the blue, a firm of solicitors in London contacted me, and asked if I would be available to work on certain aspects of the *Amoco Cadiz* stranding. I naturally jumped at the chance, because the *Amoco Cadiz* grounding on rocks off the north-west coast of France had led to the biggest pollution case in history, and this resulted in the Master, Captain Bardari, being put in jail.

My appointment was limited to the following:

> To investigate and report upon the cause or causes of, and circumstances surrounding the stranding, and, in particular, the conduct of the Master, Captain Pasquale Bardari, prior to, during and after the stranding.

At this juncture, I was also approached by a Canadian solicitor as to whether I would consider working for the Government with regard to the *Amoco Cadiz* disaster; regrettably, I had to refuse because of my involvement already, which would have led to a conflict of interest. I write 'regrettably' because the *Amoco Cadiz* legal actions lasted for a considerable time, but as I was involved only in the early part of these actions, then I would soon have to look for other consultancy work. In fact, I had been looking increasingly towards marine arbitrations in London as a future that may hold out prospect of more permanence as well as being a natural move, as much of the work I had done was associated in some way with arbitration, and I had also studied to take examinations, which, together with my experience, had led to my becoming a Fellow of the Chartered Institute of Arbitrators.

The *Amoco Cadiz* total loss and pollution off the north-west coast of France was due to a number of factors: firstly, there was a failure of the steering gear during extremely bad weather;

secondly, there was a failure of the anchors to hold the fully laden VLCC, and the salvage tug failed to hold the tanker in the storm force winds which prevailed at the time.

There was much criticism by the media of the Captain for phoning the owners, and reports that he had awaited instructions before sending for a salvage tug, but in fact, it is normal for a Master to contact his owners if he is in difficulty; but that did not stop Captain Bardari from taking what action he could under the circumstances. Papers have been written concerning the inadequacies of anchoring VLCCs, especially during bad weather; once these huge vessels go out of control, it is extremely difficult to get them back under control, and for this reason, there has to be more time spent on voyage planning and the handling of cargo on the basis that 'prevention is better than cure'.

My work on the *Amoco Cadiz* case lasted about seventy days, and as Captain Bardari was released from jail and his Master's Certificate was returned, I thought that my involvement in the *Amoco Cadiz* case had concluded satisfactorily. I read somewhere that the case in the United States courts carried on for about two years, headed by a top-notch legal team including, from the UK, Richard (Dick) Stone QC, who I worked with again later, and Kirkland and Ellis, who were involved in the Watergate case. Unfortunately, I also read that Amoco had lost the case in the United States, which cost them a huge amount of around $2 billion.

Forty-nine

WHILST I WAS continuing my training to become a Maritime Arbitrator in London in the latter part of 1980, after completion of my work on the *Amoco Cadiz* case, I was contacted by the Home Office, with regard to assisting the inquiry into the breaking in two of the British motor tanker *Kurdistan*, in ice, off Newfoundland on the 15th March 1989.

I was actually on the British Government panel of Marine Investigators and Assessors as a 'Class 1 Nautical Assessor', and this case had fallen into my area of experience, so I was duly appointed, and, in fact, was involved for much of 1981 from January to September; sitting in a hotel initially, and then in Westminster Church House.

The case was of great interest professionally because if we found that the waters in the approaches to the St. Lawrence River were unsafe for navigation in winter, this could have had very serious repercussions upon the economy of Canada; accordingly, the Canadian Government and Coast Guard service were represented at the inquiry, as were Lloyd's Register, the Classification Society, the builders and ship repairers, shipowners and cargo owners.

Not only was the case of great importance to the Canadian Government but also to Lloyd's Register, because it is they who had given the *Kurdistan* her Classification, including her Ice Classification; Lloyd's had also supervised the repairs carried out to her bilge keel, which were defective.

The general details of the disaster are as follows:

On the 15th March 1979 the motor taker *Kurdistan* ran into ice at full speed in a position to the south of the Cabot Strait. She was at the time fully laden with a cargo of heated Bunker C6 fuel oil on a voyage from Point Tupper, Nova Scotia to Baie des Sept-Îles, Quebec. There was a south-south-easterly gale to storm passing over the area, causing rough seas and a heavy swell in the open water. The *Kurdistan* was navigated out of the ice, re-emerging into open water taking the seas on her starboard bow. Very shortly afterwards, at about 13.50, the bows of the vessel paused towards the middle of a downward pitch and shuddered. Immediately afterwards oil was seen escaping from the fractures, one on each side of No. 3 cargo tanks. The vessel proceeded at dead slow ahead into moderating conditions. Tank ullages were taken and cargo transferred from No. 3 wing tanks to the empty No. 4 wing tanks. About 18.40 there was a further less noticeable sensation. The wind had by now veered to the north-west. About 20.10 Captain Green, the master of the Canadian Coast Guard vessel *Sir William Alexander*, which was proceeding to the *Kurdistan*, requested her master to rendezvous 10 miles off Low Point, Cape Breton Island. The *Kurdistan* was altered on to a course of 250° True, to reduce the motion in the vessel. About 21.30 there was a further shuddering, the bows of the *Kurdistan* rose in the air and the vessel broke in two by finally hingeing on and parting the deck plating in way of No. 3 cargo tanks.

The 41 persons on board the *Kurdistan* were all in the aft section which remained upright but with the broken deck edge submerged. The engines were stopped, the engine room was abandoned and Mayday transmitted by VHF. The Mayday was immediately answered by the CCGS *Sir William Alexander*, which was distant about 5 miles. All persons were mustered at boat stations and with difficulty the Nos. 1 and 2 lifeboats were launched. Neither boat's engines could be started and the boats drifted clear astern, leaving the chief officer, who had been lowering the No. 2 lifeboat, on board the aft section. The seas were confused and the boats out of control, but all were rescued.

Normally, the bilge keel of any vessel is not regarded as being of any particular consequence, structurally, because it has no relevance with regard to longitudinal strength and it is added to the outside of the hull on each side purely to reduce the amount of rolling. In the case of the *Kurdistan*, the bilge keel had been repaired at Smith's Dock on the Tyne and the inquiry found that the welding of the repair was not up to standard. The significance of this was that when the *Kurdistan* re-emerged from the ice edge, into which she had navigated at full speed, she ploughed into rough seas which increased the longitudinal bending moments and which all combined to break her in two.

We discovered that the very cold water (around 0°C) had affected the molecular structure of the steel, such that, because of the poorly welded bilge keel repair, had initiated a fracture in the keel that had continued right round the hull, and then she broke in two.

It was of some interest that the *Kurdistan* was carrying heated fuel oil for the first time, and the thermal stresses could have been of some significance.

Without going into the technicalities in any detail, the recommendations made as a result of this disaster should minimise the chances of it ever recurring. Fortunately, due to the professionalism of the Master, officers and crew, the *Kurdistan* was evacuated by lifeboat, in poor weather conditions, without any loss of life.

Fifty

ON COMPLETION OF my work for the Home Office regarding the *Kurdistan* inquiry, I had been appointed as a Justice of the Peace and was continuing my work as a potentially full-time Maritime Arbitrator in London. About the same time came an offer from the International Maritime Bureau (specialists in the detection and prevention of Maritime Fraud), of some work over a three-month period, on a retainer basis, in Malaysia.

I did not know much about the situation in Malaysia except that it was to supervise the inspection of a VLCC in Japan and the inspection of an offshore storage vessel *Esso Mercia*. I had no problem with either of the two vessels, so I agreed to the appointment, planning to resume my work in the UK on completion, and flew out to Malaysia in September 1981.

I met up with the Petronas Inspection and Enforcement Department on arrival and they then briefed me about my trip to Japan, to supervise the VLCC inspection, which to my surprise was none other than the *British Inventor*; so no problem there, as I already had intimate knowledge of the vessel.

Whilst arranging for flights I found out that this 'small' job had more to it than met the eye; apparently there had been front page articles in the local press, in which the Leader of the Opposition had criticised the new Government for allowing Esso Malaysia (EPMI) to illegally lift crude oil from a source, or sources, owned by Petronas, the National Oil Corporation. This was a political hot potato, resulting in a lot of pressure on Petronas by the Government. Still, I was not involved in all this political mud-slinging and set off to Japan for my inspection.

I took only two days to survey the *British Inventor,* and I returned with the report already drafted, confirming that she was suitable for conversion to an offshore storage vessel. It was at this juncture when I started to query why Petronas should go to so much expense to remove one storage vessel and replace it with another, because it would not only be very costly, but would stop production of oil at a total cost of around $200 million.

I communicated my reservations to the Head of the International Maritime Bureau (IMB) in London, advising him that I was concerned about the way Petronas were being pushed to replace one vessel for another without any reason as far as I could see; but in order to do anything about it, I would need to discuss it with Petronas' MD, YB Dato Rastam Hadi. He concurred, so I immediately made the arrangement to meet the MD.

My meeting with Rastam Hadi was an eye-opener. He was an important man in Malaysia. As MD of their biggest company and the biggest source of income, he was important to their economy and, of course, to the Government. I told him that I did not think that it was necessary to spend so much money changing the *Esso Mercia* when it could be inspected in situ, providing that I was given the go-ahead to communicate with the senior executives of EPMI, because prior to this, I had received specific instructions not to talk to them. He readily gave permission to contact anyone in EPMI, and also, on being told that I was denied access to Petronas' confidential reports and documents concerning the alleged illegal lifting of crude oil, he immediately sent out a directive to every department that everything was to be shown to me. That did not please all their 6,000 staff!

My meeting with the EPMI senior executives were most fruitful; they were all well qualified and experienced, and readily agreed with me that the *Esso Mercia* could be inspected in situ, to search for any 'secret' valves or pipelines which may have assisted illicit lifting of crude oil.

From this point, I was able to arrange a meeting between the Chairman of Petronas and the Chairman of EPMI, convincing both of them that my plan was perfectly feasible and could be carried out safely, providing that I could maintain communications with EPMI. It was readily agreed, and I was given the go-ahead to start immediately.

The next stage was to advise IMB, because instead of my very limited role originally planned, I would be required to work full-time to carry out the rather complex activities which would be required to bring the project to a satisfactory conclusion; they readily agreed.

I soon struck up a good working relationship with EPMI and planned to clean all the tanks of the *Esso Mercia* sequentially, such that we could inspect one or two at a time and yet continue to load oil from the fields offshore. There had to be a good margin of safety, which we always maintained; additionally I had insisted on an independent Safety Inspector being on board at all times. I had also invited the Leader of the Opposition, Chief of Police and Head of Customs to inspect the tanks, along with representatives from EPMI and Lloyd's Register, plus photographers, who would take photographs from the top of each tank using air-driven safety lights for illumination.

We had to set off early in the morning by fixed-wing plane to Kerteh Airport and then transfer to a helicopter for the thirty-minute flight to the *Esso Mercia*.

On arrival on board, those inspecting the tanks would carry out their tasks and then we would fly back and repeat the process until all tanks were inspected over a two-week period. The Leader of the Opposition had decided not to come, but I had met him in Kuala Lumpur and briefed him about our intentions. We did have representation from the Police and the Customs, but they did not want to go down the tanks – they stayed in the mess room.

I went down all the tanks together with Jim Seery of Lloyd's. It was difficult in some respects because it had not been possible to completely gas-free each tank, which meant that we had to wear breathing apparatus. Climbing up and down 50-foot-deep tanks, in the tropics, and then clambering over the huge strength members in the bottom, was extremely enervating. What I never let anyone know was that my asthma was causing me a great deal of distress, due I suppose to lack of sleep, high humidity, stress, or whatever, but I would not allow it to interfere with the inspections, because this work was very important. At the time, in Malaysia, the Government had only been in office for about one year, and front-page allegations of the sort that had appeared in the local press were causing unnecessary problems.

We duly completed the inspections very thoroughly, with

three sets of photographs to prove that there were no 'secret' valves or pipelines.

I was able to give Rastam Hadi a verbal report immediately, but he would have to wait another three weeks for the photographs and written report. In the meantime, having instructed all departments to release all confidential reports and papers to me, my office was nearly *full*!

All the reports had to be gone through. They mainly concerned themselves with the refineries, documentary evidence and inspections of gauges, valves and pipelines of the offshore platforms, of which there were many, owned by Petronas, but operated by Shell and EPMI.

I waded through the mountains of paper and was able to encapsulate all that they contained into one very slim report, which I duly presented to the MD, advising him that there was no substance in any of them. He was over the moon: 'That's what I thought from the beginning,' he said.

By pushing through my proposals, and successfully carrying out the inspection of the *Esso Mercia,* I had considerably reduced unnecessary criticism of the Government and saved EPMI/Petronas about $200 million. It was at this juncture that the Chairman of Petronas, Tan Sri Abdullah Salleh, said to me 'You're a useful man to have around. Why don't you join us?'

I had to point out that I was still employed by IMB and that it would not be ethical. Moreover, I realised that such a large corporation as Petronas really needed some marine expertise, because virtually all its oil and gas was offshore, and there was so much marine activity with its supply boats, chartered tankers, oil terminals and ports; and yet Petronas did not have what I considered to be essential capability in the many marine fields of expertise.

By the time my report was completed and properly distributed, my contract with IMB had expired, so I was then able to accept employment with Petronas.

Fifty-one

I WAS FORTUNATE that my overall boss in Petronas would be the Managing Director, YB Dato Rastam Hadi. He was much criticised by the Board because he authorised the payment of such high salaries to expatriates, but he was adamant that if Petronas did not then the expatriates they were employing would not stay. He was quite right, because it is always difficult to work in a foreign country; not only that, one loses other opportunities and other contacts in one's own country. The fact that expatriates have also to make suitable arrangements for families was also considered. I signed my first contract with Petronas in January 1982, with some advice from Dato Rastam Hadi: 'Keep out of politics and do everything you can for the national interest.'

Prior to my contract with Petronas, I had been living in an hotel in Kuala Lumpur. Whilst it might sound good, there is no joy in sitting alone to eat a meal or have a drink, so I was really pleased to be able to move into my own apartment, Highland Towers, in January 1982; and with a company car, good salary and allowances, life was looking up!

I had pointed out to Dato Rastam that it was extraordinary that whilst Petronas actually manned the billions of dollars' worth of offshore structures, the current system was that there could be no direct contact between Petronas and the offshore structures.

'Surely we should be able to make direct contact with them,' I pointed out. 'In fact, we need a communications centre to maintain communication with all Petronas assets.'

'Do you know how to go about creating one?' he asked.

'Of course I do,' was my response. Even though I was not a communications expert, I had been involved with communications between ship and shore for years, and had a lot of experience regarding emergency communications; so, it was with some justification and confidence in my own abilities, that I readily accepted the challenge to build a communications centre.

I was working as Marine Adviser with the Inspection and Enforcement Department, whose head was Dato Jarjis, an ex-Police Inspector; he nominated one of his staff, a quiet but likeable and intelligent chap called Zainol Said, to be over me. Obviously this system could not work well, because in order to achieve objectives one has to really push things through to the highest level and to go through a somewhat tortuous route would ensure that I could achieve very little, or that whatever I achieved would take far too long.

I suggested to a number of executives that what was needed was a Marine Department to cater for all the multifarious needs of Petronas and its offshoot, Carigali; they agreed, and asked that I submit a paper to the Management Committee. This I did, and was told to proceed with it immediately.

It was pointed out to senior management that during the years 1980/81, allegations were made by the opposition party leader concerning illicit lifting of crude oil from Petronas oilfields; this caused considerable embarrassment to the Government and placed an enormous pressure upon Petronas senior management. Initial proposals to resolve the matter were estimated to cost M$280 million, bringing in marine operational/technical expertise eliminated the need for all this cost. This alerted senior management that there was an urgent need to develop a strong marine capability, and the Marine Department was formed, with me as its Head, and the Department itself divided into six sections, viz: Safety, Environment/Pollution Control, Marine Operations, Communications, Consultancy and Research and Administration, with a total staff of forty-seven.

Whilst all the planning for the new department was in progress, I had to carry on with the work I had been instructed to do, namely, build and operate a communications centre.

I thought about it at some length because I did not want to spend money unnecessarily on something so sophisticated that it would never be used, or that would be difficult to operate. What I did know was that currently there was no way we could communicate with our many offshore structures, and some of the terminals, without asking the Production Sharing Contractors

(PSC), Esso and Shell. I also knew that great difficulty was experienced in using landlines because the numbers and reliability of these were inadequate due to the rapid expansion of the Malaysian economy and its subsequent development.

Although my status as a manager within Petronas was not really high enough to accomplish all that was required – I really needed to be on the Board – it was at least an opening to all the Government departments, especially as I had been enjoined by Dato Rastam Hadi to do all that I could in the national interest. With this in mind, I nearly always managed to meet up with the actual Head of most Government departments, including Ministers, Deputy Prime Ministers and the former Prime Minister, Tun Hussain Onn.

Once I had outlined to the Head of the Telecoms what our requirements were, the communications centre was allotted several direct lines, for various functions, almost immediately. The location for the Comcentre was ideal, on the mezzanine floor of the Petronas Headquarters, which also gave it added prestige and convenience for senior management to use in emergency.

One had to be careful to expend money wisely, and accordingly, three quotations were sought for the cost of construction and installing all the equipment necessary; the cheapest quotation turned out to be an excellent choice, with an American Technical Manager who really knew what he was doing. According to the feedback from senior management, it had been built on a 'shoestring' budget.

The Comcentre really looked impressive, and more important – it worked! On one side of the room was a huge wall map with all the Petronas offshore and onshore structures throughout East and West Malaysia and the South China Sea clearly marked. Each communication centre, located in several areas, was fitted with a light, so that any messages coming in would energise a red light, and those going out a green light. Wherever possible, connection had been by direct landline with microwave links as required, connecting locally to VHF links.

All the calls were made to and from a control panel and, in an adjacent room, all incoming and outgoing calls were automatically recorded. In the centre of the control room was a conference table and chairs.

Conceptually, the centre was to be used whenever a major emergency arose and in particular, whenever there was a major oil spill and to this end, we had a National Oil Spill Response Exercise, participants included the RM Navy, Air Force, Army, Police, Fire Department, Observers, PSC staff, etc. The exercise was very successful and well received by the media.

So that we could properly deal with most emergencies, the fire-fighting and pollution clear-up equipment in all our chartered vessels was fed into a computer so that, at the touch of a button, all details appeared on the monitor.

All the senior staff of Petronas were briefed about the operation and uses of the Comcentre, including the Minister for Oil, Dr Ongkili, who, coming from East Malaysia and knowing the difficulties we all encountered contacting Lutong in Sabah, thought he would test our capability by asking how we communicated with Lutong. As soon as he asked, a button was pressed and a voice said, 'Lutong here!' Success!

Tun Hussain Onn, the now deceased former Prime Minister, who was 'Special Adviser' to Petronas, also visited the Comcentre occasionally; he liked to chat to me at these times because he was semi-retired and, I think, somewhat lonely at times.

Although the Comcentre was very basic, it did look a little futuristic in 1982, with lights flashing, monitors giving coloured presentations, buzzers, alarms, etc., to the extent that one of the Board called it 'Hindle's James Bond Centre'!

Fifty-two

WITH THE COMCENTRE project in full swing, I was asked by the director in charge of production and Carigali to assist with the placing of insurance at Lloyd's. Apparently, someone who did not know the rules had recommended a large number of brokers to try and obtain the best price, but that was not the way it is done. Usually one broker is appointed by that firm to negotiate the best deal. So incensed had the market at Lloyd's become that one underwriter had posted a notice on his box at Lloyd's, 'If you want to talk Carigali – p— off!'

It was a serious situation because Carigali (the exploration arm of Petronas) no longer had insurance cover and for a national asset, that was not what was expected. I flew to London with the insurance managers of Petronas and Carigali, and within a day we had placed the insurance *and* at a 10% discount; so that was extremely helpful and it helped to secure my position. One has to understand that because I was the only expatriate manager out of 6,000 staff, there was a lot of whispering behind my back – not only because I was a foreigner, but because I was very highly paid, and on more than one occasion, I had found out that someone had been prying into my personnel file, checking with the Nautical Institute, amongst others; but as I was a Founder Member and a Fellow of the Nautical Institute, and had nothing to hide, there was nothing detrimental to find.

As you can imagine, it was not easy working in such a prestigious company. It was a fine balancing act; on the one hand to keep producing high profile projects but, on the other hand, to minimise the amount of publicity the Department was receiving. Often there were reports about us in the press or in the Petronas monthly magazine, *Nada Petronas*, or in other publications, because that was the raison d'être of our Public Affairs Department. Fortunately, we had the Managing Director staunchly behind us, and that enabled me to actually forge ahead with projects without spending too much time and energy looking over my shoulder!

As Petronas developed, its demand for office space increased, so we all moved to a new building called Daya Bumi, right in the centre of Kuala Lumpur, then the tallest building in town. The Marine Department occupied half of the thirty-second floor, just a nice size for our staff, which now numbered forty-seven.

One day, I was perturbed that my secretary, Lynnette, was not around, until someone told me that she was in a room designated as a prayer room. Sure enough she was there, and a little tearful because of some personal problems; whilst I sat next to her at the table, trying to console her, a head kept bobbing up and down on the other side, it was quite amusing, in retrospect; trying to console Lynnette on one side with the head bobbing up and down on the other; and it was a moment or two before I realised that the head belonged to a lady on my staff who was on her knees saying her prayers.

Lynnette was a good secretary and I always made sure that she received proper reward at the annual salary review; ultimately, she became the President's secretary.

Another of my staff, who was often underestimated, was my Administrator, Zainol Said; he used to keep me on the straight and narrow by sorting through the internal memos, which were often written in Malay. On one occasion, the head of Personnel phoned me querying why I had approved a company loan for one of the staff; as I dealt with so much paperwork, I could not remember that particular one, nor could Zainol. The incident was growing in seriousness, because, as an expatriate, I had to be doubly careful in what I did; eventually, I discovered that on the day that I was supposed to have signed for the loan I was in the UK – the staff member had forged my signature! He was dismissed.

One of my more pleasant duties was to persuade the Board to give donations to suitable bodies. For example, an annual donation was given to the Maritime Academy that trained all the officers and crew for the burgeoning Malaysian Merchant Navy; another was to one of the universities to assist with their environmental protection projects, and yet another was to protect the tourist beach at Port Dickson by introducing an 'Adopt-a-Beach' programme, whereby sections of beach were sponsored by different organisations.

At one stage, I was allowed to employ four top-quality expatriate consultants to help with the work of the different sections within the Department, thus helping to train Malaysian staff to a higher standard of excellence – bearing in mind that there were not many qualified mariners in Malaysia.

Although the main contractors to Petronas, Shell and Esso, were operators of an acknowledged high international standard, I maintained that it was time that Malaysia had its own standards. Accordingly, we drafted Malaysian standards for many of the procedures and operations involving petroleum and marine related procedures.

In our Marine Operations Section, we standardised surveys for Vessel Condition and On/Off Hire, and we introduced one of the earliest Port State Enforcement operations by inspecting vessels at Petronas terminals to ensure compliance with international and national regulations.

Our Environment and Pollution Control Section monitored contractors' compliance with the Environmental Quality Act and internationally recognised environmental regulations. Additionally, this section carried out regular inspections of oil platforms and terminals. As a result of our active involvement in all matters relating to oil pollution and environmental protection, I was given a Ministerial appointment to the Malaysian Government Environmental Quality Control Council. Of course, I was delighted that our work had been recognised at such a high level, but on the other hand, disappointed at the slowness with which governments move. I found it very frustrating trying to reduce air pollution in the cities, for example; but to be realistic, this rather slow pace of change is not limited to Malaysia, and many other governments worldwide suffer from the same malaise.

The Safety Section monitored the contractors' compliance with National and International Safety Regulations, and drew up the Malaysian Regulations to be complied with by all contractors. Officers used to inspect all the platforms and terminals on a regular basis and investigated all incidences of fire, explosion, structural damage and loss of life.

The Marine Consultancy Section carried out many Consultancy Studies concerning marine related projects throughout Malaysia, and initiated the production of hydrographic charts in Malaysia, instead of them being produced by the UK Royal Navy.

As a natural progression of the Marine Department, we became involved in all the aspects of insurance placements, supporting the Insurance Department at all levels to help obtain the best quotations. In order to succeed in this area we had to carry out in-depth surveys of all Petronas assets, such as offshore platforms and onshore terminals. Not only did we survey all these assets but also caused improvements to be made to their safe operation, and this we were able to document, and thus help reduce insurance premiums by up to $10 million.

In addition to our work with insurance departments, we had become involved with many committees on a national level: the National Environment Quality Council, National Oil Spill Contingency Committee, ASCOPE Environmental Affairs, Maritime Coordination and Enforcement Committee, Board Member of Kemaman Supply Base, SIRIM Standard Development Committee, Petronas Committee on Safety Regulations, Refinery Interplant Safety Committee, Kerteh Marine Terminal and Interplant Coordination Committee.

There were very many sub-committees and ad hoc committee meetings, and I was privileged to attend a number of such meetings in the Prime Minister's Department – the department that advises the Prime Minister.

The whole of the East Coast of Peninsular Malaysia was being developed; on the one hand, it was gratifying to see prosperity coming to the rather backward State of Terengganu, but on the other hand, it was a shame to see the natural environment being destroyed as roads and terminals were built.

I was involved in much of the development along the East Coast, in particular, the development of Kemaman as a port; in fact I was on the Board, representing Petronas' interests, as we, directly or indirectly, would be the main users of the port.

Initially, it was a supply base, a storage area for all the pipes, chemicals and equipment needed to supply all the offshore structures. A large breakwater was built to protect the harbour.

To ensure that there were no major problems that would be encountered entering or leaving the port, I piloted the first supply boat into the port and was able to write directions for the future guidance of Masters who used the port.

Once the supply base was in full swing, it was decided to build a gas terminal within the breakwater. This was a major development in which I was directly involved, culminating in the pilotage of the first gas tanker into Kemaman.

Similarly, the dredged spoil out of the harbour had been used to help build a steelworks that, in turn, needed facilities to load ships within the harbour. All the marine operational aspects were decided at our board meetings.

It was gratifying to see the development of Kemaman from a piece of waste ground to becoming a busy and successful port, with possibility of further expansion to export petroleum products.

One disappointment I encountered was that senior management had not thought it appropriate for Petronas to build and operate its own tanker fleet. Perhaps it is understandable because it took a lot of persuasion for them to accept the need for marine expertise within the corporation; subsequently, after I had left Petronas, they decided to build and operate a fleet of gas tankers.

Despite the success of the Department, I had always been instructed to train a suitable Malaysian to take over my work there. Accordingly, I recruited Commodore Albert Thong, a Royal Malaysian Navy engineer, to take over from me. He worked willingly for twelve months, attending courses, sailing on our chartered ships and receiving the best training I could possibly give him, which, on top of his many years experience in the RMN and his natural leadership qualities, ensured a smooth handover when my last contract expired.

In a way it was sad to leave something that I had built up from scratch, but it had certainly been demanding and exciting, with responsibilities throughout Malaysia at the highest level, earning me the sobriquet 'King of the South China Sea'.

Epilogue

JUST BEFORE I left Petronas, I was invited to give a lecture in Singapore by the United Nations. As the numerous small island states throughout the Pacific Ocean did not have access to the kind of sophisticated Tanker Safety Courses that were readily available in the UK and other more developed countries, it had been decided to prepare a full two-week course for all senior harbour masters in the region. In order to add some authority to the course, I had been chosen to give the keynote lecture at the end.

Over the years, I had given a number of lectures, the first of which was the initial Annual Lecture for the Nautical Institute, in London. I didn't think that it was particularly good, because, for one thing it was my very first lecture and for another, as the Nautical Institute was in its formative stages, it was not well attended, although it was well received by the press. Subsequently, I delivered lectures at London University and various other venues, which naturally improved as I became more experienced in my presentation and delivery; but the keynote lecture for the UN was the best. I enjoyed it myself and was able to incorporate the investigations I had been involved with for various governments such as the *Venoil/Venpet* Inquiry, the *Betelgeuse* disaster in Ireland, the *Thorland* disaster, and the *Amoco Cadiz* and *Kurdistan* Inquiries.

What made a lot of my work worthwhile was the unsolicited appreciation given by such bodies as the United Nations, and by the Hon. Mr Justice Declan Costello, who also wrote to me after our work on the *Betelgeuse* Inquiry, and the appreciation of Tokyo Tankers for my work on the big Globtik tankers. I can even recall two of the sailors on different ships of which I was Chief Officer, telling me, as they paid off, 'You've done a good job, Chief.' I mention these because, if there is no appreciation of one's work by those who should know, then there is very little job satisfaction in just working for a salary or fee.

This brings me to put the question that I have often been asked, 'Do you miss the sea?'

The answer to that must be 'No', because I achieved everything that it was possible for me to achieve; that is, purely from the professional point of view. But what about the separation from family? That was hard, very hard at times, and the only way I could deal with it was by working as hard as I could and saving up as much money as I could, to spend it on leave with plenty of holidays for the family; and, later on, I was in a position to give lots of really good holidays, such as sailing holidays round the Greek Islands, and of course very many to Cyprus and other areas.

By the nature of my work, I lived in many places, such as Malaysia for about seven years, Japan for about one year, Kuwait for two years and, of course, I visited many ports and islands in parts of the world not normally visited, and in an era when they were not developed. So it was, at that time, very exciting and interesting. Being able to have some of the family with me in Japan, Malaysia, Kuwait and occasionally on board ship was a plus, and I'm sure that they will always remember those exciting times.

The weather plays a big part in a seafarer's life. Needless to say, with the ship rolling all over the place, dark clouds, and huge waves crashing over the decks, one wondered what on earth one was doing at sea at all… and then the sky would clear, the sun come out, the wind drop, seas abate, and we were able to enjoy some unimaginable and wonderful sea passages with clear starry skies, the phosphorescent torpedo-like streaks of dolphins round the bow; and then would come the long awaited message, 'Land's End For Orders' – we were homeward bound.

Dora and I came to live in Cyprus in 1986. We built a villa with a decent-sized swimming pool and garden, and are enjoying the 325 days of sunshine per year and the annual holiday visits of family and friends.

It is in this rather pleasant environment that I am now writing my books; this is my second, and there are plans for three more. Whether they will be well received by the public, I do not know, but I will enjoy writing them and, who knows, I might receive a 'Well done, Chief' from somebody!

Printed in the United Kingdom
by Lightning Source UK Ltd.
109086UKS00001B/14